ORWELL'S NOSE

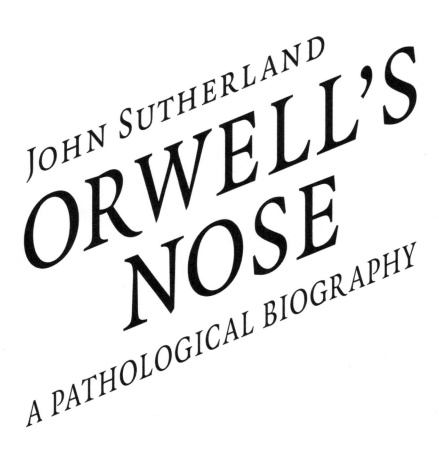

John Sutherland

ORWELL'S NOSE

A PATHOLOGICAL BIOGRAPHY

REAKTION BOOKS

Published by Reaktion Books Ltd
Unit 32, Waterside
44–48 Wharf Road
London N1 7UX, UK
www.reaktionbooks.co.uk

First published 2016
Copyright © John Sutherland 2016

Printed and bound in Great Britain by TJ International, Padstow, Cornwall

A catalogue record for this book is available from the British Library

ISBN 978 1 78023 648 3

Contents

I was damned. I had no money, I was weak, I was ugly,
I was unpopular, I had a chronic cough, I was cowardly. I smelt.

ORWELL, about Eric Blair, aetat 8

four frightful words . . . *The lower classes smell.*

The Road to Wigan Pier

A NOTE ON NOTES

The most comprehensive information resource is Peter Davison's *Complete Works of George Orwell*. Davison's twenty-volume work (prohibitively expensive) is hard to come by outside copyright and research libraries. I have access to such a library; many readers will not. For the text that follows I have used, where useful, the four-volume, widely available (Penguin) paperback *The Collected Essays, Journalism and Letters of George Orwell* (1968), edited by Ian Angus and Sonia Orwell. Its contents are chronological and indexed: dates of composition and first publication are given.

Foreword

In 1928 D. H. Lawrence, as passionate a defender of the English language as Orwell, made his quixotic attempt to liberate ('hygienise') a small lexicon of 'four letter words'. The UK finally gave way on the point, in November 1960, at the Old Bailey. I have used a few four-letter words, once (perhaps still in some places) thought offensive. Had he lived fifteen years longer, so, of course, would George Orwell have done.

Preface

Reading with the Nose

It would be hateful if things did not smell: they would not be real.
ADRIAN STOKES

Three years ago, in high hay-fever season, I lost my sense of smell. It has never returned and I'm told it never will. Of all the five senses one can expect to part with en route to sans everything, smell is the most dispensable.

And if the Freudians (and Jonathan Swift) are right that civilization is the distance *Homo sapiens* ('Yahoos') puts between his nose and his excrement, I am a more civilized person for living in my organically neutralized world. The 94 per cent of British adult women and 87 per cent of British men who use deodorants daily would perhaps agree. (These figures, taken from the Internet, seem high to those I've spoken to with the power of smell. Particularly on homeward journeys on the London Tube.)

About the same period that my nasal membranes wilted I had embarked on a reread of Orwell, in the spirit of Janeites who revisit Austen's six novels every year, just to relax into the comfort of old literary places. The writings I had known for half a century were, I found, interestingly different. Not quite as comforting. Imagine, for example, a person born with no sense of smell. Would *Animal Farm* 'read' the same way as for someone with functioning nostrils and long familiarity with the richly mixed but detectably different

aromas (cow shit, chicken shit, horse shit, pig shit) in a farmyard?
And then, at the end, Napoleon walking past on two legs with –
what else? – an aromatic cigar.

According to Norman Mailer, a fellow connoisseur, with Orwell,
of life's olfactions (or, as Mailer would call them, 'olfactoids'), there
'ain't but three smells' in the whole Hemingway *oeuvre*. Papa's fish,
to adopt the working-class insult, don't smell. Mailer's count, thrown
out, as I recall, on the Dick Cavett talk show, was not the result of
careful textual examination but nonetheless rings true.

Compare the first three richly scene-setting aromas in *Nineteen
Eighty-Four*. The story opens with Winston Smith escaping the
April cold through the glass doors of Victory Mansions. Instant
nasal attack: 'The hallway smelt of boiled cabbage and old rag mats.'
Having slogged up to his apartment on the seventh floor (the lift, of
course, is broken), Winston pours himself a reviving swig of Victory
Gin. 'It gave off a sickly, oily smell, as of Chinese rice-spirit.' He
smokes a Victory cigarette (no need to describe that acrid smell),
and is called to the Parsons' flat next door. Can he unplug the sink?
begs the harassed mother:

> There was the usual boiled-cabbage smell, common to the whole
> building, but it was shot through by a sharper reek of sweat,
> which – one knew this at the first sniff, though it was hard to say
> how – was the sweat of some person not present at the moment.

You need a nose that a bloodhound would envy to track the
perspiratory reek of someone who has been out of the house for
hours. Later, in the grim waiting room for the dreaded Room 101
trip, Winston is obliged to smell, at close range, Parsons's shit while
it is still warm and at its most odoriferous. Horrible as it is, it is
preferable to the smell that awaits Winston in Room 101.

There are many threads in Orwell's fiction. But it is interesting
to compile their 'smell narratives'. I append one for *A Clergyman's*

Daughter, along with the most smell-referential of his non-fiction books, *The Road to Wigan Pier*. The latter contains the four words that have hung like an albatross around Orwell's neck: 'The working classes smell.' The qualifications with which he surrounded the allegation are rarely quoted.

Smell narratives would be as terse as a 140-character tweet with some authors. I asked Deirdre Le Faye, the doyenne of Jane Austen studies and editor of her surviving letters, what smells there were in the six novels. Deirdre's reply was interesting and perplexed:

> Smell I think is only specifically mentioned in *Mansfield Park*, with the bad air and bad smells of the Portsmouth house. This does strike me as slightly odd, because by our standards at least, the past must have been a fairly smelly place.

The 'lady' who wrote *Sense and Sensibility* was, apparently, short of one sense.

What would the ambient smell of Jane Austen's outside world have actually been? Easily answered. Inside the house, the communal toilet sand box. Outside, horse droppings, predominantly – whether in rural Hampshire or urban Bath. The Regency world moved on four legs. Horses deposit between 7 and 14 kg (15 and 30 lb) of excrement and 9 litres (2 gallons) of urine per day where they will. There is no such beast as a house-trained horse.

Orwell, who claimed he would have preferred to have lived two hundred years ago, with his fellow 'Tory-anarchist' Jonathan Swift, might have found that equine-excremental world more bearable, attractive even, than the world he was born in. He loathed twentieth-century mechanical smells – although paraffin (his commonest source of home heating and lighting, when in the country) he found oddly 'sweet' to his nostrils, probably because of its association with warmth and light. More than most twentieth-century authors, he did a lot of reading and writing by tilly lamp, the odoriferous heater meanwhile throwing its mottled pattern onto the ceiling.

One of Orwell's perceptive observations in his 1946 essay 'Politics vs. Literature', on his most admired author, Swift, is that in *Gulliver's Travels* the morbidly naso-sensitive hero finally accepts as his ideal the horse, 'an animal whose excrement is not offensive'. It is a 'diseased' choice on Swift's part, Orwell grants. But Gulliver's first experience when he arrives in Houyhnhnmland is to be spattered with human shit. Of the two varieties, which would one prefer? Orwell was, whenever the opportunity came up, a smallholding farmer: horse shit he valued (there are diary entries recording him examining minutely the quality of recent droppings) as fertilizer. Pig shit (he hated the omnivorous pig) was useless for that purpose.

Human excrement, like that of other carnivores, is offensive. Herbivores and graminivores, like the horse and goose (an animal Orwell loved and kept, whenever he could), have inoffensive excrement (when walking in Regent's Park I have to prevent my dog from eating that variety of animal dropping. Dog shit does not attract her).

Not that it's relevant, but I've often wondered where vegan droppings would stand on the Orwellian offensiveness scale. But Orwell despised 'sandal-wearers' and 'fruit-juice drinkers' as cranks, and they would not have attracted his nasal interest. He despised, as he told his working-class friend the aptly named Jack Common, 'eunuch types with a vegetarian smell'.[1]

The reasons Orwell, ruinously for his health, spent the best years of his adult life in Burma, are hard to disentangle. But one was surely the call of the nostalgic curries, and the fading but still pungently mingled scents of sandalwood, rattan and teak (the most long-lastingly odoriferous of woods) in the Anglo-Indian house he was brought up in. He could not, joked his friend the critic Cyril Connolly, 'blow his nose without moralising on conditions in the handkerchief industry'. Or sniff, one suspects, his mother's vindaloos and chutneys, without wondering about the subcontinent and the ethics of colonialism.

There were indeed intoxicating aromas to be found in Burma for a young man. And if Orwell's description of his hero, John Flory's, lovemaking in *Burmese Days* is to be trusted, erotic nasal stimulus was a major part of the oriental package. Flory, as he embraces his house concubine, Ma Hla May, is aroused: 'A mingled scent of sandalwood, garlic, coconut oil and the jasmine in her hair floated from her. It was a scent that always made his teeth tingle.' Tingling teeth is a fine detail. And it is not metaphorical. The trigeminal nerves connect nasal and dental sensation. The English working class (as Orwell would have overheard many times) glorify the 'knee trembler' (sex, *faute de mieux*, standing up, in an alley – Orwell describes it in *The Road to Wigan Pier*). Tooth tinglers are less common with the cold wind whipping round your bare ankles – damned uncomfortable, but relatively smell-less.

Compare aromatic Burmese copulation with the whiffiness of the whore Winston Smith recalls using in *Nineteen Eighty-Four*:

He seemed to breathe again the warm stuffy odour of the basement kitchen, an odour compounded of bugs and dirty clothes and villainous cheap scent, but nevertheless alluring, because no woman of the Party ever used scent, or could be imagined as doing so. Only the proles used scent. In his mind the smell of it was inextricably mixed up with fornication.

Whorish filth, for Orwell (who is known to have used common prostitutes at various stages of his adult life), was as powerful as sandalwood. It too 'allures', like the rotten apple that Schiller kept in his desk drawer to revive his literary inspiration when it flagged. Fresh apples don't get the teeth tingling.[2]

Orwell's discrimination of the sniff reaches a pitch of sheer nasal virtuosity, as in the following, ascribed to George Bowling, on one of his time trips back to Sundays in his childhood Lower Binfield (Orwell, of course, is describing the church of St Mary he attended, as a child, in Henley-on-Thames):

> How I could smell it! You know the smell churches have, a peculiar, dank, dusty, decaying, sweetish sort of smell. There's a touch of candle-grease in it, and perhaps a whiff of incense and a suspicion of mice, and on Sunday mornings it's a bit overlaid by yellow soap and serge dresses, but predominantly it's that sweet, dusty, musty smell that's like the smell of death and life mixed up together. It's powdered corpses, really.

In his essay on Swift, 'Politics vs. Literature', Orwell rhapsodizes on 'the gloomy words of the burial service and the sweetish smell of corpses in a country church'.

Biographers are sometimes surprised that Orwell, who claimed to have embraced atheism aged fourteen, should have insisted on being buried in a country church rather than the 'sanitary' option of cremation. He wanted, one surmises, to leave the world accompanied by his personal decaying smell as he had entered it, *inter urinas et faeces*.

'Lower' Smells

Only the proles used scent.

Adrian Stokes, in his curious essay 'Strong Smells and Polite Society',[3] notes that for the English 'decent' classes all smells are bad smells. Particularly those emanating from the human (sweating, perspiring or, with 'ladies', glowing) body.

And what Stokes (an artist who chose to live the life of a peasant) calls, with an irrepressible patrician sneer, 'politeness' entails suppressive cultural inhibition. The English have, with a sense of national self-righteousness, never developed any aesthetic cultivation via the nose. For the French, by contrast, the pleasure of the 'bouquet' is an essential preliminary to the enjoyment of wine or liqueurs. The French value an 'art' of smell. Watching a Frenchman drink a fine vintage, and his British counterpart down a pint of bitter, is a lesson in national difference.[4]

Suppression of smell is, for the British since the puritan revolution of the seventeenth century, 'moral'. Even cultural revolutionaries find it difficult to shake off this nasal puritanism. D. H. Lawrence, for example, fought valiantly, in *Lady Chatterley's Lover*, to liberate four-letter ('dirty') words for writers' creative use – fuck, arse, shit, piss. 'Hygienising', he called it. There is one four-letter word not on the liberated Lawrentian lexicon – 'fart'. It is beyond hygienization. Why? Because as Richard Hoggart insisted in the 1960 trial (to the shattering discomfiture of the prosecution), 'Lawrence is a puritan.' And in that silence about flatulence one hears, distantly, his evangelically inclined woman, immortalized as Mrs Morel, saying, 'No, please *no* Bert; that word is so *vulgar.*'

Orwell did not read *Ulysses* until 1933, when his cosmopolitan lover, Mabel Fierz, smuggled him, at the risk of both their prosecutions, a copy of Joyce's prohibited book. Among the legally offensive passages was the description of Bloom 'asquat the cuckstool . . . seated calm above his own rising smell'. Joyce, of course, wrote the bulk of *Ulysses* in France.

The flatulent virtuosity of 'Le Pétomane', the French *artiste du fart*, could, one feels, have originated nowhere but at the Moulin Rouge where Joseph Pujol, as a rousing finale, would nightly ejaculate an anal *Marseillaise*. In English theatres and cinemas, it was 'God Save the King'. Standing to attention, buttocks decently clenched.

Henry Miller

Orwell's obsessive relationship with smell created odd cultural comradeships: principally with Swift, Salvador Dalí (the one artist he wrote an essay on) and Henry Miller.

His decades-long fascination with the author of *The Tropic of Capricorn* is, on the face of it, odd. It was not a casual thing. One of the few times Orwell fell foul of the law was for illicitly having a smuggled collection of Miller's Paris-published *oeuvre*. He wrote about and referred to Miller many times, and went out of his way to visit him. What principally drew him was not the 'pornography' (as then defined – Miller is now an American classic) but the sensory extravaganza on interesting French stench, from the gripping second sentence of the first tropic onwards: 'Last night Boris discovered that he was lousy. I had to shave his armpits and even then the itching did not stop.'

As Orwell wrote, in his first tribute piece to Miller, he creates a Paris permeated with:

> the whole atmosphere of the poor quarters of Paris as a foreigner sees them – the cobbled alleys, the sour reek of refuse, the bistros with their greasy zinc counters and worn brick floors, the green waters of the Seine, the blue cloaks of the Republican Guard, the crumbling iron urinals, the peculiar sweetish smell of the Metro stations, the cigarettes that come to pieces, the pigeons in the Luxembourg Gardens.[5]

More specifically, *the smell of it*. Orwell found in Miller the most congenial nasal Francophile. A brother of the nose. The company of Cyrano.

Outside the whale. Henry Miller, Orwell's idol.

Orwell's Smell-talent

One seemed always to be walking a tight-rope over a cess-pool.

Orwell was born with a singularly diagnostic sense of smell. He had the beagle's rare ability to particularize and separate out the ingredients that go into any aroma. One memorably odoriferous passage, never forgotten by anyone who has read the account ('Such, Such Were the Joys') of Eric Blair's (as he then was) awful prep school, describes the ablution ordeal that the pupils had, daily, to endure at St Cyprian's. It centred on 'the slimy water of the plunge bath':

> and the always-damp towels with their cheesy smell: and, on occasional visits in the winter, the murky sea-water of the local Baths, which came straight in from the beach and on which I once saw floating a human turd. And the sweaty smell of the changing-room with its greasy basins, and, giving on this, the row of filthy, dilapidated lavatories, which had no fastenings of any kind on the doors.

The 'cheesy smell' of the towels? An odd adjective, one might think. But it's not. The 'aromatographer' (not, one suspects, a crowded specialism) Avery Gilbert has devoted himself to 'olfaction – the strange and wonderful world of smell'. He offers a precise analysis (as Orwell's is a precise description) of the exclusive masculinity of the cheese-on-towels smell. In a recent study,

> researchers . . . spent three winters collecting droplets of fresh sweat from volunteers in the sauna. It turns out that women have far higher amounts of the MSH precursor than do men, which means women (or rather the bacteria that love them) can liberate significantly more of the sulfur volatiles that smell like

tropical fruit and onions. Male BO, in contrast, tends to smell cheesy and rancid.[6]

That gender-distinct odour is something that only a nasal virtuoso would pick up on. Orwell qualifies as just such a virtuoso of the nostril.

Nose or Nez?

For eight-year-old Eric Blair, St Cyprian's was a traumatizing culture shock, beginning with the affront to his young nose. It was not a wholly English nose, which was a major part of the problem.

Eric Blair was half French. He was brought up by a French mother in the expatriated absence of his English father, in his form-ative first seven years of life. The Blair household, by the Thames, was, behind its walls, as Gallic as a household along the Loire. His essen-tial Frenchness was efficiently camouflaged in later life by an ultra, almost theatrical, English carapace. Close friends, such as Anthony Powell, saw through it. For those not close to him he was as 'English' as the legendary Major Thompson (played by Jack Buchanan in *The French, They Are a Funny Race*, 1955).

Orwell's 'toothbrush' (pubic hair of the upper lip) and unflowing locks ('short back and sides, please' – in later life he would perform it himself with kitchen scissors) were the kind uniformly adopted by young English men in the early twentieth century, to proclaim that they were no Oscar Wildes (Francophile and worse). 'Nancies'? Orwell despised them, viz. the (outrageously homophobic, by today's standards) opening chapters of *Keep the Aspidistra Flying*. The 'tash' also served as a barrier between the nose and the smelly world outside.

Photographs bear out the fact that no great author was less the dandy than George Orwell. A cadaver with suits that hung like an unwashed shroud is the usual verdict of friends such as the dapper

Malcolm Muggeridge. Gordon Bowker notes amusingly that in
his Jura period Orwell actually carried a scythe and shotgun around
with him – looking like something out of Ingmar Bergman's
The Seventh Seal. But as a small and rather touching filial tribute
he chose poodles, the dandy's pooch, as his favoured domestic pet
(his mother, Ida, had bred them). One poodle, in later life, he called
'Marx' – the closest he ever got to reading *Das Kapital*, as Bernard
Crick, never one to admire Orwell as a political thinker, sourly
observes.

Maternal, Gallic influence meant that young Eric was wholly
unacculturated to the nasal shocks of St Cyprian's and their under-
lying ideological meaning. If there were a word that summed up the
ethos of schools like the one his parents sent him to, it was 'manly'.
The above 'plunge bath', for example, would have been 'bracingly'
chill. The testicle-shrivelling 'cold bath' or 'shower' is, for the English,
a moral, not a sanitary thing. It forms 'character'. In *A Clergyman's
Daughter*, the heroine, Dorothy, takes a cold bath at 5.30 every
morning to purify her mind and tame her body. The English shiver
into virtue. Warm baths, the pupils at St Cyprian's would have been
ritually warned, led to the downfall of the Roman Empire. No such
fate should befall England's dominions.

Nations, societies and groups founded on a bedrock of puritanism, like the UK and U.S., take up arms (up to the very armpits
themselves) against smell, as militantly as Christians going to war.
In the hazy picture that Christians traditionally have of the place,
hell is horrifically odorous. Its smell (like rotting eggs but worse) is
fearful. In an illuminating book, *Why Hell Stinks of Sulfur: Mythology
and Geology of the Underworld* (2013), Salomon Kroonenberg traces
our conviction that those of us condemned to suffer eternal damna-
tion will have our noses punished, while devils go at our rumps with
pitchforks, and the large worm feasts on us as the whim takes it.

Heaven (with all those freshly laundered white robes) is as odour-
free as we would like our inconveniently odoriferous bodies to be.

We spray every dubious carnal pit, hole and suspect warm place. Perhaps, we fantasize, the tiniest 'fragrance' is permissible 'up there' – the 'odour of sanctity', for example, which hovers over the rotting flesh of those destined for beatitude when mother church gets round to it (Orwell's first – incense-laden – primary school was run by nuns).

Miltonic Stench

Cosmic stink/fragrance merits a short digression. Orwell discovered *Paradise Lost* when he was sixteen. He read, in a small tutorial group at Eton, the whole poem aloud. 'It sent', he later recalled, 'shivers down my backbone.'[7] Another tingler.

Anyone who, like Orwell, knows the poem will recall how extraordinarily, and theologically, smelly it is. There is no mystery as to why Milton should have been so sensitized. He was blind and his other senses were sharpened in compensation. To take one of many examples, the following typically extended Miltonic simile describes Satan's (the fiend's) use of seductive odour (Milton, puritan that he was, did not approve of perfume. Or Satan):

> now gentle gales
> Fanning their odoriferous wings dispense
> Native perfumes, and whisper whence they stole
> Those balmy spoils. As when to them who sail
> Beyond the Cape of Hope, and now are past
> Mozambic, off at sea north-east winds blow
> Sabean odours from the spicy shore
> Of Arabie the blest, with such delay
> Well pleased they slack their course, and many a league
> Cheered with the grateful smell old ocean smiles.
> So entertained those odorous sweets the fiend
> Who came their bane, though with them better pleased
> Than Asmodeus with the fishy fume,

That drove him, though enamoured, from the spouse
Of Tobit's son, and with a vengeance sent
From Media post to Aegpyt, there fast bound.
(*Paradise Lost*, IV, 156–71)

There are no fewer than six different smells described in these dozen lines.

When, by contrast, in Book V the archangel Raphael comes to Eden to warn Adam and Eve, he shakes his wings and exudes a decently 'heavenly fragrance' – no deceptive Sabean odour or fishy fume.[8]

Holy/Unholy Smell

Smells, one agrees with Milton, are charged with religious significance. According to the *Washington Post*, over 90 per cent of Americans, adult and teenage, use deodorants as a gusset tribute to the puritan fathers of the nation. Most do so 'religiously' around the time when puritans would say their morning prayers. These applications are laboratory-designed to 'kill' smell – at source. They are also implausibly accused of killing their too-enthusiastic users. But a few cancers are, surely, a small price to pay for national odourlessness.

One can fancifully draw up a list of objects and rituals that define the cultural distance created by 21 miles of channel. The bidet; the caporal cigarette with its North African 'bite'; the stale incense of the country church at noon on a hot day in Provence; the olive-oil tang wafting from the adjoining street café; the open street 'pissoir' on a warm night; the fragrance that, to this day, wafts with dry, offshore winds over the Côte d'Azur from Grasse; the 'bouquet' of its perfumeries; the mouth-watering aroma of café express and fresh croissant; the memory-stirring madeleine.

Only French culture could produce such triumphs of *art nasale* as Huysmans' *Le Gousset* (in his *Croquis Parisiens*) – an extended rhapsody on the woman's armpit: 'no aroma has more *nuances*.' Research (there's not much in this area) has discovered that it is maternal armpit odour that draws the baby to its food supply underneath.

To summarize: for the Americans, it's purifying deodorant; for the French, enriching fragrance. For the English, as the German cynic von Treitschke put it, 'soap is civilization.' The 'Great Unwashed' is a very different concept from *sansculottes* or *Lumpenproletariat* or white trash. That 'cleanliness is next to Godliness' has been drilled proverbially into English children for centuries. The hope of resurrection requires a carbolic bar in one hand and the Bible in the other. Salvation is hinted at by the premier soap of Orwell's day (and mine), 'Lifebuoy'. sos. Soap saves souls.

In later life the rule is: 'Working classes sweat, gentlemen perspire, ladies "glow".' Class and gender are subtly involved in our engagement with smell. And, of course, selfhood.

Olfactory Narcissism

Most people enjoy the sight of their own handwriting as they enjoy the smell of their own farts.

w. h. auden

Gordon Bowker argues that Blair/Orwell sought out 'evil odours . . . as if to rub his own nose in them to exorcise his demons through self-inflicted suffering'. But there seems to be interest, and on occasion relish, in his fascination with smell.

One suspects that Blair/Orwell was of that sexual group of paraphiliacs for whom Freud could only devise a French term – renifleurisme; male erotic gratification from the covert sniff.[9] Freud developed the theory and practice of the renifleur in his case study of the 'Rat Man' (an appropriate pseudonym for Orwell). Shoes and underwear are the two popular fetish objects for the active renifleur.

Both, of course, must have been used, and must still reek with the spoor of their owner.

A relevant literary comparison comes to mind. Orwell, as has been said, was late coming to James Joyce – in 1933, as he was writing *A Clergyman's Daughter*. He must have been struck by the idea that Joyce was as connoisseurial about sexual smell as he was. A 'smell narrative' of *A Portrait of the Artist as a Young Man* would be as lengthy as any novel of Orwell's.

In *Portrait*, Joyce observes that smell is the primal sense the newly arrived human being uses to make sense of its extra-uterine environment. Freud calls this the 'anal stage'. It is vitally important for the newborn child to recognize the smell of the milk-giver, and to clamp onto it. The autobiographical *Portrait* opens with little Stephen, two years old, 'all ears' under the table as his family argues. He thinks: 'When you wet the bed first it is warm then it gets cold. His mother put on the oilsheet. That had the queer smell. His mother had a nicer smell than his father.'

It is a few years later that more complex sensory discrimination is cultivated. In his Swift essay, Orwell recalls the child's 'horror of snot and spittle, of the dogs' excrement on the pavement, the dying toad full of maggots, the sweaty smell of grown-ups, the hideousness of old men, with their bald heads and bulbous noses'. It's a little coming of age, and a toe-dipping plunge into the universal cesspit. The child, of course, whatever its dislike of the 'sweaty smell of grown-ups', has grown, over the years, to be fond of its own ('my') smells and treats them as treasured properties, privately and, usually, shamefully as it grows older. Hence Auden's remark above about one's own farts. Other people's are mephitic.

James Joyce records the olfactory narcissism ('my smell, right or wrong') more indulgently than Orwell. There remained enough Catholic in the Irish writer to absolve himself of this little carnal indulgence. Most interesting in *Portrait* is the passage describing Stephen's self-mortification, in his religiously fanatic period. He

determines to bring 'each of his senses under a rigorous discipline'.
Sight and hearing are relatively easy. But

> To mortify his smell was more difficult as he found in himself
> no instinctive repugnance to bad odours whether they were the
> odours of the outdoor world, such as those of dung or tar, or
> the odours of his own person among which he had made many
> curious comparisons and experiments.

His most intimate body odours are dear to him, because they are his
own. But what is implied by 'many curious comparisons and experi-
ments'? It requires an inward holding of the nose to pursue that
question.

Joyce, an unashamed coprophiliac (as, one can conjecture, was
Orwell – hence his recurrent use of the word 'faecal'), was driven
to ecstasies of erotic excitement by female soiled knickers. He once
disclosed that all he needed to come to climax was a sniff of his wife
Nora's underwear. In one of the famous 'dirty letters', he rhapsodizes,

> The smallest things give me a great cockstand – a whorish
> movement of your mouth, a little brown stain on the seat of your
> white drawers, a sudden dirty word spluttered out by your wet
> lips, a sudden immodest noise made by your behind and then a
> bad smell slowly curling up out of your backside.

Joyce's 'dirty letters' were not published until half a century after
Orwell's death.[10] It's interesting to speculate what the latter would
have made of passages like the above. There might well have been
fraternal sympathy.

Madeleines and All That

> When from a long-distant past nothing subsists, after the people are dead, after the things are broken and scattered, taste and smell alone, more fragile but more enduring, more unsubstantial, more persistent, more faithful, remain.
>
> MARCEL PROUST, *Remembrance of Things Past*

Comparisons with the so-called 'Proust Phenomenon' (as psychologists call it) – *temps perdus* recovered via the smell of a teacake – are not out of place when discussing Orwell's fiction. As his amiable 'Tubby' Bowling puts it in *Coming Up for Air* (we first encounter him in the family 'lav'), the past is a very curious thing:

> It's with you all the time. I suppose an hour never passes without your thinking of things that happened ten or twenty years ago, and yet most of the time it's got no reality, it's just a set of facts that you've learned, like a lot of stuff in a history book. Then some chance sight or sound or smell, especially smell, sets you going, and the past doesn't merely come back to you, you're actually IN the past.

Science is as interested in the Proust Phenomenon as literature is. In what is claimed to be the largest ever investigation to date,

> the National Geographic survey gave readers a set of six odours on scratch-and-sniff cards. From a sample of 26,200 respondents (taken randomly from over 1.5 million responses), 55% of respondents in their 20s reported at least one vivid memory cued by one of the six odours and this fell to just over 30% of respondents in their 80s, remarkable proportions with such a small number of odours.[11]

In his essay 'Music at Night' (1932), Aldous Huxley foresaw, with a shudder, cinemas of the future in which 'egalitarians' (Huxleyese for 'proles') will experience the total sensory barrage of 'talkies, tasties, smellies, and feelies'. In the manuscript of *Nineteen Eighty-Four* Orwell also played with the idea of 'smelloscreens'. Roll on, say I. Orwell and Joyce will be rich sources for this madeleine for the people.

The Sour Smell of Politics

> To see what is in front of one's nose needs a constant struggle.
> ORWELL (1946)

Orwell's socialism is a battleground, best avoided by those who do not wish to find themselves in a slough of hot-tempered tedium. One thing one can safely say is that his political thought is common-sensical and that the Orwellian 'smell test' is central to it. Who but Orwell would diagnose the current (1936) malaise of socialism nose-first, as a malodour? 'Socialism, at least in this island, does not smell any longer of revolution and the overthrow of tyrants; it smells of crankishness, machine-worship, and the stupid cult of Russia. Unless you can remove that smell, and very rapidly, Fascism may win.'[12] It is hard to think of it inspiring a rousing call ('We Must Reform our Smell, Comrades!') at the annual Labour Party Conference. But it is echt Orwellism.

Orwell trusted the 'smell test', and made crucial changes in his life on the strength of it. When he came back for good, after five years in Burma, 'one sniff of English air' confirmed that he had done the right thing. The nose knows. One inhalation, and he decided he was never going back.

Orwell was, elsewhere, raised to heights of mirthful satire by the odour of left-wing 'crankishness':

It would help enormously, for instance, if the smell of crankishness which still clings to the Socialist movement could be dispelled. If only the sandals and the pistachio-coloured shirts could be put in a pile and burnt, and every vegetarian, teetotaller, and creeping Jesus sent home to Welwyn Garden City to do his yoga exercises quietly!

Beaujolais Socialism

The money stink everywhere
Keep the Aspidistra Flying

Another kind of socialism – which Orwell repudiated more angrily – was the hypocritical, silk sheets, variety. There is a telling episode in *Keep the Aspidistra Flying*. Gordon Comstock (a 'moth-eaten', short-arse, prematurely burned out, talentless, self-punitive caricature of Orwell himself) bullies his rich magazine-proprietor friend and patron, Philip Ravelston, into accompanying him into a working-class pub. Ravelston is an ungrateful caricature of Richard Rees, the 'socialist baronet' and proprietor of *The Adelphi*. It was 'Dickie' who assisted Orwell into authorship, publishing the nucleus of articles that became his first book, *Down and Out in Paris and London*.

Comstock drags his rich best friend into the awful-smelling spit-and-sawdust boozer. What follows is usefully summarized via its 'smell narrative'. 'A sour cloud of beer seemed to hang about [the place]. The smell revolted Ravelston.' They are served two pints of 'dark common ale' ('mild', for those who can remember the sickly-sweet-smelling swill). The air is 'thick with gunpowdery tobacco-smoke'. Ravelston catches sight of a well-filled spittoon near the bar, averts his eyes and thinks, wistfully, of the wines of Burgundy.

The two friends have their usual argy-bargy about socialism. Ravelston tries, vainly, to explain Marx. What does Marx mean, Comstock snorts, in the stinking 'spiritual sewer' to which £2 a week has consigned him? 'He began to talk in obscene detail of his life in Willowbed Road [his fifteen-bob-a-week lodgings]. He dilated on the smell of slops and cabbage, the clotted sauce-bottles in the dining-room, the vile food.' 'It's bloody,' murmurs Ravelston several times, in feeble sympathy. Bad-tempered, and with a belly full of bad beer, the two men go out into the now night-time street. The discussion drags on. If you're poor, says Comstock, those who are not poor hate you – because you have a bad smell: 'It's like those ads for Listerine. "Why is he always alone? Halitosis is ruining his career." Poverty is spiritual halitosis.'

Perverse, thinks Ravelston, with an automatic sniff. Desirable women won't look at you, complains Gordon, now in full cry. You have to buy sex from women who smell as bad as you (there's a later scene when, very drunk, Gordon does just that). Ravelston thinks, inwardly, of his fragrant mistress, Hermione, as wholesome to her lover's nostrils as a 'wheatfield in the sun'. 'Don't talk to me about the lower classes,' she always says whenever he brings up his damned socialism. 'I hate them. They SMELL.' She must not call them the 'lower classes', he objects mildly (tacitly agreeing with the smell point). They are the 'working class'. Very well, she says, 'But they *smell* just the same.'

The two men go their separate ways: Comstock to his 'slops and cabbage' in Willowbed Road; Ravelston by taxi to his flat, where a sleepy Hermione is waiting for him, curled voluptuously, half-dressed, in an armchair. 'We'll go out and have supper at Modigliani's,' she commands (in other words, Quaglino's in Piccadilly, London's best restaurant). In the taxi she lies against him, still half asleep, her head pillowed on his breast. The 'woman-scent' breathes out of her. Philip inhales it, sensually, thinking of his favourite corner table at Modigliani's and of sex, trying not to think of that vile pub with its hard benches, stale beer-stink and brass spittoons.

Outside Modigliani's a beggar importunes them for money: 'A cup of tea, guv'nor!' The request is half-coughed through 'carious teeth'. Halitosis. Spittle. Phlegm. SMELL. Hermione forbids Ravelston to give this human offal a single penny. Ravelston obeys. His socialism is a paper and print thing. He loves the people – but not their smell. He and Hermione dine, expensively, on grilled rump steak and half a bottle of Beaujolais. A feast to the nose and the palate.

Orwell's feelings towards Rees and his kind were deeply confused. He was grateful enough for favours given to name his son (Richard Blair) after the socialist baronet who so helped his early career and whom he made his literary executor. He liked the man. Who could not? Everyone who knew him liked him. Yet Orwell hated Rees 'for what he was'. Rees/Ravelston's kind of socialism, well meant as it might be, *smelled* wrong to Orwell because it had the aroma of expensively scented sex, French cuisine and newly washed underwear, after the morning bath fragrant with its expensive Selfridges-bought 'salts'. Where, then, was the healthy 'smell' of socialism to be found? Not in that 'hotbed' of theory, the LSE, dominated by the Laski faction – those incorrigible abusers of plain English (half-gramophone, half-megaphone, all phoney) and sympathizers with Moscow. Not in the brimming chamber pot under the working-class Wigan breakfast table. Not in what is called, in *Aspidistra*, the 'money stink' that leaks, like furtively broken wind, from the well-meaning, well-bred rich, like Ravelston.

It is found in two places, one deduces from Orwell's writing. One is the naked coal miner, hundreds of feet underground, his finely muscled body exposed in the murky light: 'but nearly all of them have the most noble bodies; wide shoulders tapering to slender supple waists, and small pronounced buttocks and sinewy thighs, with not an ounce of waste flesh anywhere.' Around them the 'fiery dusty smell' of their work place. It is a 'real' smell. The stench of honest labour and erect manhood. The other location where socialism smells 'right' is the trenches of wartime Spain. 'I suppose I have failed to convey more than a little of what those months in Spain meant to me,' says Orwell in the epilogue to *Homage to Catalonia*:

'I have recorded some of the outward events, but I cannot record the feeling they have left me with. It is all mixed up with sights, smells, and sounds that cannot be conveyed in writing.' Orwell's nose can do more than most, but it cannot put into words what it knows, on the senses, is right, and what is wrong.

And what, one wonders, would socialism smell of now, in the second decade of the twenty-first century, were Orwell and his diagnostic nose here to sniff it for us?

Personal

Nineteen Eighty-Four is at the top of teachers' list of books 'every student should read before leaving secondary school'.

NATIONAL ASSOCIATION FOR THE TEACHING OF ENGLISH, July 2015

My acquaintance with Orwell occurred on 19 December 1954 – I can date it as precisely as my wedding days.

Nineteen Eighty-Four was published, by Orwell's most loyal publisher, Frederic Warburg, on 9 June 1949. It sold brilliantly but by the autumn of 1954, three years after Orwell's death, reprint sales had steadied to 150 a month; just sufficient to keep the novel in print. It was not, as now, a novel that the schoolteachers of England were advised to drill into their pupils like imams in a madrasa.

All this changed with Nigel Kneale's 'horror' adaptation, put out by the BBC on Sunday evening, 12 December 1954. With it the novel's rise to supersellerdom took off like a Guy Fawkes rocket from a milk bottle. The fact that it was the first novel in which the arch-villain is a television set must have helped. BB was watching Winston. When, then, would the BB(C) be watching us?

My family home couldn't yet run to a 'goggle-box'. I missed out on the first broadcast but, inflamed by playground gossip ('rats! eyeballs!'), I was careful to book a place with a better-off friend to see the repeat, a week later. It wasn't actually a repeat in the modern sense, there being no video technology then. The cast, troupers all, went through the whole thing again.

The production starred Peter Cushing as Winston Smith (the eighty-year-old Churchill, after whom he is named, was currently prime minister, which added a resonance). Cushing's constipated, haunted look would be carried over into his portrayals of arch-agents of light versus darkness in Hammer Horror films of the 1960s. There was a preliminary Auntyish warning that the programme was 'unsuitable for children or those with weak nerves'. This had the predictable effect of gluing even the most susceptible viewer (including, of course, fifteen-year-old schoolchildren like myself) to the screen, their nerves pinging like over-wound violin strings.

The dramatization (still available on YouTube, as a muzzy TV-grab from the surviving 35-mm film) opened with a clanging overture based on Holst's 'Mars' and the monitory voiceover: 'This is *one* man's alarmed view of the future' (not, that is, Lord Reith's view). There followed a Wagnerian montage of atomic explosions before the opening scenes in Minitrue (an institution inspired, as we dimly apprehended, by the BBC's Broadcasting House). And so, with the competent performance level of a good provincial repertory company, the narrative rolled on, for one hour and 47 minutes, to rats and eyeballs. Orwell's bleak ending was respected by Kneale (as it was not in the CIA-financed animated film of *Animal Farm* that also came out in 1954; or the CIA-financed American version of *Nineteen Eighty-Four*).

The effect of the 1954 dramatization of *Nineteen Eighty-Four* on the population – soon, they were informed, to become telescreen-enslaved citizens of 'Airstrip One: Oceania' – was electrifying. Susceptible housewives, who had lived serenely through the Blitz, were reported (apocryphally) to have died of shock watching the 'H[orror] Programme'. On 15 December five Conservative MPs put down a motion deploring 'the tendency evident in recent BBC programmes, notably on Sunday evening, to pander to sexual and sadistic tastes'. A less pompously inclined weather forecaster began his bulletin with 'Stand by your sets, Citizens, bad news coming up.'

Television lives by viewing figures. Those for *Nineteen Eighty-Four* were, for a live drama, unprecedented. The tally (seven million) was exceeded only by that for the coronation of Queen Elizabeth the previous year. 'Big Brother is watching you', 'doublethink', 'thought-crime' and the 'two-minute hate' became catchphrases. They still are.

The 1954 televization jump-started Orwell's upward progress to his present status as the Cassandra of his time. All time, perhaps. As the estate's literary agent, Bill Hamilton, reported in January 2015: 'Interest in Orwell is accelerating and expanding practically daily . . . We're selling in new languages – Breton, Friuli, Occitan – Total income has grown 10% a year for the last three years.'[3] With some difficulty (it's not yet on Google Translate) I've discovered that the Occitan for 'Big Brother Is Watching You' is 'Gròs Hrair T'espia'.

Not only has *Nineteen Eighty-Four* lasted, selling nowadays better than ever; it is, we're told, a work of biblical importance. In November 2014 a list was drawn up on behalf of YouGov (or 'You the People Govern', an interesting example of what Orwell calls 'Newspeak'), asking a representative two thousand members of the reading public what they thought were 'the most valuable books to humanity'. The top ten were as follows:

1) The Bible (37 per cent)
2) *The Origin of Species* (35 per cent)
3) *A Brief History of Time* (17 per cent)
4) *Relativity: The Special and General Theory* (15 per cent)
5) *Nineteen Eighty-Four* (14 per cent)
6) *Principia Mathematica* (12 per cent)
7) *To Kill a Mockingbird* (10 per cent)
8) The Qur'an (9 per cent)
9) *The Wealth of Nations* (7 per cent)
10) *The Double Helix* (6 per cent)

Nineteen Eighty-Four is judged more 'valuable to humanity' than the Qur'an. Not everyone (probably not two billion everyones in the Islamic world) would agree. But few would disagree with the assertion that Orwell 'matters'. It is a pity he did not live to enjoy the vast revenue (the copyright is still in force for another five years) and join his rich friends on equal terms. What Orwell – who is recorded as giving away his meagre ration-book coupons to the deserving during the war – would have done with great wealth is a nice speculation.

I devoured *Nineteen Eighty-Four* in the days following the 1954 broadcast and had read all the principal works by the end of 1955.[14] Any relationship such as mine with Orwell has been enriched by Penguin's handsome, budget-price reprints (Allen Lane was a staunch admirer); by the four-volume *The Collected Essays, Journalism and Letters of George Orwell* (Secker & Warburg, London, 1968), edited by Ian Angus and Sonia Orwell; and, climactically, by the twenty-volume *Complete Works of George Orwell* (1998). This last was the life's work of Peter Davison. His efforts took seventeen years and required a sextuple bypass to complete, he told the launch party under UCL's cupola, fifty yards from where Orwell had died. Few literary critics would pay the price that Davison did.

The posthumous biographical situation has been troubled. In the will made three days before his death, Orwell forbade biography. His widow, Sonia, whom he married on his deathbed, would be a ferocious guardian of the flame. It may be that Orwell had that prohibition in mind when he made her his 'future widow', as he bluntly put it. It may be, as Gordon Bowker shrewdly suggests, that she insisted on it, as a kind of prenup/post-mortem. In the years after her husband's death, Sonia slammed the door in the face of any serious life-writer (as they are now called) by appointing the deeply unserious Malcolm Muggeridge, in 1955, as the 'authorized biographer' – with the implicit understanding that he would do nothing. He did nothing.

The first biographers to do something, Peter Stansky and William Abrahams, were forbidden by Sonia to quote any in-copyright material and were denied access to literary remains. Friends and family were instructed not to cooperate. A ferocious anathema was published in the TLS when their book appeared. Sonia was convinced that they had somehow cheated her. But working as they did, shortly after Orwell's death, the American biographers had access to living sources. Their work, hampered as it was, has been foundational in the personally vouched-for witness it supplies.

Nonetheless, Stansky and Abrahams were stumped, as all biographers have been, by strange turns in Orwell's life. Why, having excelled at prep school, did he slack at Eton, closing off access to privileges that, with some effort, were his for the taking? Why did he, already sceptical about Empire, enrol and serve for five years in one of the most brutally exploited and neglected of the Crown's colonial territories? And then, why did he come back, an Etonian, God help us, and plunge into the down-and-out depths of London and Paris?

Born into a class neurotic about sanitation, what was it about dirt that so fascinated and obsessed Orwell? He went to Spain, as many of the militant left did, but why volunteer for a Fred Karno's Circus outfit like the POUM? Anarchists are damnably efficient terrorists but they do not make good soldiers of the line. What on earth does 'Tory anarchism', as Orwell called it, mean? Where, precisely, did Orwell's 'socialism' lie? Was he, come to that, really a socialist? Did he love the working class (the 'animals' of *Animal Farm*) or did they, particularly their porcine (trade union) leaders, disgust him to the point of nausea? Did he ever tell the low-life characters he dossed and tramped with, and the miners he accompanied, that Mr Blair was writing about them, unflatteringly, under another name? Why, in the last year of his life, was he so desperately keen to marry? Why, on his deathbed, was he so insistently desperate that there should be no biography when so much of his writing was infused with autobiography?

Why did he, the creator of Big Brother, compose his 'list' – a *lettre de cachet* – denouncing people who thought they were his friends to one of the more sinister British secret-service agencies?[15] One could extend the questions, but it is enough to say that his life is wreathed in enigma.

My Orwell Problem: And Yours? 'VH'

The problem is small – relative to what is unproblematically great in Orwell's achievement. But it is troublesome. One could call it 'VH' – the vein of hurtfulness in his fiction to those who did nothing to deserve cruelty.

Examples are legion. How could he, for example, write that cruel description of a son's callous indifference at his father's funeral in *Coming Up for Air*, as his own father was dying of cancer? (Luckily Richard Blair went to his burial having read only a glowing review of the novel.) His mother and sisters (particularly) had sacrificed their life chances for Eric's expensive, and apparently wasted, start in life (as his father sacrificed a painfully large chunk of his income). It was not an easy thing for a family of four on £450 a year to send a child to Eton. Resourcefully, in 1933, Orwell's mother and sister Avril set up a tea room and bridge club, 'The Copper Kettle', in Southwold's Queen Street, where the family was then living. The café was a success and won them respectful affection from townspeople, along with good trade from summer holidaymakers. The Blairs' Southwold tea room is scornfully rubbished in *A Clergyman's Daughter*. In fact Avril did very well out of the Copper Kettle and her locally famed cakes. She even bought herself a new car with the profits. Orwell himself could not, for most of his life, afford motorized transport better than second-hand motorbikes. Avril had some right to be proud of her small achievement. What, then, did she and her mother (who ran the Copper Kettle bridge club) make of passages in *A Clergyman's Daughter* like the following (Knype Hill is, transparently, Southwold):

> The two pivots, or foci, about which the social life of the town moved were Knype Hill Conservative Club (fully licensed) . . . and Ye Olde Tea Shoppe, a little farther down the High Street, the principal rendezvous of the Knype Hill ladies. Not to be present at Ye Olde Tea Shoppe between ten and eleven every morning, to drink your 'morning coffee' and spend your half-hour or so in that agreeable twitter of upper-middle-class voices [it goes on lengthily in this vein].

The scorn shocks ('Ye Olde Tea Shoppe'?) When he wrote this, Orwell, a thirty-year-old layabout, was out of work in his parents' house, convalescing from pneumonia, at the very period the women were setting up their brave venture. He evidently disapproved.

When, after the publication of *A Clergyman's Daughter*, he was on his uppers, his rich, aristocratic and ever-obliging friend Richard Rees helped find him a stop-gap job in a bookshop in Hampstead – then, as now, the most intellectually active enclave in Britain. The bookshop, a local institution at the corner of Pond Street and South End Road (there's a Daunt's nearby now) was called the 'Booklovers' Corner'. The branch of Le Pain Quotidien that has replaced it in this degenerate age has a plaque commemorating Orwell's fifteen months' service as an assistant and manager in the shop.[16] The first fifty pages of *Keep the Aspidistra Flying* revolve around Gordon Comstock's wage slavery in Booklovers' Corner – unnamed in the novel. The proprietor in the novel is Mr McKechnie, a white-haired and white-bearded 'dilapidated' Scotsman (a nation Orwell peculiarly disliked). He is a chronically lazy, penny-pinching, stupid, rabidly teetotal, snuff-taking ignoramus who underpays and exploits Gordon before firing him for a night on the town that landed him in jail.

The actual proprietor of Booklovers' Corner was Frank
Westrope. A founder member of the Independent Labour Party
(with which Orwell would affiliate himself a couple of years later),
Westrope had been imprisoned for years as a conscientious objector
during the First World War. His conduct was gallant. He was still,
in the mid-1930s, under surveillance (as was Orwell when he worked
in the shop) by MI5. He was no teetotaller. He would certainly have
been indulgent to, and amused by, a youngster as bright as Orwell
(it was by this name that Eric Blair introduced himself to Westrope)
who went on the razzle and found himself up in front of the beak
next morning. Westrope's wife, Myfanwy, had thrown herself into
the suffrage movement. It would not, until 1928, fully emancipate
women.[7] The kindest of landladies, she gave Orwell a bedsit around
the corner, rent-free for six months, and intimated that she would
turn a blind eye if he invited girlfriends in (this was freethinking
Hampstead). He did. Noisily, according to later complaints (he was
running at least two women – 'compartmentalized', as one of them
later complained – during his months at the shop).

In the novel, Gordon pigs it in wretched lodgings: his ogre of a
landlady's ears are always suspiciously cocked to hear any creaking
bed springs in the rooms of her 'paying guests'. Then it's 'pack your
bags and get out, you filthy fellow'.

Booklovers' Corner also had a 'tuppenny library' of current best-
sellers. Good-Bad Books, as Orwell called the best of them. These,
however, were not, all of them, the best bad books. They were tat
of the Ethel M. Dell and Edgar Wallace kind. Before Allen Lane's
Penguins came on the scene in 1936, 'tuppenny' loans were a profitable sideline. Even Boots the Chemist lent them. Orwell is scathing
in *Keep the Aspidistra Flying* about the clientele who patronize the
800 volumes of 'soggy, half-baked trash' Gordon is in charge of.
Dowdy, ill-smelling women, so-called 'book lovers', come in, looking
like 'draggled ducks nosing among garbage', with their insatiable
appetite for Ethel M. Dell's romantic slush and the loathed Warwick

Booklovers' Corner: Gordon Comstock's hell.

Deeping (author of *Sorrell and Son*, 1925). Similarly held up for scorn are timid smut hunters (how Lawrence's *Women in Love* will disappoint them!) and 'nancies', delicately fondling books about ballet. There is not a single admirable customer in the hateful bookshop Gordon superintends, and no 'Hampstead Intellectuals'.

Victor Gollancz, the publisher of *Keep the Aspidistra Flying* – soon to launch, in 1936, his Left Book Club (in which Orwell would later publish *The Road to Wigan Pier*) – had a high regard for his fellow socialist Frank Westrope and for Hampstead intellectuals generally. When Gollancz pointed out to Orwell that the depiction of Frank (and, indirectly, his wife) was derogatory and possibly libellous, the author replied, in honest innocence, how could that be? Mr McKechnie is Scottish, has a white beard and takes snuff. Frank Westrope was clean-shaven, English and did not take snuff. Case closed. No malicious intent whatsoever. Orwell, so clear-headed about so many things, never seems to have worked out what libel and its consequent criminal damage were. If there was one place in London where a book like *Keep the Aspidistra Flying* was likely to be read (did Westrope display it in the window?), it was bookish Hampstead. What customers, thereafter, would be encouraged to browse and buy from the Westrope establishment with the imputation hanging over them that they were so many draggled ducks, smut hounds and nancy boys? And knowing that the superior young man behind the desk was looking at them with secret contempt, which he would put into print?

Why did Orwell hurt in this way (as he surely did) the Westropes, who had offered him nothing but kindness? What had the kindly Richard Rees, who got him the Booklovers' Corner job (a life saver), done to deserve the lampoon of himself as Ravelston in *Keep the Aspidistra Flying*? Or the literary critic William Empson in *Nineteen Eighty-Four* as the big-brained buffoon Ampleforth? To find yourself in Orwell's novels, said the woman he first loved, was to feel torn limb from limb.

The Two Mistresses of George Orwell

> You might find it interesting to be a writer's widow.
> ORWELL's proposal to his second wife, Sonia

Orwell's depiction of his first wife, Eileen (as Rosemary), in *Keep the Aspidistra Flying* is disparaging.[18] Much more so is the fictional portrait of his second wife. It is accepted that Julia in *Nineteen Eighty-Four* 'is' Sonia. Hilary Spurling titles the memoir of her friend *The Girl from the Fiction Department*. It's how Winston Smith first identifies his future lover.[19]

In *Nineteen Eighty-Four* Julia works in Pornosec (the 'Muck Factory'), engaged in churning out 'the lowest kind of pornography'. Sonia Brownell (later 'Orwell' – she took his pen name in marriage rather than 'Blair') was, in fact, a long-serving co-editor, with Stephen Spender and Cyril Connolly, of the most distinguished literary magazine of the 1940s and early 1950s, *Horizon*.[20] It was no muck factory. Among the galaxy of writers it published was George Orwell. Sonia later worked as an editor at Weidenfeld & Nicolson, where she is credited with 'discovering' the novelist Angus Wilson. She had sound literary, and even better artistic, taste. Anthony Powell depicts her, admiringly and infinitely more kindly than does Orwell in *Nineteen Eighty-Four*, as the efficient Ada Leintwardine in *Books Do Furnish a Room*.

For her lovers, Sonia Brownell was not merely a beauty ('the Venus of Euston Road' – she was sketched by an admiring Picasso and Lucian Freud) and a gratifyingly easy lay (allegedly Connelly would pimp her out to potential backers of his magazine), but an intellectual equal. The love of her life was not Orwell, but the philosopher Maurice Merleau-Ponty. She formed lifelong friendships with such other French intellectuals (her command of French was perfect) as Georges Bataille, Jacques Lacan (later the darling of deconstruction) and the *roman nouveau* novelist Marguerite Duras,

Sonia Orwell (left), the Venus of Euston Road, at work in the *Horizon* office.

whose work Sonia translated and who honoured her with yet another friendly depiction in her fiction.

In *Nineteen Eighty-Four*, Julia is depicted as an intellectual dolt. She falls asleep when Winston Smith reads *The Theory of Oligarchical Collectivism* out loud to her. It is beyond her feeble brain. Sonia

Brownell, by contrast, had no difficulty, we understand, grappling with Merleau-Ponty's *Phénoménologie de la perception*, or Bataille's *Histoire de l'oeil*. Julia's one virtue in *Nineteen Eighty-Four* is that she has a politically rebellious vagina, which she uses like an anarchist's indiscriminate bomb. Winston raves about the organ's voracity. 'Listen,' says Winston, 'The more men you've had, the more I love you. Do you understand that?' Was Sonia's highest claim to Orwell's respect that she had been, over the course of her life, rampantly promiscuous? A living vagina dentata? Sonia had not liked Orwell, when healthy, as a lover. She was one of the 'once in a lifetime with that man is quite enough' party. She was not, the evidence suggests, the 'gold-digger' some biographers have portrayed her as. She would have been the least competent gold-digger in literary history. She died so penniless that her friends Francis Bacon and Hilary Spurling had to kick in for her funeral. The reason she married Orwell, I suspect, was that she respected what he was – a great writer. And serving the writing and art she most admired was her self-imposed mission in life. Stephen Spender liked to tell a story about Sonia that is probably apocryphal but which contains an essential truth about the woman. She was spending a weekend

> in the country with Connolly's friend Dick Wyndham, a leathery, lustful satyr who pursued her round his garden until she dashed into the pond. 'It wasn't his trying to rape me that I mind,' she gasped when the writer Peter Quennell fished her out, 'but that he doesn't seem to realize what Cyril stands for.'

She married Orwell because of what he stood for. Literary greatness.

Particularly hurtful in Orwell's depiction of Julia was O'Brien's casual answer to Winston's question, 'What have you done with Julia?' O'Brien smiles: 'She betrayed you, Winston. Immediately – unreservedly.' Sonia never betrayed the man whose name she bore.

Why, one wistfully thinks, could Orwell not have portrayed a more loyal and clever Julia/Sonia in his last novel? It would not have hurt, in either sense – hurt the novel, or hurt her.

The Dam Breaks

Finally, in 1974, Sonia relented and broke the dying Orwell's prohibition. The pressure had become irresistible. She invited Bernard Crick to write an 'authorized' biography. Crick was the editor of *Political Quarterly* and an LSE-trained political scientist with no outstanding literary-critical qualifications. He was mystified at the summons. Sonia was reportedly won over by a review in which he had called Orwell a 'giant with warts' and by his unrelenting attacks on the then prime minister, Harold Wilson.

Crick took as his guiding thesis the premise that Orwell's great, and achieved, mission had been to turn political writing into art. The subtext, for hard-nosed Crick, was that Orwell's fine words buttered no political parsnips. Himself a no-nonsense writer, Crick had no pretension to any art whatsoever. He was sadly lacking a 'literary touch', sighed Frank Kermode, reviewing the resulting biography.[21] True enough. What political scientist trusts 'literature'? Crick, it was clear, saw Orwell as a political ignoramus.

Sonia did not like one bit this line of biography that she had unwittingly commissioned. Crick was determined that his portrait would be 'external'. There would be no psycho-biographical nonsense. And he would be Solomonic in his judgements. He acid-tests for falseness such ubiquitously quoted (late-life) declarations as: 'From a very early age, perhaps the age of five or six, I knew that when I grew up I should be a writer.'[22] In their milestone four-volume *Collected Essays, Journalism and Letters of George Orwell* Sonia and her co-editor, Ian Angus, use that sentence as their epigraph. This was the dominant Orwellian 'fact'. It was as if a fairy godmother had come to little Eric Blair's cradle, waved a wand and uttered

'Be a writer, my child.' But does it, Crick wondered, if you give it a moment's thought (and recollect your own career aspirations aged five), ring true? A train driver, perhaps. But a 'writer'? By his own account, little Eric was only months past bedwetting. Orwell was, Crick concluded mildly, 'laying it on a bit thick'. He peeled off many other layers of thickness. Leaving what? Not enough to keep admirers of Orwell happy.

Least of all the woman who had 'authorized' Crick. There was much in his account to vex Sonia – and not merely his antipathy to literariness and refusal to take anything Orwell wrote at face value. He chronicled, without moral judgement, Orwell's apparent indifferent attention to his first wife, as she died on the operating table of something he never seemingly inquired about (uterine cancer). And, along the way, there was his wayward, sometimes 'rough', sexuality, of which telling glimpses were on record. Crick glimpsed and recorded, with a cold, camera-like eye. And, unflatteringly to his patroness, he recorded the string of women to whom Orwell impulsively proposed when he knew for a fact that he was dying. Sonia came in at about number five.

Crick's authorized biography saw publication, belatedly, in 1980. A mortified Sonia's last weeks, petulant, alcoholic and broke, were anything but sweetened by the account she had brought into being. Crick's task had been complicated, at every step, by his fallings-out with Sonia. Her touchiness is immortalized by her vitriolic, much-quoted outburst across a dinner table when Crick queried one of the most frequently cited 'facts' about Orwell and Empire: 'Of course he shot the fucking elephant. He said he did. Why do you always doubt his word!' Crick, predictably, is highly sceptical about the elephant-icide, although he valued the famous essay as a brilliant allegory of the rotten core of colonial power.

Orwell inspires moral nobility in his admirers. Crick, not a rich man, made over his royalties to found the Orwell Society and its annual prize.

Orwell in his NUJ picture, 1930s.

Other, less self-restricting, full-life biographies followed. They went, some of them, very psycho-biographical. Gordon Bowker, the most intrepid, promised that 'the main thrust of [my] book will be to reach down as far as possible to the roots of [Orwell's] emotional life, to get as close as possible to the dark sources mirrored in his work.' But all the biographers have been obliged, in the main, to chew over the same old facts, from their subject's first recorded word ('beastly') to the fact that his coffin was six inches too long for his grave. He was always an awkward customer.

Orwell remained shadowy. Maddeningly, for someone who had worked at the BBC, there were no voice or pictorial recordings (he had a 'flat', toneless voice, we are told, croakier after he was shot in the throat in Spain), no moving film and very few photographs of the man. No revealing private journals. Reviewers of Davison's mountainous *Collected Works* concluded that their sense of Orwell had been usefully solidified, but not overset. And the enigmas remained. Still remain. It was almost as if, like Winston Smith, he had a memory hole beside his desk. Stansky and Abrahams had called their quick-off-the-mark biography *The Unknown Orwell* (1972). They, and their successors, could have called it 'the unknowable Orwell'.

The most informative of the post-Crick biographies are currently the third generation (following the work of the Americans Stansky and Abrahams, Michael Shelden and Jeffrey Meyers) by D. J. Taylor and Gordon Bowker, both published in 2003. As a novelist, Taylor lets his imagination loose more than the others. Among Orwell's scrawled final words in his hospital notebook are: 'At 50, every man has the face he deserves.' He never made that age, but what does that rueful, moustached, expressionless face in the few photographs that survived tell us? Taylor was imaginatively speculative about that. He presents, I think, the 'living' Orwell as well as anyone will ever be able to. Paul Foot, in a haughty review of Taylor's biography (it annoyed him as being insufficiently engaged politically), was rude. What next, he asked, a biographical meditation on 'Orwell's bum'?[23]

Actually, that might be interesting, if lifelong scars remained on the traumatically caned buttocks. They might explain a lot about the punitive and self-punitive Orwell.

For me, Taylor's and Bowker's are the biographies to start from, as on their part they started from Crick. Their accounts have been added to, and complicated, by new tranches of correspondence that have more recently come to light. John Rodden has been illuminating.[24] Critical verdicts are in on all the half-dozen or so biographies: mine are supererogatory other than that I have drawn on them gratefully.

What I offer here is an approach from oblique, self-indulgent angles. The relationship of coarse fishing (that smelliest of sports) to Orwell's notion of civilization, for example, may be thought a little too fine-drawn. But the indirect approach can sometimes pay off, as in John Ross's illuminatingly medical *Orwell's Cough* (2012). George Orwell's bum may, I concede, be an obliquity too far.

The Life

I wasn't born for an age like this.

'Why I Write' (1946)

Orwell was born Eric Arthur Blair in Bengal, India, on 25 June 1903, the first and only son of a 46-year-old 'assistant sub-deputy opium agent, 4th grade', on £600 p.a., nine years off retirement and five into late marriage. Pooter in a sola topi, Richard Blair is remembered by his son as a remote 'elderly man forever saying "don't"'. Kids can live with that. What young Eric found beyond bearing was his father's taking out his false teeth, and placing them in a glass on the family table, before eating.

A few months after Eric's birth the family returned 'home'. That they were fleeing an outbreak of plague he probably found piquant in later life. Plague-free since the fifteenth century, Henley-on-Thames was where they settled in 1904 and stayed for ten years. Young Eric liked the place more than anywhere else he would live.

With his family safely taken care of, Richard Blair went back to do his duty (giving grants to Indian poppy farmers to stupefy Chinese addicts, a filthy business) while clambering, at snail's pace, towards 'First Grade Deputy Agent', before the mandatory retirement (given the exhaustions of colonial life), aged 55, in 1912. He was away from England for his son's first eight years of life, apart from three months' furlough (in which he impregnated his wife with a third, certainly unwanted, child, Avril).

Separation was very bearable for Eric and his mother. As Crick relates, one of the few revealing things one knows about Ida Blair is that her usual term for men was 'beasts'. At a very early age, as he recollected, Eric overheard his mother's view of sex, talking to women friends of a similarly independent mind. He could, Orwell apparently felt, write a story, founded on the impression he received that women did not like men:

> they looked upon them as a sort of large, ugly, smelly and ridiculous animal, who maltreated women in every way, above all by forcing their attentions upon them . . . the picture of it in his mind was of a man pursuing a woman, forcing her down and jumping on top of her, as he had often seen a cock do to a hen. All this was derived, not from any remark having direct sexual reference – or what he recognized as a sexual reference – but from such overheard remarks as 'It just shows what beasts men are.'[1]

Eric's first recorded word is not 'ma-ma' or 'da-da', but 'beastly'.

It would have been possible for wife and husband to reunite in India (entrusting Eric to the care of a British boarding school, as other Anglo-Indian parents did), but they did not. Orwell's most formative years were fatherless. He was, by way of compensation, over-mothered. Ida Blair, née Limouzin, was eighteen years younger than her husband, whom she married on the rebound. She was, by blood and cultural background, French-colonial (she had no English passport until late in life, and no desire for one). One of the very few things one knows about her is that she had suffragette sympathies.

Both parents were the offspring of families that had, over the generations, come down in the world. D. J. Taylor traces the paternal Blair heritage from the great-great-great-grandfather who was an earl, through gentry, discreet owners of slaves in the distant Caribbean (Orwell's great-grandfather Charles Blair), high-ranking

Ida the proud mother, with, probably, Avril.

soldiers and sailors and clergymen, to, in the twentieth-century descendants, a few perilous notches above shabby genteel. Orwell is eloquent on that miserable social station in *Keep the Aspidistra Flying*.

Ida's family had been, for three generations back, in the Franco-Burmese teak trade. 'Blood timber', it has been called, for the colonial rapacity of the industry and its indifference to the country it was ruinously deforesting. The rapacity extended beyond timber. Orwell had illegitimate Eurasian relatives on the Limouzin side.[2] (Did Richard Blair console himself with native women in the long years of absence from his family?) The international teak industry changed during the late nineteenth century as forests were bought up by multinationals and as iron took over from the material of which large ships had been made for centuries. The Limouzins did not adapt to changing commercial circumstance, and the clan was falling apart when twenty-year-old Ida married the 39-year-old low-flyer Richard Blair in 1896.

They met and married in a station in the hills of India, away from the heat and the dust, where she was teaching and he was on his annual summer leave. They then moved down to the heat and dust and, probably, a less grand lifestyle than she had been brought up with. Ida's father, Bowker notes, was absent from the wedding – evidence that he disapproved of the age gap and Richard's mediocrity. Whatever romance there was in the marriage was left, one suspects, a fading memory in the cool hills of the northwest.

The parental Blairs have been called 'mismatched', but both, manifestly, were prepared to make painful financial sacrifices for their only son to 'rise'. It was not just their pain. The investment in Eric meant, necessarily, neglect for the two girls, particularly the younger child of the 1907 furlough, Avril. She was destined for that dreariest of fates, being the 'spinster' daughter, helping around the house, an 'old maid' carer of her parents when they were elderly.

Richard died in 1939, Ida in 1943, Eric's elder sister Marjorie in 1946. Avril stayed in Southwold (where the Blairs had resettled, in 1921) – running, after 1933, a tea shop – over the years her family still required her service nearby. For Avril Blair life was probably the superintendence of whatever sink she was nearest, full of other people's dirty crockery. Eric left and came back to the hated Southwold only when broke or at a very loose end. After Orwell's death (and the leaving of his literary estate to his second wife), Avril (not the stepmother, Sonia) took over as carer for his son, young Richard, as she had cared for the old Richard. I remember hearing her on the radio, in the mid-1950s, saying how, as a little girl, she played French cricket with George, but he would never give up the bat. Orwell expresses uneasiness about the way the world – and (one can conjecture) he – treated Avril. But he evidently chose to leave her nothing directly in his will. She was the last of the family, dying in 1978.

The eldest, clever, daughter, Marjorie, broke away early and married a family friend who, on what slender evidence survives, never had much time for uppity Eric. In the seven full-length biographies, the indexes make only bare passing reference to Marjorie, who seems to have been a woman of spirit, as well as clever. The three Blair women knew Eric best: what they knew, we never shall.

Ida determined, when Richard returned in 1912, that there should be no more children, or the beastly act that went into the making of them (separate bedrooms). What went on behind doors in the Blairs' many houses is, again, forever unknowable. Nonetheless, there is an interesting moment in *A Clergyman's Daughter*, explaining the heroine's lifelong horror of sex:

> And yet, though her sexual coldness seemed to her natural and inevitable, she knew well enough how it was that it had begun. She could remember, as clearly as though it were yesterday, certain dreadful scenes between her father and her mother – scenes that she had witnessed when she was no more than nine years old. They had left a deep, secret wound in her mind.

Orwell was, like Dorothy, aged nine when his father retired in 1912. Attempts to reclaim 'conjugal rights', that male right to legally rape an uncooperative spouse, may have been witnessed, or heard behind closed bedroom doors. Richard, it seems, did not get his rights. The retired paterfamilias could, henceforth, find his pleasures on the golf course. There is some wispy recollection that women found his hopeful extramarital gallantries – like those of Mr Warburton in *A Clergyman's Daughter* – unwelcome. Like D. H. Lawrence's Mrs Morel, Ida's 'lover', henceforth, was her gifted son. She had perceived, astutely and from the start, that those gifts were literary and precocious. It was she who took down, to his 'dictation', his 'first poem', composed 'at the age of four or five'. 'I cannot remember anything about it', he much later recalled, 'except that it was about a tiger and the tiger had "chair-like teeth" – a good enough phrase, but I fancy the poem was a plagiarism of Blake's "Tiger, Tiger".'[3] My fancy is that it was *Little Black Sambo*, the story of the little Indian boy who is chased by tigers and runs so fast around a palm tree that the chasing tiger finally expires into a pool of ghee. Sambo's loving mother, Black Mumbo, uses it to cook delicious pancake. It would be an interesting fact, though, if Mrs Blair had indeed read the Swedenborgian Blake to her four-year-old. But hard to picture.

No detailed account of the mother–son relationship has survived. Virtually all the many letters Eric is known to have written her are lost. She would surely have kept them, but after her death in 1943 he must have destroyed them, as he destroyed a lot of records of his life. As *Nineteen Eighty-Four* testifies, 'privacy' was, for him, indivisible from freedom.

It was Ida who planted the seed that would flower into George Orwell's most influential essay ('Politics vs. Literature') by giving little Eric a copy of *Gulliver's Travels* on his eighth birthday. He in fact found the present and devoured it, from beginning to end, the night before (by candlelight, and furtively, one supposes). In the Swift essay, he offers a vignette of the eight-year-old Eric Blair's increasingly bleak view of the world. The quote is worth repeating:

A child, when it is past the infantile stage but still looking at the world with fresh eyes, is moved by horror almost as often as by wonder – horror of snot and spittle, of the dogs' excrement on the pavement, the dying toad full of maggots, the sweaty smell of grown-ups, the hideousness of old men, with their bald heads and bulbous noses.

With his bucket of cold water ever at the ready, Crick suggests that the book must have been a children's 'expurgated' version, without the Laputan totalitarianism and the Yahoo projectile diarrhoea. Nonetheless, it is pleasant to indulge a pretty picture: young Eric creeps downstairs, middle of the night, and is careful not to rustle the paper. Joy! The very book he was asking for. He goes back to his room and reads by night light (he has night terrors – will do as long as he lives). He comes, eyes devouring the page, on the passage in which, in Lilliput, little Gulliver gets out of bed for the nocturnal 'natural necessity'. Eric has a 'gesunder' (goes under the bed) as well. Horror! Two giant rats are running up the bed-curtains 'smelling backwards and forwards on the bed'! One of them comes sniffing at his face – 'these horrible animals' are about to attack his face. But he draws his tiny sword and disembowels one. The other scampers off. Eric will not sleep that night, and the horror (rats 'smelling' your face before biting) will remain with him till he dies.

Orwell calibrated his family's social standing, with contemptuous exactitude, as 'lower-upper middle class'. His wilfully preferred company when he was old enough to choose was either the very low (like the illiterate Irish tramp Paddy)[4] or the very upper classes, such as David Astor or Richard Rees: both very rich, generous and inexhaustibly patient with their difficult and chronically penurious friend. There were no poor people at his two funerals. And he rests, for all time, in the same churchyard as one of the richest men in England: David Astor.

Eric's first school experience was at a nearby convent school, Sunnylands, run by Ursuline nuns who were forbidden to teach in France because of their doctrinal severity. With the exception of young Eric Blair, apparently, it was an all-girls, French-themed establishment. His elder sister, Marjorie, went with him. It was Ida's choice, clearly (Richard was in India). Among the women and girls, Eric experienced the stirrings of what would be in later life an uncontrollable libido. The object of his first love/lust fantasies was a pubescent girl called Elsie. The name has a working-class resonance:

> My friends were the plumber's children up the road, and we used sometimes to play games of a vaguely erotic kind. About the same time I fell deeply in love, a far more worshipping kind of love than I have ever felt for anyone since, with a girl named Elsie at the convent school which I attended. She seemed to me grown up, so I suppose she must have been fifteen.[5]

The phrase 'a far more worshipping kind of love than . . . felt for anyone since' is odd. And the age difference is odder. Since Sunnylands (lovely name) was an infant girls' school, Elsie must have been a skivvy. Orwell immortalized Elsie as the hero's first love in *Coming Up for Air*. That Elsie works not in a school but in a draper's shop. As usual, there is a triggering reference to smell. In a passage oozing the lust of yesteryear, George (Bowling) reminisces:

> You know the atmosphere of a draper's shop. It's something peculiarly feminine. There's a hushed feeling, a subdued light, a cool smell of cloth, and a faint whirring from the wooden balls of change rolling to and fro. Elsie was leaning against the counter, cutting off a length of cloth with the big scissors. There was something about her black dress and the curve of her breast against the counter – I can't describe it, something curiously soft, curiously feminine. As soon as you saw her you knew that you could take her in your arms and *do what you wanted with her* [my italics].

The last words strike an ominous note, as does the 'curiously feminine' smell of a draper's shop.

The 'plumber's children' were of a lower class than the Blairs. Eric was forbidden by Ida to play with them – but clearly did. One recalls Stephen Spender's rueful poem 'My Parents Kept Me from

Children who were Rough'. Young Stephen, a 'good' child, did as he was told. Wilful young Eric did not. The proles always knew fascinatingly more about sex than their betters.

Little Eric had little love for the nuns; perhaps they were too free with their ferrules. In later life Orwell was oddly vengeful about Sunnylands. He recalled in a letter of 1931 to Brenda Salkeld, a clergyman's daughter (who resolutely refused his amorous advances), that when he was a schoolchild

> we had a story that after Robin Hood was done to death in the Priory, his men raped & murdered the nuns, & burned the priory to the ground. It seems this has no foundation in the ballads – we must have made it up. An instance of the human instinct for a happy ending.[6]

The 'happy ending' remark is, on the face of it, breathtaking, particularly since Orwell was writing to a teacher, Brenda, at St Felix School, Southwold, whom he hoped to marry. He proposed to her twice; the surmise is that she never slept with him, despite his urgent requests.

Orwell recorded turning atheist aged fourteen. But Gordon Bowker suggests that the Ursulines implanted in the child Eric a lifelong sense of sin on the Jesuit principle, 'give us a child until he is five and he is ours for life.' Catholic imagery and iconography crop up regularly in Orwell's writing, as in Winston Smith's crazed fantasy about the dark-haired girl from the Fiction (that is, Pornosec) department, whom he thinks to be an agent of the Thought Police:

> Vivid, beautiful hallucinations flashed through his mind. He would flog her to death with a rubber truncheon. He would tie her naked to a stake and shoot her full of arrows like Saint Sebastian. He would ravish her and cut her throat at the moment of climax.

Orwell's unleashed imagination can sometimes terrify and suggest Freudian slips. 'Beautiful' hallucinations? Unlike coevals such as Graham Greene and Evelyn Waugh, there was never any likelihood of Orwell's 'going across'. His attitude to the Catholic Church swung between contempt and paranoid fear. Bowker traces it back to the Ursuline influence.

Around these formative five to six years, there occurred another traumatic event, the first of Eric's recorded encounters with the 'cane'. It happened as he was walking along the street in Henley with his mother. She stopped to talk to a 'wealthy local brewer', who was also a magistrate. He pointed angrily to a tarred fence, vandalized by chalk drawings, one of which was by little Eric:

> The magistrate stops, points disapprovingly with his stick and says, 'We are going to catch the boys who draw on these walls, and we are going to order them SIX STROKES OF THE BIRCH ROD.' (It was all in capitals in my mind.) My knees knock together, my tongue cleaves to the roof of my mouth, and at the earliest possible moment I sneak away to spread the dreadful intelligence.

On this occasion he escaped.[7]

St Cyp's

> If one is looking for a factual account for life at St Cyprian's, this is not the place to seek it.
> PETER DAVISON, on 'Such, Such Were the Joys'

Eric Blair, at eight years old, was manifestly 'bright' and was expertly home-tutored by his adoring, former schoolteacher mother. There were no canes in the Blairs' house in Vicarage Road.[8] With his mother's help and resourcefulness, Eric gained admission to a 'prep' school, St Cyprian's, aged eight. Foreigners are invariably surprised by the English middle- and upper-class practice of entrusting their barely toilet-trained offspring to the care of remote institutions while they look so well after their dogs. Orwell in fact was older than some other entrants at his boarding school, recruited as early as six. It still happens. Foreigners are still astounded.

On the face of it, 'St Cyp's', as boys called it, was well chosen. It stood in handsome grounds in Eastbourne, on the Downs, and advertised its spacious, salubrious, airy setting, facilities and premises. From birth, young Eric had shown clear evidence of pulmonary weakness; ozone-laden breezes would be tonic – what the doctor ordered. Since Florence Nightingale's revolution, the British were fanatical believers in fresh air: a freezing gale whipping across the sleeping child at night was supremely health-giving. The French have always disagreed on that point.

The fairly newly opened St Cyp's had in twelve years gained a formidable reputation under the energetic management of a young couple, the Vaughan Wilkeses, for getting its pupils into 'top' public schools. First-class tickets for life, or, as Cyril Connolly wittily put it, 'hotting boys up . . . like little Alfa Romeos for the Brooklands of life'.[9] Lewis Chitty Vaughan Wilkes taught classics; his wife, Cicely, was the driving force in the marriage and the running of the school. She taught, to sixth-form level, English, History and French. The 'filthy old sow', as Orwell called her (he never liked pigs, and liked her even less), was in fact 37, and the mother of five children – a sizeable litter – when Eric arrived. The boys nicknamed Mr Vaughan Wilkes 'Sambo' (he was, presumably, swarthy in his youth) and her 'Flip' for her flippy-floppy bosom. More docile pupils (most of them, in point of fact) called her more fondly – but still with an eye on the bosom – 'Mum', as presumably did her own children.[10]

Demonstrably (the school honours board displayed the fact) 'Mum' could bring her pupils up to Eton and Harrow entry standard – or, if they were not that bright, get them into one of the less galactic public schools, such as Uppingham. Orwell describes one luckless lad, who failed the lowly Uppingham exams first time round, being flogged into exam competence like a 'foundered horse'. One St Cyprian, a school contemporary of Orwell's, Alaric Jacob, glows in memory of Mum's pedagogy:

> Her classes in English verse would have done credit to an Oxford tutor; by the time I was twelve I was well grounded in poesy and could write a sonnet or an ode that would not have disgraced a much older boy.[11]

Orwell himself became a published schoolboy versifier (see below) under her hand.

Flip had no recorded higher education. Lewis Vaughan Wilkes was a Perse School and Oxford man, dark blue to the core. The couple had met when both were employed at another Eastbourne school, she as a matron, he an assistant master. He (b. 1869) was six years her senior. Flip was the daughter of a stockbroker, and there was, presumably, money enough in her family to found St Cyprian's and get it off the ground. It was soaring by the time Eric Blair arrived.

The fees, £180 p.a., were far beyond the Blairs' means. Richard's salary peaked at £650 p.a. in service, and he would, after 1912, be pensioned on £200 less. But Ida wangled half-fees for Eric. She was helped by the fact that her brother Charlie Limouzin lived in Eastbourne and, a hero on the local links, played golf with Lewis, captain of the club. A vigorous man even in middle age, Wilkes believed in *mens sana in corpore sano* – and so, of course, should his boys. The fact that his wife had family in the Indian service may also have helped Ida's petition. In return for the commuted charge, Eric was expected to reimburse St Cyp's by gaining entry to a top public school. He was 'scholarship fodder'. Cyril Connolly, who was at the school when Eric arrived, offers a pen portrait of the St Cyp's new 'flier': 'Tall, pale with his flaccid cheeks, large spatulate fingers and supercilious voice, he was one of those boys who seem born old.'[12] And manifestly not strong on the *corpore sano* front.

Cyril (nicknamed 'Tim' at school, after Dickens's Tiny Tim) was himself no oil painting and even less athletic than Blair. Short and podgy, he had, through life, a facial resemblance to an insatiably lustful frog. But he was possessed of quick wit and mischievous charm. He was 'winning'. And he, like Eric, was 'scholarship fodder'. The two of them would be chums for life. It would be Connolly, as editor of the wartime magazine *Horizon*, who published many of the essays that made Orwell's name as a socio-political commentator.

Henry Longhurst, later the famous golfer (did he swing his first clubs with Lewis?), came to the school three years after Blair, whom he cordially hated:

> We were transported from Eastbourne Station in a charabanc run by a gas balloon on the roof and met at the door by the most formidable, distinguished and unforgettable woman I am likely to meet in my lifetime. This was Mrs L. C. Vaughan Wilkes or 'Mum', the undisputed ruler not only of about 90 boys but of a dozen masters and mistresses, a matron, under-matron, several maids, a school sergeant, a carpenter, two or three gardeners, Mr Wilkes and their two sons and three daughters.[13]

Orwell was singularly ungrateful for the start in life St Cyp's would give him and the sacrifices his parents (and, involuntarily, his education-denied sisters) made for 'the hope of the family'. Late in life, when he was furious about pretty well everything, he wrote a scathing and mendacious 15,000-word memoir of his St Cyprian's schooldays, 'Such, Such Were the Joys'. Those days were not, as Orwell records them, enjoyable. The chronicle begins with eight-year-old 'Blair', newly arrived (with the statutory six pairs of pyjamas), being beaten for bedwetting. He had been continent for 'four years'.[14] It was, one may conjecture, biological shock. The convent, at which he was earlier educated, was all girls (bar him) and run by nuns. It was, to this point, the upbringing of a 'sissy'. The beating, if we credit his 35-year recollection, was sadistic. He was flogged not once, but three times. Flip threatened publicly to get the whole sixth form to make a 'gauntlet' and thrash him up and down the length of the dormitory if he soiled another pair of sheets and stained the mattress (that detail always went down badly with prospective parents). When young Blair was overheard by Flip boasting, tearfully, that the second thrashing didn't hurt *that* much, he was sent back for more of the same. But

> this time Sambo laid on in real earnest. He continued for a length of time that frightened and astonished me – about five minutes, it seemed – ending up by breaking the riding-crop. The bone handle went flying across the room.
> 'Look what you've made me do!' he said furiously, holding the broken crop.

Blair was left a small, snivelling lump of boy – but it was shame, not the crop, that hurt most.

St Cyp's, as Orwell records, was not, like some private schools, a sexual hothouse. But this third whipping has something orgasmic about it – a lachrymose, and unusual, ejaculation of a kind. As often with him there is a hint of flagellophilia (five minutes' 'earnest' flogging 'does not hurt'? What does it do, then?) – the 'English Vice', as the non-English complacently call it.

Snobs to the core, the Wilkeses, Orwell recalls, encouraged arrant snobbery in their ninety impressionable charges. They would never, he surmised, have thrashed the bare arse of a boy whose 'pater' earned £2,000, or who owned three miles of river and rolled up on speech days in a chauffeur-driven Daimler, 'tipping' all and sundry. Connolly, who spent vacations in the family home, Clontarf

Castle, was not entirely spared the cane, by his own account, but his buttocks were only lightly and infrequently touched (he never, apparently, invited Eric home with him – a fact that may have galled). Eric was, as he claims, publicly shamed by being reminded, in front of Daimler-owning-class schoolmates, that he was a 'half-fees boy'. As often with Blair/Orwell, one sees him as someone who thinks that his problems would be solved by money, while despising the stuff and its 'stink'. He was a dreadful bore on the subject of money, one of his later friends complained. So may some readers.

Sambo was the flogger. Flip administered even more painful tongue-lashings. She blew hot and cold, mixing treacly friendliness with psychopathic sadism, as does the schoolmasterly O'Brien in *Nineteen Eighty-Four*, 're-educating' Winston ('He had the air of a doctor, a teacher, even a priest, anxious to explain and persuade rather than to punish'). Her harshness, Connolly said, 'pierced like a rapier'.[15] He was cannier at dodging the thrusts than Blair. And, of course, he wasn't a half-fees boy.

A long charge sheet is drawn up by Orwell against St Cyp's: vomit-inducing food (he claimed still to taste the vile porridge decades later); foul lavatory and bathing conditions (turds in the bathwater, as well as the open-door unflushable wc); pointless learning based on mnemonic 'facts, facts, facts'; and Latin, forced into the brain with the pedagogic equivalent of a pneumatic drill. 'Cramming' was the word. Any mistake might mean being sent 'outside' for a summary touch of the cane, then back to 'where we left off'. Cane–cram–cane–cram. So it went.

Stansky and Abrahams visited Mrs Wilkes in her retirement (a widow from 1947, she died in 1967) and found her, over the tea and cakes, a very nice old duck. Yes, she remembered young Blair, the ingrate. 'A very small boy, with a very large chip on his shoulder', she mildly called him. Mum was proud of the school she and Lewis had made (it burned down in 1939, Orwell was delighted to hear), and had reams of grateful testimony from former pupils. Several had even chosen to get married in the place where they had been so happy, and former pupils had routinely sent their own children there. There was a memorial blue plaque to 'Mum' where the school had been.

Wartime, when young Blair was in residence, 1912–17, had been difficult for schools. Mrs Wilkes's husband (never dynamic, by all accounts) was, in his forties, too old to serve, and slowing down, and she had lost most of her male teachers to the war. Servants were hard to come by; rations were tight. She had five children of her own, a staff to manage, and a full teaching load. Many parents, with a father in the services, needed reduced 'terms' (and drastic reductions if they were killed or disabled). Former St Cyp's boys were being killed – sadly commemorated in morning assembly. All this seemed to have passed young Blair by, so disturbed was he by the scummy quality of the bathwater.

It is argued by Crick that Orwell's account was conceived in 1938, as a riposte to Connolly's milder account of the school ('St Wulfric's' – the school was still in business) in *Enemies of Promise*. Connolly went so far as to describe Flip, Orwell's 'old sow', as a 'warm-hearted and inspired teacher'. He was, of course, chronically fork-tongued. Others, who have studied the evidence, argue for a post-war composition of 'Such, Such Were the Joys' and finishing touches in 1948, when Orwell submitted it to his publisher. A typescript was shown to Mrs Wilkes by Fred Warburg shortly afterwards. She pronounced the essay a 'tissue of lies'. The publisher, prudent like all their kind (or constitutionally 'gutless', as Orwell liked to think), duly had the piece 'legalled'. The lawyers identified thirty-plus actionable paragraphs in the face of a mass of wholly credible pro-Wilkes testimony. Any publisher of the piece would be lucky to survive on the right side of bankruptcy. The essay was put to the side and not published until after Flip breathed her last, aged 91.

A chorus of Cyprianites vouched for the fact that their beloved school did not live by the cane, like some latter-day equivalent of

Thackeray's Dr Birch's Academy, or Wackford Squeers's establishment. Of course there was corporal punishment: in what 'good' Edwardian school wasn't there? Orwell himself, when briefly a schoolteacher in 1932, is recorded as 'keeping a large stick by his desk' and using it 'fairly often'. One boy he beat recorded his buttocks being so badly bruised that he couldn't sit down for a week.[16] Boys were born to be beaten. But Orwell's description of a St Cyp's pupil being publicly thrashed for fifteen minutes was preposterous. Neither was it Mum's practice, the pro-school faction protested, to mortify pupils by sneering at their parents' income. She had a short fuse, no one denied that (she may have been menopausal in Blair's last years at the school), but she was a terrific teacher. The honours board proved it. Orwell's later doctrine of 'windowpane' prose can be traced back to 'Mum'. One of her favourite exercises was to get her class to précis, or rewrite, bad writing with the simplicity, and eloquence, good English required. The St Cyprian confutation of 'Such, Such Were the Lies' continues to this day.[17]

Bernard Crick, the 'authorized' biographer, was confronted with the awkward fact that he couldn't trust what George Orwell wrote about Eric Blair. What does an ethical biographer do in that situation? Hums and hahs. The wetting of the bed, Crick ventures, is probably 'laid on a bit thick', but some lesser incontinence perhaps happened. 'Five minutes' of flogging, even with a right arm fortified by long drives down the fairway, was a trifle improbable. What are we talking about – '200 of the best'? But again, there was probably a lesser beating, magnified by hypersensitivity and indignation. One should make judicious use of the get-out-of-biographer's-jail card, Crick suggested, of 'semi-fiction'. 'Semi-fact' might have been more like it. The pro-Cyprians had no problem at all with blowing 'that human turd' Crick's wishy-washy defence out of the water. Orwell, had he not, had called the essay 'autobiography' when he sent it to his publisher? Answer that, Crick. And in the original typescript, Orwell used (outrageously) the real names of staff and pupils. And his own, of course: except that he did it, hiding, coward that he was, behind a pseudonym. The only possible defence for his lies was 'tubercular mania'.[18] There is no evidence, however, that Orwell, when he completed the essay, was 'manic', although he was certainly tubercular. So why did he perpetrate what he must have known to be untruths? One explanation is Connolly's, that junior schools are 'incubators of paranoia'. If anyone starts talking about their school-days, just switch off until they've stopped. And if he, Connolly, said (as he did) that St Cyprian's was 'well run and did me a world of good', don't believe him, either.

Floreat Etona and After

To say a great deal about Eton is not to say much about Orwell.
BERNARD CRICK

Orwell cruised to a full scholarship to Eton, along with his chum 'Tim' Connolly. It was lucky for the Blairs that he did, since it was scholarship or nothing. As one of the elite fifteen 'Collegers', his fees (around £200 p.a. with incidentals) would be a sixth of those paid by the majority of unscholarly Etonians. Richard Blair would have been stretched on his £450 p.a. pension.

The progress he had made at St Cyprian's had been a credit to the hated place. His name was, doubtless, painted on the honours board. He had come far in this educational hothouse, where the only thing that mattered was passing exams. His first weekly letters home (around twenty survive) are primitive. His later letters are of full adult quality. His extracurricular reading was similarly adult in his last years at the school. He and Connolly were caned (inevitably), he records, for clandestinely reading Compton Mackenzie's *Sinister Street*, a novel with sex in it and probably as offensive to the Wilkeses for its satire of the prep school (Randell House) the hero attends. A book worth a caning.[19] Another book enjoyed by Eric and Tim, provoking a tug of war as to who could read it first, was H. G. Wells's collection of short stories *The Country of the Blind*.

Both boys cultivated an interest in what Orwell would later call, and praise as, 'Good-Bad Literature' that made you think about 'things'. In later life he wrote a couple of influential essays about novels that were frowned on but which had more good in them than those one was made to read.[20] There were also Bad-Bad Novels – something enlarged on, sneeringly, in Gordon Comstock's ordeal as custodian of a 'tuppenny library' in the opening chapters of *Keep the Aspidistra Flying*. The value of Good-Bad novels, as George Bowling says in *Coming Up for Air* (he steeps himself in them during the boring watches of his war service), is that they foster 'a kind of questioning attitude' – scepticism – about the official view of the world. They are healthily seditious.

This interest of Orwell's and his essays on Good-Bad Literature (along with his other classic essay on boys' comics) have been plausibly credited as the seed from which the modern academic discipline of Cultural Studies has grown. A list of Good-Bad Books, for Orwell, would include: *The Singing Bone*, R. Austin Freeman; *Dracula*, Bram Stoker; anything featuring Sherlock Holmes or Raffles; H. G. Wells's 'scientific romances'; *Rain*, Somerset Maugham; *King Solomon's Mines*, Rider Haggard. Top of the list would be Wells's *History of Mr Polly*. Jack London's *People of the Abyss* would be level pegging. Bad-Bad Books would be anything by Ethel M. Dell; *No Orchids for Miss Blandish*, James Hadley Chase; *Sorrell and Son*, Warwick Deeping. Edgar Wallace held an ambiguous position between the categories. Connolly did his bit for Good-Bad Books by introducing Raymond Chandler to English readers, as editor of *Horizon* in the 1950s.

Orwell had been at St Cyprian's for two years when war was declared in summer 1914. Caught up in the mass euphoria, he penned a sub-Kitchener ('Your Country Needs You') ode for the occasion. It would be his first publication, printed in the family's local newspaper, the *Henley and South Oxfordshire Gazette*. D. J. Taylor suggests that Ida sent it to the paper. Quite plausibly she also co-wrote the thing, on patriotic fire with the Hun's invasion of her ancestral France:

> Awake! Young Men of England
> Oh! give me the strength of the Lion,
> The wisdom of Reynard the Fox;
> And then I'll hurl troops at the Germans
> And give them the hardest of knocks.

This bugle call in verse does not sound like the work of a ten-year-old. Nor is the sentiment 'Orwellian'. Blair's enthusiasm for his school's Officer Training Corps over the years that followed was less than tepid. It was, he later said, 'a mark of enlightenment' to be slack on parades. No hard knocks for cadet Blair. Whether it was a momentary patriotic spasm, or his mother's invisible (*aux armes, vos jeunes!*) hand, Eric Blair's name was at the bottom of the doggerel. He was 'in print'. On the outbreak of the Second World War he strove to remember, *in toto*, what he recalled of the First World War. 'Margarine' was the word that came to mind. That does indeed sound Orwellian. It's a nice speculation as to what he would have done had he been born three years earlier. Would he have answered the call (conscription after 1916)? Or would he have 'dodged', using the wholly legitimate excuse of a dodgy set of lungs? The merest whiff of mustard gas would probably have killed him.

Orwell asked his mother for two copies of the paper containing his poem, for Mrs Wilkes to admire. She read it out ('well done, Blair!') at the school assembly and pasted it in her scrapbook; she would show it to Stansky and Abrahams fifty years later. At school, at St Cyp's and at Eton (where his silence on the subject is recorded), Blair kept angrily quiet about his own father, who, having retired aged 55 in 1912, answered the call and joined the colours

Blair family portrait, c. 1914. Eric has a pronounced unmilitary air. Ida leans away from her husband, using Avril as a barrier. Richard has the bearing of a major-general, at least.

('Awake! Old Men of England'). It was the occasion of a family photograph.

Richard gained fame, of a kind, over the next five years as the oldest 2nd Lieutenant in the army. Meanwhile, eighteen-year-old ensigns were dying in their thousands at the front. Some of the wounded may have had their pain deadened by the opium that Richard had helped to produce (not all of it went to stupefy the Chinese addict). There was another, gloomier honours board at St Cyprian's, and at Eton, commemorating gloriously 'fallen' former pupils. 2nd Lt Blair was a minor inconvenience to the War Office, and a major embarrassment for his son. At one point Richard was officer in charge of pack mules in Marseilles. A donkey-driver. All this with the humiliating single pip on his shoulder. He retired from military service in 1919, having done his bit. One feels for him. Eric Blair didn't. In one of his few comments, to one of his few close friends at Eton, Orwell dismissed his father, cruelly, as a man who 'didn't do much of anything'. He also confided that he increasingly found Ida 'frivolous'. What does Philip Larkin call it? 'A son's harsh patronage'.

Over the war years, the Blairs, less Eric and Richard, and with Marjorie serving (dashingly, as a Woman's Legion dispatch rider), moved the family home to Earls Court, London. Ida took up a job in the Ministry of Pensions. She may, Crick hints, in the relaxed moral mood of wartime, have taken a lover – male or female. She was still in her thirties when the war started, and unencumbered with domestic duties or her husband's nocturnal attentions. During the disturbances of moving and war, Eric was lodged with the Wilkeses over the vacations – a kindness (unacknowledged by him) on their part. He would have registered the Zeppelin raids, London's painful introduction to modern warfare. As he would later say, there is nothing like a bit of civilian bombing to shut up the Home Front Colonel Blimps.[21]

The entrance exams for Eton, which Eric and Connolly took in 1916, centred on Latin and Greek. Orwell never had any problem with languages. As he casually divulged in a late essay, he had mastered at least seven in the course of his life, two dead. He could talk as fluently with a Burmese priest as with a French *poule* or a Spanish *compañero*. His multilingualism was, however, never shown off in obedience to that Orwellian fifth rule of good writing: 'Never use a foreign phrase, a scientific word, or a jargon word if you can think of an everyday English equivalent.'[22]

The five Etonian years, 1917–22, are one of the mysteries of Orwell's life. He was primed to fly high at the school, and he flew just about as low as an Etonian scholar could. He resolutely 'slacked' (his word) and 'dodged' (one of his teachers' words). It was the first of many *non serviams*.[23] In his second year, after much chopping and changing of classes and subjects, he came 117th out of 140 in his year. He was never one for academic field specialism, and paid the price. 'Skimming' might have been a more appropriate word than 'slacking'. 'Bright boys teach themselves,' Crick sagely reminds us.

Dished by Gow; Damned for Doggerel

In the final school examinations for his year ('elections', as they were called), Eric Blair came 137th out of 168. The shame was such that Andrew Gow, his longest-serving tutor, told Richard, when he came to enquire what should be done with Eric, that it would be a 'disgrace' to Eton, specifically the top dogs' college, even to allow Blair to apply to Oxford or Cambridge. Lesser institutions (say London University, or Manchester) were unthinkable. Eton would have had to raise a 'Dishonours' board. As regards higher education, Gow might as well have worn a black cap.

It is preposterous on the face of it to have suggested that an Eton scholar, by no means at the bottom of the class, could not, with some judicious cramming, have won an Oxbridge scholarship. Orwell was one of the cleverest boys in England. Why did Gow deliver this death sentence? Andrew Sydenham Farrar Gow (1886–1978) was the son of a public-school headmaster. He got a double first at Trinity College, Cambridge, in Classics but, when Blair came his way, was having difficulty getting the fellowship back there, something that he wanted above all things in life. As his tight-lipped entry in the ODNB records:

He applied four times for permanent posts in Cambridge, but was each time unsuccessful; it was feared that he would alarm and discourage his pupils, particularly the weaker sort. Indeed Gow's appearance was formidable, an uncompromisingly Scottish kind of countenance being set off by bushy eyebrows and side-whiskers, and anything like conceit or pretentiousness on the part of a pupil might provoke a wounding sarcasm.

The rejection letters from Cambridge cannot have softened Gow's schoolroom sarcasm. A 'bachelor and a half' (as Paul Johnson archly called him), Gow liked the friendly company of favourite pupils, out of school hours. Barely thirty, he was nicknamed 'Granny Gow' for his effeminacy and for his solicitude to those favourites.

Gow was Blair's Classics tutor. They were necessarily close, but they didn't like each other at all. 'Granny Gow' could not have been unaware of homophobic sneers against him by the 'manlier' boys. Orwell was not tolerant – at any period of his life – of 'nancies'. What Freudians called reactive suppression has been suspected, and there is a fleeting reference to one crush at Eton. Blair wrote a scurrilously homophobic limerick that was printed in one of the school's papers. It opens: 'Then up waddled Wog [i.e. Gow backwards] and he squeaked in Greek / "I've grown another hair on my cheek."' No need to ask which cheek is alluded to. Gow was a hairy man – down to the hirsute buttock, apparently. The lines are an allusion to the outrageously homosexual Cleisthenes tearing the hair out of his rump in Aristophanes' *The Frogs*. The verse in the school magazine was anonymous, but Gow – who probably dreamed in Greek – would have had no difficulty in uncovering the rascal who wrote it and what it implied. But he could not rush off to the Provost, M. R. James, and demand condign retribution without the career-endangering query: 'Do *all* the boys *know*, Andrew?' James, it has been suspected, was himself discreetly homosexual. One can speculate that Gow used certain texts (such as *The Frogs*) in his small classics translation group to observe how receptive boys were to various Hellenic and Roman improprieties.

The early biographical birds, Stansky and Abrahams, interviewed Gow, and recorded him recalling a warm relationship with Blair, perceiving 'under the shyness and surliness . . . an authentic intelligence'.

As with other pupils, Gow said, they had private tutorials in Gow's room, where groups of four or five boys would read aloud their personal writings. A fondness for Eric Blair is implied. Did Gow, in this relaxed atmosphere, venture some kind of pass? What he told Stansky and Abrahams makes all the odder the account of Richard visiting Eton, to be told by Gow to remove his son entirely from the British higher education system, lest he somehow disgrace Eton. Richard, a man used to obeying orders, got the message, and cut off any further family monetary sacrifice for Eric: no longer the hope of the Blairs.

From now on, Eric would have to pay his own way. And that meant the colonies. Richard would, of course, have relayed to his son Gow's devastating report. It cannot have been a pleasant conversation. According to Jacintha Buddicom, Eric's first sweetheart, her family put pressure on Richard to get Eric to university, whatever the cost. He wanted 'so much' to go, she recalled to Crick in 1972. 'But Mr Blair was adamant.' Gow had delivered a death sentence. It was revenge for the doggerel.

Orwell offers a scathing pen portrait of Gow as 'Porteous' in *Coming Up for Air*. The actual name is borrowed from the tutor who gets Kit into college in *Sorrell and Son*, a novel Orwell loathed for its grovelling worship of the English class system. In Orwell's novel, Porteous is the public-school friend, and unofficial mentor, of the intelligent but unschooled hero. He is a kind of one-man prep school: a crammer, or freelance tutor. Bowling routinely turns to Porteous for worldly advice but, finally, he discards him:

> I watched him leaning up against the bookshelf. Funny, these public-school chaps. Schoolboys all their days. Whole life revolving round the old school and their bits of Latin and Greek and poetry . . . And a curious thought struck me. HE'S DEAD. He's a ghost. All people like that are dead.

How Much of Eton Did He Take With Him?

If St Cyp's was a 'prep school' preparing 'scholarship fodder' for the (anything but) public school, what was Eton preparing its pupils for? Power, influence and 'achievement', as currently defined (at the moment this achievement includes prime ministership and screen stardom; *floreat Etona*). Connolly, on arrival at the school, realized that 'This was the place for me', and played the system with the expertise of a card sharp. He attached himself, courtier-like, to those schoolfellows whom he could amuse, and who could be useful to him in years to come.

Evidence is scant as to what Orwell's game was. He certainly wasn't a truckler. He and Connolly remained friends but ceased to be bosom friends, Connolly going so far as to say that he hardly ever saw Eric at Eton. Orwell evidently chose not to be easily seen. He adopted the pose of *flâneur* outside the Etonian whale, but close enough to know it better than did those who were swallowed up like so many Jonahs. 'Aloof' is Connolly's description in *Enemies of Promise*. He himself had the aloofness of a social tapeworm. There seems to have been some slight friction over a joint crush on some pretty junior boy.[24] Connolly slyly accused Blair of being the purer of the two of them. By which he meant timid.

After St Cyprian's, Eton clearly suited both young men, in their different ways. Stansky and Abrahams shrewdly note that Orwell never dwells in his writing on periods of his life when he was happy(ish). This seems to have been one such. Like Connolly he was pleased to discover, he said later, that Eton 'had a tolerant and civilized atmosphere'. Even for bolshy Eric Blair. Despite war there was a reasonable level of creature comfort, much less corporal punishment than at St Cyprian's, and nearby rivers – flowing water, which Eric Blair always loved (hence 'Orwell') more than the tidal ocean, which he found 'dull'. The streams and pools were teeming with fish, and many of the anglers were in uniform. Blair caught and cooked arm-long pike, the largest of them. Pike flesh is (to my palate) muddy: but it was more fun than rugby. He doubtless, as I did as a child, boiled the head to show off the terrifying teeth.

A transparently disapproving Crick (grammar school and LSE) describes the peculiar internal institutions of Eton: 'elections', 'wall-games', 'Collegers vs Oppidans', 'dry bobs', 'wet bobs', 'Pop', etc. Orwell, he implies, was in Eton, but not of it. Eric 'led his section behind a distant haystack and in shirtsleeves read them *Eric, or Little by Little*, whose ethic he detested so cordially, [and] read it with mock seriousness for the whole of a long and undisturbed summer afternoon'. Author Dean Frederic Farrar's 'ethic' was that of a public-school headmaster (which he was): children must obey their elders or go to perdition – down the little-by-little path to becoming 'a bad lot'. Self-abuse was identified, discreetly, as a main cause of juvenile downfall. Victorians had a holy horror of masturbation – tolerated as the prophylactic practice of Onan is in Holy Writ. It's sanctioned if nothing better is, so to speak, at hand. Orwell surely masturbated. Boys' schools, then and now, floated on a sea of frustrated juvenile sperm.

Orwell, it is well recorded, had, like many boys, his porn stash – Donald McGill 'dirty postcards', in his case. They were aphrodisiac to middle-class lads, even until the 1950s. I remember one I found oddly arousing: burly gym instructor to busty lass – 'You'll take your physical jerks under me tonight.' Eric Blair began collecting McGills at about the age of twelve. They were available at newsagents in seaside Eastbourne (not Henley). Not all newsagents would let children buy them, but some would, particularly stands round the pier.[25] The McGills incarnated Orwell's 'Sancho Panza' view of life: fornicating, farting, feasting and generally having fun. Eric's 'calf love', at this period, was Jacintha Buddicom, a family connection, in Henley. In a friendly, late-life and deliberately foggy memoir, *Eric & Us* (1974), Jacintha recalled him, in his very early teens, showing her a selection of his less naughty McGill items. The hot ones he kept in a manila envelope, for private use.

Etonian rebel
with drooping fag
and bathing togs,
probably 1916.

Orwell had other unofficial passions. A lifelong sufferer from
nightmares, he loved horror stories, particularly Poe. The Provost of
Eton, when he was there, was M. R. James. James arrived at Eton,
his first and last love, the year after Blair had, and superintended the
school until 1936. In 1918 his *Ghost Stories of an Antiquary* (1904–12)
were famous. Orwell, as D. J. Taylor says, 'was addicted to M. R. James'.
James's horror stories may have inspired Orwell to go himself into
dark, supernatural places. He and a schoolfriend, Steven Runciman,
made a voodoo doll of a pupil (an elder brother of the novelist Henry
Green) whom they particularly disliked. First the boy sustained an
injury, then he died. Orwell was always a dangerous man to cross.

There is a surviving picture of Eric Blair at Eton that is revealing. Unusually for him, he has his guard down in front of the lens. He has a floppy sun hat, rolled-up swimming togs under his arm, and a fag drooping from his mouth (doubtless the 'lucifers' are in his bags). He had found his lifelong deodorant.

An Etonian, Whatever

I'm a public school man. That means everything.
'CAPTAIN' GRIMES in Evelyn Waugh's *Decline and Fall*

Stephen Spender's 'Orwell was the least Etonian Etonian ever to come out of Eton' is witty but, to borrow one of Orwell's favourite terms, 'bollox'.[26] In his later career Orwell might as well have had the old school tie tattooed on his chest.

Orwell's higher journalism is one of the glories of English literary culture. But it is illuminating to look behind the crystalline, classless prose to his patrons. The first such patron was Richard Rees, the 'socialist baronet' (and millionaire) who published Orwell's finest early articles, such as 'The Spike', and the much-reprinted 'A Hanging', in *The Adelphi*. The last was the multimillionaire David Astor, who published a hundred of his finest later articles in *The Observer*. Rees and Astor had four things in common: they were hugely rich, they were top people and they were Etonians. And, fourthly, they were unfailingly helpful to Orwell. *Horizon* – the magazine that sold massively during the war, giving Orwell his largest readership for such articles as 'Raffles and Miss Blandish' (1944, a paean to 'old-school' values) – was edited by Eric's friend Cyril Connolly, an Etonian, and funded by the margarine millionaire Peter Watson. Watson? Another Etonian. Oh, and Raffles? Etonian, of course.

These editors did more than lick Orwell's prose into shape and open doors for him. They were patrons, in an eighteenth-century sense of the word. It was the radical baronet, Rees, who made the introductions that brought Orwell (like Rees himself) into the Spanish Civil War: two Etonians fighting for republicanism (which, if victorious, would have eliminated the Spanish equivalent of their class like rabbits at harvest time). When Orwell went to Wigan in 1936, observing with a jaundiced eye the grubby fingerprint in the margarine and the overflowing chamber pot under the kitchen table, he had in his pocket letters of introduction from Rees. Mine owners did not allow emaciated London journalists of leftist views with bad coughs to go into their deepest tunnels as it took their fancy (to write not entirely friendly articles). Orwell was always good at using friends like Rees as invisible social lubricant. Rees's services, as a source of support, are acknowledged – with, as has been said, a somewhat ungracious portrait – in the character of Ravelston in *Keep the Aspidistra Flying*.

One doesn't know how much Orwell cost Astor (not that it would have made the slightest dent in his fortune), but it was a large sum. It was all done on a friend-in-need basis. An Etonian friend. The two men became hobnobbingly close when Astor got in touch, admiringly, after reading Orwell's 'The Lion and the Unicorn', with its gripping first line: 'As I write this, highly civilized men are flying overhead trying to kill me.' During the Second World War Astor served spectacularly well against the highly civilized enemy, as did Rees; Astor was in 'intelligence' during the war. There is speculation that he introduced Orwell into that murky world.[27] Astor gave Orwell a free range to contribute 'as he pleased' when he (Astor) took over *The Observer* after the war, making it the most politically influential paper in the country. The relationship went well beyond an ever-open editorial door. When Orwell did a kind of Robinson Crusoe, in 1947, to live a crofter's life in the Hebrides, it was on an island, and estate, that Astor owned. Astor was immensely and discreetly helpful during Orwell's dying days – arranging the poignant marriage and country funeral. He was the widowed Sonia's pillar of strength. He chose to lie with Orwell in All Saints' graveyard, Sutton Courtenay. Etonians in life, Etonians for eternity.

Wealthy as he was, Astor was enriched by Orwell in ways that mattered more than money. (He had a charmingly vague notion of real life sometimes. Famously, when he was editor of *The Observer* a colleague had to explain to him what a mortgage was.) I met Astor once only, at an Orwell Trust committee meeting. Someone observed that the archive was on a sound footing, for a year or two at least. 'Orwell said [that] the most immoral thing a man can say', Astor mused, half to himself, 'is "it will see out my time".' Then the committee, bracing itself morally, Orwell's posthumous instruction ringing in their ears, proceeded to the next item on the agenda.

One other small episode illustrates the Masonic Etonian network that invisibly supported George Orwell. In 1938, he wanted to write what would be the most ambitious novel he had hitherto attempted. *Coming Up for Air*, it would be called. Unfortunately, he was having difficulty with air himself: his lungs were in collapse. Doctors recommended clean, warm, dry foreign air. He was acutely hard up at the time. It was out of the question. An Etonian Orwell barely knew, L. H. Myers, heard about his plight. He advanced, anonymously, £300 (around £10,000 in modern currency) for Orwell to go away and write. He and his wife went to Morocco, the air did him no end of good, and the novel, his best, was written. It was years before Orwell knew who his benefactor was. By then Myers had committed suicide and repayment was impossible.

Would Etonians like Rees, Astor, Connolly, Watson and Myers have been, en masse, as consistently and constructively generous to a chronically down-and-out Harrovian or, God help us, a grammar school boy? Orwell may have hated it – Gordon Comstock, his alter ego hero, sternly refuses handouts from Ravelston/Rees – but he took the help gladly, lastly a cool £1,000 to set up his 'independent' farm on Jura. Without his Etonian comrades, pulling all together, posterity would not have George Orwell or care about someone called Eric Blair.

The book-publishing world ('trade', as Jane Austen would have called it) was something different. Eton did not flourish in the British book trade. Orwell's books were, every one of them, put out by brilliant mercantile Jews: Victor Gollancz, Fred Warburg and Tosco Fyvel. The one Anglo-Saxon publisher he repeatedly tried, T. S. Eliot, turned down his first book (*Down and Out in Paris and London*) and *Animal Farm*. There was something about Orwell Eliot didn't like.

It's not worth wasting words on the tediously repeated, and wrong-headed, charge that Orwell did not like Jews. Orwell was not, at his most Orwellian, anti-Semitic.[28]

The King's Policeman

In order to hate imperialism you have got to be part of it.
The Road to Wigan Pier

I loved Burma and the Burman and have no regrets that I spent the best years of my life in the Burma police.
ORWELL in a late letter, quoted in Stansky and Abrahams

Burma ruined my health.
'Autobiographical Note' (1942)

Orwell left Eton without completing his last term. Cyril Connolly, always the shrewder of the two, had bagged a plum scholarship at Balliol. He was currently on a grand tour of the Continent – broadening his mind, as the phrase was. And his posterior (never svelte). Would the cadaverous Orwell recognize the fat-cigar-smoking frog he was, when, years later, they met, Connolly wondered? The next station in his life after Eton and Oxford would be Brideshead.

Orwell's other close Eton companion, Harold Acton, was also Oxford-bound. He would have three years to 'become' himself

– as a precociously published poet, aesthete and half the original of Anthony Blanche. He distinguished himself with a night-time reading, through a megaphone, of Eliot's recently published *The Waste Land*. The performance is immortalized in Evelyn Waugh's *Brideshead Revisited*. The other half of Blanche, Brian Howard, another Etonian contemporary of Blair's, was also at Oxford. 'Bright Young Things', they were called. The world was their oyster.[29]

There were no oysters for Eric Blair. He had hit life's buffers very early, it seemed. The colonies were traditionally where middle-class children who had no better choice were deposited. A 'finishing school', it was jested, for those who were finished before they had even got started. The word 'exile' hovers over biographical accounts of Orwell's next five years, 1922–7. The word has an element of truth. The choice of what to do next was not entirely his. Three years short of the age of majority, without private means, he was still – if not for much longer – subject to his father's authority. 'India' was decreed.

Without a degree, and 'friends', the elite track in the India Office was closed to Eric (dashing what had been his father's fond hope). He would never be a viceroy's personal secretary. His mother's family had been three generations in the Burmese teak industry, and at times rich. But the industry was now monopolized by multi-nationals, and the Limouzin clan was a spent force. The premium required to get Orwell in was thousands more than the Blairs could afford, or his mother's relatives nowadays wangle. He could, however, opt for the Indian Police Service, Burmese branch. He had maternal relatives in that country. It was a home-from-home posting that would mollify his parents. It would not, however, get him any glory at his school. IPS Burma was not a line of work that was crowded with Etonians, as his reference letter snidely implied. Richard could just about stretch to the required initial expense (around £200, Crick records). There was a very decent salary in prospect: the IPS would yield a qualified assistant superintendent as much as £600 p.a. Eric would no longer be a drain on the Blair household, and he might even repay something of what he owed his father. There was also another reason for his getting out of England.

A Close-run Thing

> I took hold of her.
>
> *Coming Up for Air*

For a nineteen-year-old chronically starved of oats, as were most young males of Orwell's class and time, the prospect of exotic 'oriental' sex was alluring. He was certainly having no luck with the English variety.

He had, for five years, been courting Jacintha Buddicom, a friend since childhood in Henley. A bright young girl, Jacintha had missed out on any chance of higher education. Her prospects were sacrificed so her brother Prosper (aptly named) could go to Oxford. This was the sister's lot (Avril and Marjorie Blair's, as well). But she was nubile. Marriage would be her career. Orwell offered to marry Jacintha and carry her off as a memsahib to Burma. He was throughout life impulsive with proposals of marriage. She was inclined. The families, who had smiled at the relationship over the years, could be talked round – although perhaps a longish engagement would be prudent. His financial and career prospects in the IPS were hopeful once he settled in.

Throughout his life Orwell found open, deserted places in the wild wildly aphrodisiac. There was something, one guesses, about the ambient smell that, via his supersensitive nose, triggered a rush of uncontrollable desire. He dreamed like Winston Smith of Edenic love in the 'golden countryside' – a dell, glade or meadow in the woods – where the act of love would be as natural as the bluebells and birdsong. Julia and Winston achieve it – just once in their lives. So, just once in his life, does George Bowling with his Elsie:

I chucked my hat on to the grass (it bounced, I remember), knelt down, and took hold of her. I can smell the wild peppermint yet. It was my first time, but it wasn't hers, and we didn't make such a mess of it as you might expect.

Bowker recalls an odd but revealing exchange with Anthony Powell in which Orwell asked him (seriously) if he found parks sexually arousing. When Tony looked perplexed – 'Why parks?' he enquired – 'Nowhere else to go' was the answer.

If a friend like Arthur Koestler was, as the ladies who knew him agreed, NSIT (not safe in taxis), Orwell was not safe with grass

The teenaged Jacintha Buddicom, Eric's sweetheart.

under his feet. And if he encountered resistance, it was, perversely, the woman's fault. (He blamed Jacintha, in one of the three letters he sent her, for 'abandoning' him to Burma – and its sexual delinquencies, presumably. A wife would have kept him straight.)

Orwell's first recorded attempt at love al fresco was, by contrast, a total mess. It was on a walk with Jacintha in the countryside round Rickmansworth, where both the Blairs and the Buddicoms were holidaying, in the heat of late summer, some fifteen months before his departure for Burma. His life was at its point of change. The young couple doubtless talked of 'relationship': what they would do with their lives. Marriage? They may have kissed. There was in the air the redolence that excited Eric, as the wild peppermint excites George Bowling into 'taking hold' of Elsie. Fifty years later, Jacintha recalled in a letter to a friend what had then happened to scupper everything. She was five foot nothing. He was over six feet tall, twelve stone and honed into athletic condition by the high-contact,

Husky Orwell, back right. Wall game at Eton.

all-barging sport he played at Eton – the wall game. Open space
had its usual effect on Orwell. She resisted; he attempted bodily
persuasion. She broke free with bruises and torn clothing. Luckily
for him she kept quiet. Had Jacintha Buddicom, a young woman of
impeccable virtue, gone, weeping, to the local police station, Eric Blair
might well have faced Wandsworth Prison rather than Rangoon.[30]

Marriage was henceforth off the cards. The five-year love affair
ended with a mystifying chill. Jacintha did not go to Burma as his
bride, did not apparently write to him (apart from one cool letter)
and went out of her way never to meet her former sweetheart again,
even though, when he came back five years later, he had a hopeful
engagement ring for her in his baggage.

In later life Jacintha admitted that Eric was the only man she
had ever loved. He had ruined it. She was not, she later said, ready –
aged 21 as she had been on that awful day – to go 'all the way'.
Or even, one suspects, some of the way. She would live almost twice
as long as him but never married and after the assault closed her
mind on him. As late as 1949 she did not even know that 'her' Eric
was the George Orwell everyone was talking about. When she read
the account of Winston and Julia's lovemaking in the country in
Nineteen Eighty-Four, which incorporated background elements of
their disastrous summer walk, meaningful only to her, she felt torn,
'limb from limb'.

What happened in that Hertfordshire countryside was an act
of crass inexperience on Eric's part. He was no freebooting Alec
D'Urberville, ravishing a helpless maiden in the woods. And young
Blair should have remembered another of his favourite novels,
The Way of All Flesh, whose hero, Ernest Pontifex, attempts what he
attempted on the body of a wholly respectable young woman (tries it
on with force) and goes to prison for it. Eric Blair dodged the bullet,
but it was an added reason for wanting to get out of England.

Kitting Up

The Blairs had moved from Henley to something less expensive,
but more congenial to Richard, in Southwold on the Suffolk coast,
during the same period Eric was leaving Eton, in December 1921.
They were perhaps feeling the financial strain (it would make for
difficulty until, five years on, Ida inherited some family money).
Eric was duly enrolled with a 'crammer' in Southwold. There was an
Anglo-Indian retiree colony in the town and a small establishment
for their offspring taking the India Office exams. Orwell doubtless
relished Southwold's briny air and green spaces. He hated its character, however, as an Anglo-Indian graveyard whose occupants wouldn't
have the decency actually to die (his own father would live there until
the age of 82). It is described, venomously (with location replacement)
in *Burmese Days*:

> the special nature of the hell that is reserved for Anglo-Indians.
> Ah, those poor prosing old wrecks in Bath and Cheltenham!
> Those tomb-like boarding-houses with Anglo-Indians littered
> about in all stages of decomposition, all talking and talking
> about what happened in Boggleywalah in '88! Poor devils, they
> know what it means to have left one's heart in an alien and
> hated country.

One of the fascinating features of Orwell's fiction, read in the context
of his life, is its savagery (the 'vein of nastiness'). His father and
mother ('prosing old wrecks') would not merely have read this; they
would have felt it was written with them specifically in mind.

Eric contrived to get himself expelled from his crammer (an
establishment run by an 'old Indian hand') for a childish prank
– posting a dead rat as a birthday present to a local town official
whom he and another wayward pupil had, for no particular reason,
taken against. It would be another source of embarrassment for his

father. Quite a lot has been written about Orwell and *Rattus rattus*: they crop up frequently before their starring role in *Nineteen Eighty-Four*.[31] The expulsion did not matter. At least, not to him. He was sufficiently 'crammed' by the best education England could offer to pass any lowly tests for the branch of colonial service he was destined for. Classics (judged as essential in the tropics as quinine) were again prominent, and he came near the top of his intake in them. To his credit Orwell, as far as I can see, rarely drops a single Latin word, or phrase, in his mature writing, where, as the fourth rule of his good writing decrees, a good English equivalent is to hand. 'You forget your Latin and Greek within a few months of leaving school,' he said.[32] But enough remains, and 'having' Latin and Greek wafting around you like the aroma of Imperial Leather was, like the Masonic handshake, an infallible sign of a gentlemanly background.

Having made the life-changing downward step from King's Colleger to king's policeman, Probationary Assistant Superintendent Blair (a title almost as Pythonesque as his father's) prepared to grow the obligatory toothbrush moustache and take up the white man's burden. At this stage of life he loathed Kipling, whose poetry he had adored at school. He could have said no. Bowker suggests he went to Burma because, with England behind him, he could wrestle with his 'demons' and explore his 'dark side'. Perhaps. But Eric Blair was also a fun-loving youngster (hence the rat prank), an eighteen-year-old who had barely torn the Eton collar off his neck. There was quite a lot of light side in him. He could now, in another absurd uniform, play the pukka sahib (in his by now well-honed 'cynic' style) and even go on 'tiger shoots'. He chose to do so on a motorbike, wielding a pistol. The Burmese forests teemed with big game. The big cats had little to fear from Eric Blair other than noise. But he seems to have been a dab hand at rat shooting.[33]

Bowker is a perceptive biographer, but Orwell's important career moves were usually perversely driven. And he was surely, in acquiescing to this twist in his career, driven by intellectual curiosity about England's biggest historical thing, Empire. To find out about that would be to find out about himself. Bengali-born, his English homes (particularly after Richard's retirement and the nostalgic clutter – not least conversation – he brought with him) were a kind of Indian sarcophagus. In *Coming Up for Air*, George Bowling (the seed merchant's child) says, 'The very first thing I remember is the smell of sainfoin chaff.' With infant Eric, it was probably Burmese teak furniture, a wood whose smell lasts as long as the wood itself. The pharaoh's tomb-like quality of the Anglo-Indian home is described, in a virtuoso Betjemanesque rhapsody in *Coming Up for Air*, by smellmeister George Bowling, whose faded wife is Anglo-Indian. (The passage can have given little pleasure to his mother; his father, dying of cancer, did not read it.)

> As soon as you set foot inside the front door you're in India in the eighties. You know the kind of atmosphere. The carved teak furniture, the brass trays, the dusty tiger-skulls on the wall, the Trichinopoly cigars, the red-hot pickles, the yellow photographs of chaps in sun-helmets, the Hindustani words that you're expected to know the meaning of, the everlasting anecdotes about tiger-shoots and what Smith said to Jones in Poona in '87.

What, Orwell was curious to know, was behind this 'racket'? How to explain the great confidence trick tiny England had pulled on the world: staining more of it Britannic red on the map than any other imperial power in history – including Rome and the Mongols. And, with the prescience that marks every stage of his life, he foresaw – or rather felt, as some animals are said to feel, through the soles of their feet, earthquakes before they come – that the British Empire was doomed. He would live, short as his life was, to feel the first puffs of the wind of change that would blow the British Empire into the dustbin of history, a smiling Gandhi clamping the lid down on the Raj for ever.

There must have been gloomy Decline and Fall conversations at home in Henley. Five years before Richard retired in 1912, Britain agreed to reduce, annually, the Indian opium export to China. It was effectively ended in 1916. It had brought in 20 per cent of India's colonial income at its height. Richard had served imperial drug-dealing for forty years. Now there were editorials in the newspapers calling it a source of national shame. Teak – blood timber – had similarly declined as the source of Burma's principal industry. Its glory days were when Britannia ruled the waves by virtue not just of hearts of oak but of planks of that wonderful Burmese timber, the ideal material for sail-driven vessels. The arrival of the ironclad – rivet, steel and steam – had hit the teak business hard. If the Empire wasn't making money, what future did it have?

Almost as soon as Orwell arrived in Burma, a fictional character, embodying the doom of Empire, began to take form, embryonically, in his mind – 'John Flory'. He is not a police officer but a drunken, sexually incontinent, facially disfigured, morally withered, cowardly (he dodged the war) teak merchant, keenly aware that he is raping the country of its irreplaceable natural resources (mature teak takes a century to grow), abusing its women and denying its people independence. But he is too weak to free himself from being what he knows he is – a thief, a rapist and a third-class conquistador. That insight, the intrinsic corruption of what his life is, ages the 35-year-old Flory. In the published version of *Burmese Days*, in an extremity of shame, he shoots himself. In an earlier plan, in an extremity of self-disgust, he drinks himself to death.[34] Flory had come to Burma aged nineteen, Orwell's age, a hopeful youth. In his darkest moment, Orwell doubtless foresaw those options for Assistant Deputy Superintendent Eric Blair, fifteen years on. He would, in the event, avoid the terminal 'bullet or bottle' dilemma and choose instead flight after five years. He had found out what he needed to. How the racket worked.

It would take him nine years to hone, with much rewriting, his first-written, third-published novel, *Burmese Days*, into shape, sweating off the malarial influence of Somerset Maugham, *A Passage to India*, Kipling and Conrad. In the fifth chapter of its final version he was in a position to distil his Burma experience, and his realization of what the Empire actually is, into eight frigid words – 'a despotism with theft as its final object'. Thievery is felonious. What made the Empire over which the sun never set more sinister to the thoughtful observer was its invention of 'thoughtcrime' to hold itself together. The colonists were mentally tyrannized, the natives (proles) physically tyrannized. The Empire, once you bought into it, was a world in which

> free speech is unthinkable. All other kinds of freedom are permitted. You are free to be a drunkard, an idler, a coward, a backbiter, a fornicator; but you are not free to think for yourself . . . In the end the secrecy of your revolt poisons you like a secret disease. Your whole life is a life of lies.

Despotism by thought control. Orwell would think more about that.

Burma

> In Burma there is a joke that Orwell wrote not just one novel about the country, but three: a trilogy comprised of *Burmese Days*, *Animal Farm* and *Nineteen Eighty-Four*.
>
> JULIO ETCHART, *Katha: In the Footsteps of Orwell in Burma* (2010)

Orwell was wryly self-deprecating as a novelist, prone to call a work on which he'd laboured for years 'bollocks'. *Burmese Days* he described as a novel principally about 'landscape'. Equivalent to saying *Animal Farm* is about animal farms.

Knowledge, the Burmese novel affirms, can be achieved only at the cost of a lifelong, incurable 'bad conscience'. The price paid is irremovable, like the stain on Flory's face. (Flory averts his head so the birthmark is not visible, as Orwell habitually averted his head in conversation, because of anxiety about bad breath.) In Burma, to pick up Bowker's point, if Orwell wrestled with anything 'demonic', it was the paradox he struggled with all his life. Call it the Jonah paradox. Do you understand the nature of the whale inside the belly of the beast – or outside, from a safe distance? At this stage of his life Orwell's belief was that you could get to Empire's dark heart (as Conrad decreed in his famous novella) only from inside. If, that is, you nodded your head in apparent assent (as does Flory) to conversation in the 'Kipling haunted club' ('they're dirt'; 'greasy little babus'); if you (yourself) punched a coolie in the face ('everyone did it'), or had some muscled sepoy lash the Burman's bare arse with bamboo canes till they splintered, *pour encourager les autres*, and violated a nation's most desirable women at will, deluding yourself that you had a sovereign right to do so. And all this was for the sovereign himself, long may he reign, toasted at least once every night, standing to attention, 'eyes front', in the club.

Orwell confided to an Indian friend, fifteen years later, that he had done 'terrible things' in Burma.[35] One can be fairly confident that these things went beyond killing the occasional wayward elephant. In *The Road to Wigan Pier*, Orwell recalls a moment of clarity. One of his sub-inspectors was bullying a suspect. An American missionary was watching:

> The American watched it, and then turning to me said thought-fully, 'I wouldn't care to have your job.' It made me horribly ashamed. So that was the kind of job I had! Even an ass of an American missionary, a teetotal cock-virgin from the Middle West, had the right to look down on me and pity me!

This rings true. The implication is that a 'teetotal cock-virgin' can take the moral high ground, for what it's worth, but only a participating drunken, bullying rapist can 'know', inwardly, what Empire is doing to Burma. And what was that? Orwell momentarily pictures himself as the cane-wielding Sambo Wilkes.

Rule by Cane

One thing which Dickens seems to have recognized, and which most of his contemporaries did not, is the sadistic sexual element in flogging.

'Charles Dickens' (1940)

Orientals can be very provoking.

GEORGE ORWELL, ironically (one hopes) justifying 'bullying' – that is, flogging – in *The Road to Wigan Pier*

Anyone who has read *Burmese Days* remembers two scenes. Both centre on the odious club bigot, Ellis, who is given to such sage thoughts on colonial rule as: 'Bambooing's the only thing that makes any impression on the Burman. Have you seen them after they've been flogged? I have. Brought out of the jail on bullock carts, yelling, with the women plastering mashed bananas on their backsides.' It goes, in the novel, beyond words. Ellis, his imperial cane swinging, meets five high-school boys and sees on them 'a row of yellow, malicious faces – epicene faces, horribly smooth and young, grinning at him with deliberate insolence'. He suspects they are Nationalists. There has been a recent outrage. His blood is up. So is his cane: 'There was about a second during which Ellis did not know what he was doing. In that second he had hit out with all his strength, and the cane landed, crack! right across the boy's eyes.' The boy is blinded. He will grin no more, greasy little babu.

Orwell was observed, in November 1924, at a Rangoon railway station, crowded at 4 p.m. by high-school boys. He was on his way

The Gymkhana Club, Rangoon. Sahibs only.

to the exclusive ('white only') Gymkhana Club. A Burmese witness recalled:

> One of the boys, fooling about with his friends, accidentally bumped against the tall and gaunt Englishman, who fell heavily down the stairs. Blair was furious and raised the heavy cane which he was carrying, to hit the boy on the head, but checked himself, and struck him on the back instead.[36]

This is nothing in comparison to what Ellis is described doing, but Orwell, in his 'fury', could well have overreacted with his 'heavy cane' (it was not a mere 'swagger stick'). Perhaps on other occasions he did. He would not, one can be sure, have done it at Waterloo station.

The Indian police were not universally firearmed; the cane was sufficient for crowd control, which was principally what worried the authorities. Riot too quickly mutated into 'mutiny'. The police cane is used to this day on the subcontinent – one of the few respected legacies of Empire.

Ritualized caning is interwoven with hierarchy in the British private and public (ill-named) school sectors. Masters routinely carried canes in Orwell's day. With seniority, sixth-form 'prefects' were privileged to carry them (at St Cyprian's, as well as at Eton). Orwell was known as a gentle flogger. But he wielded the cane, nonetheless.

There were persistent rumours in the years after his death, usually whispered in drink (as it was to me), that Orwell was a flagellophile. He derived, that is, a fetishized sexual thrill from the whip and from being whipped – the English Vice, as it's called. His astute remark about Dickens in the epigraph above is suggestive. Whatever the truth of it, there is an impressive rack of bum-whackers described in Orwell's fiction and non-fiction. Prominent is Sambo's riding crop, the horsewhip traditionally used by angry parents of dishonoured daughters. When it was broken on young Eric's buttocks, Wilkes replaced it with a 'rattan' cane. More 'whippy' than the traditional willow cane, rattan lasted longer and the 'cut' it gave was sharper. Mr Simmons, the angry magistrate, threatened to 'birch' the young offender (Eric Blair, if he but knew it). The 'birch' was favoured in prison until the 1960s. It was made up of a bundle of twigs and, on the bare buttocks, was exquisitely painful. In Burma, it was the bamboo cane ('the only thing that makes any impression on the Burman', as the obnoxious Ellis says). In Orwell's last novel, *Nineteen Eighty-Four*, the whip is modernized into the rubber truncheon – whippier and more brutal. Winston Smith is truncheoned for days on end to soften him up for the electrified rack.

Up with the Workers?

The caning episode at the Rangoon station is dated, precisely, to 1924. Let's shift scene, hypothetically, to May 1926. Had he been back home on leave that month, what would serving policeman Blair have done in the Great Strike? Would he, like his Etonian friends

Connolly and Acton (and their Oxford chum Evelyn Waugh), have enrolled as a uniformed Special Constable to be armed with truncheons, and the right to use them, against bolshy mineworkers, their arms' skill honed by their cane-swishing years in the sixth form? Or would Eric Blair, as an early manifestation of the 'anarchist' principles that would take him to Spain, march with the downtrodden masses, cobblestone in hand? Dreaming spires or Wigan Pier? Where would his loyalty have been?

The section on the 1926 cataclysm in Chapter Fifteen of *The Road to Wigan Pier* is, for Orwell, surprisingly hazy. The General Strike, he says, was the fault of the apparatchik trade union leaders, not the salt-of-the earth miners who, like the animals in Jones's farm, are misled and bamboozled by their more intelligent, selfish leaders. It is not a satisfactory analysis and is uncharacteristically evasive. The best guess is that, had Eric Blair been in London in April 1926, he would have retreated into his habitually 'cynical'

Rangoon, c. 1923. Note the length of the canes, and tall Orwell.

observation posture, and watch it pass to see what happened. Then
decide what to do. And probably do nothing.

Sex

> There's a Burma girl a-settin', and I know she thinks o' me.
> RUDYARD KIPLING, 'Mandalay' (1892)

The American firm Harper first published *Burmese Days* a year or
so before Gollancz plucked up the courage to put it out in Britain.
The Americans perceived that the novel reeks of sex. Male readers'
erections, not the grim analysis of British Empire, were what would
make it saleable in the u.s. Perhaps issue as a drugstore paperback,
in the Erskine Caldwell mode, would suit it best.[37] Paperback covers
for the drugstore market, barely the right side of pornography, were
duly commissioned. For the drugstore trade sex, as much as you
could get away with, was a prime selling point. For Orwell sex was
a painful biological problem for which the 'East' was a solution.
Burma was commonly regarded as the biggest brothel in the Empire.

Still an angry 'cock-virgin', one guesses, Orwell had left for
Rangoon, and six months' training in Mandalay, in October 1922.
He confided to his Eton friend Harold Acton in later life that in
Burma he had got all the sex he didn't get in England: from the
'Jewish whores with crocodile faces' in Rangoon,[38] one supposes, to
exquisitely aromatic doll-like live-in concubines in remote up-country
stations. Bowker suggests that even the bored wives of colleagues
may have been curious to sleep with an Etonian. Crick hints at
a Eurasian child, which, if one is fanciful, may be an explanation
for Orwell's precipitate resignation (an act that lost him a sizeable
amount of payment).

Attractive boys were also of sexual interest to Eric Blair. He was,
he recalled later, attracted by the androgynous beauty of the dominant Burmese race – the 'Burman'. He came to relish the attentions

of his young native servants ('boys') when they handled his naked body 'intimately' while bathing and dressing him. Their male bodies, golden, not boiled-beef red, were not disfigured by pubic hair (how did he know that?). 'I felt', he recorded later in *The Road to Wigan Pier*, 'towards a Burman almost as I felt towards a woman. Like most other races, the Burmese have a distinctive smell – I cannot describe it: it is a smell that makes one's teeth tingle – but this smell never disgusted me.'

The White Man's dominance in any sexual act was, over these exile years, ingrained into Orwell's sexuality if one credits one of the women testifying to what he was like in bed. Like a 'Burmese Sergeant Major', was her verdict.[39] She could at least have commissioned him. The first generation of biographers were skittish about Orwell's half-confided sexual activities in Burma, suggesting that it was boastfulness. Later biographers grant that he did what he said he did, and possibly more.

Sterility

A question that is relevant here concerns Orwell and venereal disease. If he whored (as the evidence suggests he did), sometimes drunkenly, and was wholly averse to 'French letters' (one of his crotchets), the risk of infection must have been high. In a letter of 1934 – seven years after coming back from Burma – he confided to a girlfriend that he '"was incapable of having children" because he had "never had any"'. Orwell also confided his doubts about his fertility to Pamela Warburg, the wife of his publisher, and to his friend Rayner Heppenstall.[40] It was a refrain with him. In a letter in 1945, to another woman friend, he wrote: 'I am also sterile I think – at any rate I have never had a child, though I have never undergone the examination because it is so disgusting' (it simply requires a sample of semen, onanistically produced). His disinclination to be examined and, if necessary, medicated leads one to wonder if lingering venereal disease was the reason. The pre-antibiotic treatment of such infections was genuinely disgusting.

In Orwell's marriage, Crick notes, although 'it takes two to make a child' he always blamed himself specifically for the lack of children. Other reasons for his sterility, linked to his lifelong pulmonary disorders, have been hypothesized by J. J. Ross.[41] If someone as occasionally reckless as Orwell did not pick up a 'dose', he was lucky. But similarly, if he were promiscuous, unwilling to use condoms and, in his five years of marriage, desperate for children, his infertility is strange.

Service

The luxurious, waited-on hand and foot lifestyle that Orwell's profession enjoyed would be available only after the two years' training and probation at Mandalay. It involved learning smatterings of native languages (in which cadet Blair excelled; language bonuses would swell his salary) and familiarity with colonial law (in which he was conscientious). Indian clerks would do the hard grind. For ADS (Assistant District Superintendent) Blair, too, it would be mainly deskwork. Apart from the dubious elephant, there is no record of Blair's shooting anything – other than literary magazines from England, which, when they were too 'socialist', like *The Adelphi*, he used for pistol target practice (that's the best way to deal with Bolshies). Ironically, a few years later *The Adelphi*, under his friend Richard Rees, would be the first magazine to take some of his important early, anti-colonial non-fiction – 'A Hanging', notably, one of the two very fine articles to come out of his Burmese service.

Orwell would spend four-and-three-quarter years in the tropics, in a service buoyed up by the Empire's indelible sense of racial superiority over the Burmese 'niggers'. They were, particularly the junior Buddhist priests, 'evil little beasts'. And dangerous. To be alone in a Burmese crowd was, for a white man, to be glared at, spat at and cursed. The opening section of 'Shooting an Elephant' rings true on this score:

> In Moulmein, in Lower Burma, I was hated by large numbers of people – the only time in my life that I have been important enough for this to happen to me. I was sub-divisional police officer of the town, and in an aimless, petty kind of way anti-European feeling was very bitter. No one had the guts to raise a riot, but if a European woman went through the bazaars alone somebody would probably spit betel juice over her dress.

Orwell never took well to baiting. And there is some truth in Conor Cruise O'Brien's epigram: 'Although he condemns imperialism he dislikes its victims even more.'[42] Their own king had been taken from the Burmese people. They did not love the English king. There were no durbars in Burma. The best jobs open to 'natives' went to the more trustworthy Indians – whom the Burmese hated even more than they did the English. When, years later, *Burmese Days* was published, it would coincide with bloody anti-Indian riots.

One of the things that does not ring true in 'Shooting an Elephant' is that ADS Blair would have leapt into his Ford car, Winchester rifle in hand, to go, like Tom Mix, to kill the marauding beast. He would in reality have organized a party, supervised by Indian subordinates, to keep the crowd in order with slashing canes while the disturbance was dealt with. One should not always believe what Orwell writes about Orwell.

ADS Blair, *Burmese Days* suggests, could bear Indians. But he despised his 'own kind', the 'sham' English gentleman strutting among the 'natives' who could, thanks to the privilege of imperial power, pretend to be what it would take three generations, and a lot of money, for them to become in England. Orwell knew himself to be a cut above them. He had the old school tie to prove it. The more he saw of what they were doing, the more he hated the 'Jews and Scots' – merchants and industrialists who were raping Burma of its natural resources. Their legacy would be a desert when the last of the teak had been felled, the last drop of oil pumped out and the last rupee extracted from the British-owned rice cartels (they were largely run by Jewish merchants who were as British as Eric Blair). Scottish engineers built and ran the huge new oil refinery at Syriam. Steam and motorized transport, good roads, railways and port facilities in the Bay of Rangoon made Burma in the 1920s an efficient exporter of the other country's rich resources. It was for that reason, principally, that the country's transport system had been constructed – for the colonists' pockets.

Blair was revolted, at a more visceral level, by the 'other ranks', salt-of-the-earth Tommy Atkinses of whom he was, from time to time, in charge. There were two battalions of hugely bored British soldiers in Burma in his day (about half the manpower of Britain's current army) and ten battalions of Indian troops. Lower-class smell, fomented by the damp heat and foetid barrack-room conditions, was their prime offence. The 'steam of their sweating bodies', he later wrote, 'made my stomach turn'.

Eric Blair was at this stage of his life, he later said, 'both a snob and a revolutionary'. There are times in his life when one would give anything to be near him, listening to him talk – when he cared to. This is a time when one would not much want the company of ADS Blair. Even less, of course, he yours. He was working towards a complex and unusual attitude, composed of complex dislikes and intolerances. You could loathe imperialism but you could also loathe the natives ('evil spirited little beasts') whom it tyrannized. And, most complicatedly, you could dislike yourself for being a 'cog' in this horrible, vastly efficient machine. As regards colonialism, Orwell was like those heroic doctors who, in the interests of medical science, infect themselves with, say, Ebola. There is, as at other times in his life, a perverse nobility to his actions. But one has to struggle to make sense of it.

Police State

Where there aren't no Ten Commandments.

KIPLING on Burma, 'Mandalay' (1892)

I hated the imperialism I was serving with a bitterness which
I probably cannot make clear.

The Road to Wigan Pier

The country of Burma, annexed piece by piece from larger India,
was oddly undefined. It did not have behind it the centuries that
had brought the British and Indians into a working relationship
and which was like intermarriage writ large. Burma was ethnically a
jigsaw, fragmented into cultural, tribal, religious and local sub-entities.
It was ruled, after 1923, by 'diarchy'. That is to say, it was run by
Indian satraps and owned by the British. The 30,000 'whites' and
one million Indians comprised an oligarchic tier over twelve million
Burmans who had no significant input into the way 'their' country
was run. Indian labourers were manageable; Burmese labourers were
rebellious. Similarly docile Indians dominated the lower ranks of
the professions (Veeraswamy, in *Burmese Days*, would have been one
of a host of Indian doctors), courts, hospitals, jails and police force.
The British sahibs liked Indians: charming folk, McGregor says in
Burmese Days, 'provided they are given no freedom'. The whites and
Indians detested the Burmese masses, who were regarded by their
diarchic masters as surly, cunning and intractable.

In the nineteenth century the IPS had been notoriously corrupt,
'saturated with corruption from end to end, and . . . an instrument
of private danger rather than of public protection'. Lord Curzon said
that, and it was he, the viceroy of India in 1902, who set out compre-
hensively to reform the service as Peel had reformed the English
police forces. Curzon's first imperative was that it should be a 'service
composed of gentlemen'.[43] Not, of course, the kind of gentlemen

who became viceroys of India, but decent enough fellows. And it was Curzon who realized that if the subcontinent (which then included Burma) were to be kept orderly – to facilitate its efficient plunder by the mother country – it was a modern police force, not the army, which would do the necessary. During Orwell's years of service there were twice as many police as boots-on-the-ground soldiers (called a 'reserve' force, to be used only in emergency).

Burma was renowned as the least populated province of British India (apart from Assam) yet the most criminal. It was shaken by periodic 'storms' of crime. There was just such a storm raging when Orwell arrived. These eruptions were taken very seriously by the authorities as fore-tremors of rebellion. Despite the much-repeated slogan 'we hold India by the sword', it was the formidably efficient police force that did the necessary holding in the last four decades of colonial rule.[44] The ratio of full-time police to population was one per 750. For comparison, the current UK figure is one per 60,000. In the last forty years of their colonial existence, India, Ceylon and Burma were police states – the first, and among the most efficient, the world has known. The techniques, if not inspirational (one suspects they must have been studied), would be refined in a ghastly way by the Gestapo and NKVD.

It is a vulgar error to think that Orwell set out to be some oriental version of the local Southwold bobby or London's Metropolitan copper. Those with a love of Good-Bad Books who gave the IPS a moment's thought may have called to mind 'Sanders of the River', with his Maxim gun, bringing civilization to the grateful savages who survived his slaughter. It is pleasant – in an Edgar Wallace dream world – to fantasize about ADS Blair heroically bringing down with his trusty Webley some kris-wielding dacoit about to do his worst to a white woman; or pursuing criminals through the jungle. But as reformed by Curzon, the IPS was an intelligence service; at its heart was a unit known as the 'Political Crime Department'. The Burmese police force, like its parent Indian force, was not primarily an instrument for maintaining law and order but one for gathering intelligence and nipping any possible uprising in the bud. Internal espionage ('IPS is Watching You') was its reason for being.

It was lack of intelligence that had led to the 'Mutiny' of 1857. That lesson was learned. In 1906 a CIB (Criminal Investigation Branch) had been established in Burma. It was a clearing house for intelligence to be referred up. It had free-ranging powers and became a 'cornerstone of the surveillance and intelligence powers of government'. The gathering of 'intelligence' was diffused, at local level, to DIDs – District Intelligence Departments – which operated networks of paid informants and, in villages, 'watchmen'. They had the responsibility to detect and the power to arrest. The prime aim was to identify potential insurgents. With its off-books spies, the ratio of population to police personnel would have been in the low hundreds. But the arterial information channels were 'native' – Burmans spying on Burmans. In Orwell's last posting, there were some twenty Europeans ('whites') in a population of hundreds of thousands over a land area of a thousand square miles. It was none-theless efficiently 'policed', and obsessively 'watched'.

It would be naive to suppose that Orwell had not genned up on what the IPS was, and what his responsibilities as an officer would be. He had eight postings in his five years, most of them to country districts (the population of Burma was principally dispersed, in the country's vast territory, into a mosaic of disparate villages, typically tribally endogenous). He was not moved around because he gave dissatisfaction, but because he was good at his job: a competent spy in policeman's uniform. He was shrewd, fluent in native languages and observant, and could write the kind of clear English that made for a good analytic report.

During officer Blair's tenure, truly terrible things were being enacted. He helped to enact them. The Criminal Tribes Legislation was brought into Burma in 1924 (it had been in force in India since 1911). Its powers were brutal: villages, communities and ethnic groups

(myriad in Burma) could be summarily judged to be collectively
criminal and relocated; members of the groups could be summarily
arrested and tried – on emergency trumped-up charges, if necessary.
(What crime has the condemned man committed in 'A Hanging'?
We are never told.)

Two of his postings clarified what would be Blair's indissolubly
contrary feelings about the country, and what his own country had
done to it. One was his six-month post in Syriam. It was the site
of the largest oil refinery in the Empire, a gleaming testament to
British (specifically Scottish) industrial achievement. The plant
processed seven million gallons annually. India, with its vast spaces
and population, depended on 'Burmah Oil Company' fuel, sucked,
vampirically, out of the neighbouring country's soil. For miles around
Syriam, the luscious Burmese countryside was a hideous, poisoned
wasteland. The fumes killed vegetation, infected residents and did
officer Blair's lungs no good at all. The oil, like the mature jungle
teak, was irreplaceable. When it was exhausted, all that would be left
– for millennia – was soil pollution. Syriam was valuable enough to
be protected by a standing force of British troops whom, from time
to time, Orwell helped command. He disliked their sweaty smell but
he positively hated the chemical stench of the refinery (ill-named).
Orwell lived to read about Syriam being destroyed in 1942 by the
retreating British, who had built it, lest it fall into the hands of the
invading Japanese. The irony must have given him rueful pleasure.
He would have liked to have been there with the torch himself.

His last posting was in Katha (the 'Kyauktada' of *Burmese Days*)
in the far north of the country, at the end of the railway line: the
fringe of colonialism. The unviolated landscape entranced him. In
the novel, Flory goes into the jungle, swims in its pools, wonders
at the Edenic wildness. It teems with life but the British do not
belong here. There is a poignant moment in the novel when Flory,
who has earned a furlough in England, decides he cannot go back.
Burma (specifically Katha) is too beautiful, and has become a part

of him. It would be like tearing the only decent part of himself out of his body. Orwell, however, did go home, before his five-year term of service was up, on the pretext of sickness. He intended to leave for good – unless, he may have forlornly thought, he could persuade a forgiving Jacintha to come back with him as his memsahib. The option remained open for a month or two. There was the added factor that his years in Burma had, as with Flory, aged him: 'When he left home he had been a boy, a promising boy and handsome in spite of his birthmark; now, only ten years later, he was yellow, thin, drunken, almost middle-aged in habits and appearance.' The youthful bloom had withered. It had, with Eric Blair, taken only half as long as with Flory. He would, however, wait awhile before telling his parents or the authorities about the drastic step he had in mind.

The Anarchist Spasm

Orwell came home with a stopover in Marseilles. There were street demonstrations in the city against the impending execution, by electric chair, of Nicola Sacco and Bartolomeo Vanzetti on 23 August. The Marseilles event was one of several worldwide street protests. The Italian-born anarchists had been convicted (probably railroaded, Orwell and others believed) of a bomb outrage against a bank seven years earlier. Followers of the extremist Luigi Gallean, Sacco and Vanzetti believed that domestic terrorism was the only way an entrenched capitalist system could be overthrown and replaced. The politics of the deed. And the bomb.

Incidental as it was, the Marseilles event planted in Orwell a spasmodic sympathy with anarchism, which proposed total internal war against the state as the only solution. That sympathy was to erupt at moments of political despair in his life, when anything other than the surgical 'bomb' was deemed hopeless. It seems to be connected with his occasional suicidal tendencies. Consider, for example, what Winston loyally swears to do in his recruitment to the 'Brotherhood' (a favourite anarchist term) by O'Brien, in *Nineteen Eighty-Four*. Will he murder and betray Oceania to foreign powers? 'Yes,' Winston asserts:

'You are prepared to cheat, to forge, to blackmail, to corrupt the minds of children, to distribute habit-forming drugs, to encourage prostitution, to disseminate venereal diseases – to do anything which is likely to cause demoralization and weaken the power of the Party?'
'Yes.'
'If, for example, it would somehow serve our interests to throw sulphuric acid in a child's face – are you prepared to do that?'
'Yes.'

Stop the novel at this point, and picture a narrative in which Winston Smith, in the interest of 'weakening the power of the party', actually does go around spreading VD, throwing acid in children's faces and murdering innocent bystanders in his good cause. Call it 'Nightmare on 1984 Street'. But how else can Big Brother be overthrown? The kind of vote that kicked Churchill (on whom Big Brother is partly based) out of Downing Street in 1945?

At moments of hopelessness (and there were plenty during the writing of *Nineteen Eighty-Four*), Orwell embraced the anarchist nihilism of Mikhail Bakunin as the only solution. He joined the Republican forces in the Spanish Civil War in 1937, at a time when the struggle looked increasingly hopeless. He fought there, and damn near died, under the red-and-black flag of POUM, the romantically ineffective anarchists, against the twin totalitarianisms of Fascism and Stalinism.

The strangest ebullition of Orwell's normally quiescent anarchism was during his service, as an NCO, in the Home Guard during the Second World War. The government, Orwell realized excitedly, was giving guns, grenades and bombs to the people. An armed populace could, surely, mobilize itself to overthrow and replace the government by acts of domestic terrorism. Or so, for a month or two, he fantasized. It's amusing to fancy a kind of revolution via *Dad's Army*: Captain Mainwaring on the barricades, Private Pike passing the ammunition. His Trotskyist supporters (Christopher Hitchens, for example) are embarrassed by this Orwellian flight of anarchist fancy.

Over the years Orwell's interest in anarchism was fanned and kept alight by his friend and intellectual antagonist George Woodcock.[45] His belief in it as the only way came and went, sporadically, like a bout of malarial fever.

Down-and-out

The prole suffers physically, but he's a free man when he isn't working.

Coming Up for Air [46]

When Orwell came back from Burma in the summer of 1927, the question 'what will Eric do?' hovered over the cramped Southwold household like a black cloud. It would hang there for seven lean years. Once the hope of the family, Eric was now a double-dyed failure – at Eton and in the Indian Police Service.

Orwell intended, without consulting his family on the matter, to resign his five-year commission prematurely on the pretext (fabricated) of illness – a touch of dengue fever, which he could easily have shaken off with some rest and recuperation in Rangoon. No one is recorded as seeing any sign of the ailment's symptomatic jaundiced complexion or falling hair. The Blairs could not rejoice in Eric's coming home. Marjorie, now married, had gone to live in the north and had a family of her own. Avril, whose prospects in life had been cruelly narrowed to pay for her brother's, was caring for her parents. At 22, her marriage chances looked remote. Richard was now verging on seventy, and cranky. A good cook, Avril was selling homemade cakes for the summer tourist trade to help with the family's straitened finances. Accustomed for four years to servants waiting on him hand and foot, Eric would drop cigarette ends on the floor at home and expect someone else to pick them up. Avril, the picker-up, remembered that, resentfully, decades later. Decades later, of course, she was still picking up his dog-ends in Jura. Her role in life.

There intervened at this point a very strange event. Orwell visited the man at Eton who had effectively dished his prospects, to get 'advice' on what next he should do next. It may have been at Richard's insistence. What is odd is that Andrew Gow invited Orwell to come and stay a day or two with him. After nine years of trying, the unhappy schoolteacher had finally got his Trinity fellowship. Competition had been thinned out by the war. A heart murmur had excused him from service. He is reputed to have replied, when someone asked why he was in civilian clothes, that he was the civilization others were dying for. My grandfather lost an eye in the First World War; I'm glad it went for a good cause. Gow's advice on Blair's career prospects had not hitherto been helpful, nor had Blair written to Gow since leaving Eton. In the interview Crick had for his biography with the retired don (still resident at Trinity) in 1976:

> Gow remembered little about the visit, except that Blair came to tell him that he had resigned from the Burma Police, was thinking of pursuing a literary career, but wanted to take advice first. 'I seem to remember', Gow said, 'that as he seemed fairly determined and had nothing else in mind, I said, in a rather non-committal way that he might as well have a try.' He stayed the night in college [at Gow's expense, presumably] and Gow

remembers that he sat him next to A. E. Housman at High Table, who asked him about Burma. It is hard to interpret this incident.

Hard indeed. Orwell at Trinity, surrounded by what would later be called the Homintern, was a fish out of water. But it is relevant that before the Second World War MI5 employed mostly former Indian policemen. Orwell, to indulge the most far-fetched of speculations, may have been viewed as a possible recruit. The reason these men were desirable as spooks is that their police work was that of a police state – surveillance and espionage. Orwell might be a prospect.

Gow, having got there, would, limpet-like, never leave Trinity. He taught Classics, published little (not imperative in those days at that place) and held extracurricular seminars for favourite students (his rooms were now sumptuous). He was a friend of fellow fellows such as Housman in the 1920s and master spy Anthony Blunt in the 1930s, and his favourite student was that other master spy, Guy Burgess. In short, was Gow sounding Blair out for something in behind-the-scenes 'intelligence'? If so, it went nowhere. But at least Orwell met his idol, A. E. Housman.

Women Problems

I don't think he really liked women.

BRENDA SALKELD, one of Orwell's longest-lasting lovers

There had been virtually no correspondence between Orwell and Jacintha over the five years he had been away. He nonetheless had hopes. He had come back from Burma with an engagement ring. How he proposed to support a wife (unless by return to Burma) is not clear, but the problem did not arise. Jacintha wanted nothing more to do with him. He assumed it was because of his brutishness in the fields. He did not know, and never would, that while he was away she had borne an illegitimate child. Worse still, the father had absconded. The child had been discreetly adopted out of the country. It was this disgrace, not the attempted rape, that meant Jacintha could not welcome Eric home as her lover, even if she were inclined to.

'They never met again,' John Rodden records bleakly, 'and Blair never knew the real reason why he had been rejected.'[47] With an effort of will Jacintha closed her mind on him. She went to her grave regretting that she had not taken the risk of marrying Eric on his return from Burma. She wrote, in a letter long after his death: 'He had ruined what been such a close and fulfilling relationship, since childhood, by trying to take us the whole way before I was anywhere near ready for that.'

Over the next few years, as he came and went to the town, young Blair cut a poor figure in Southwold, a place he cordially disliked. Nor – at the time and for all time, it would seem – did Southwold like Eric Blair (or, come to that, his alter ego George Orwell). A hundred years after his birth, the local *East Anglian Daily Times* commemorated Southwold's most famous literary son sourly:

> A literary giant who 'loathed' the small-town conservatism of a seaside town in north Suffolk is being remembered in the centenary year of his birth. But according to his sister Avril Blair, . . . he 'loathed' the town. He is remembered as a rather dishevelled unshaven figure, dressed in suits handmade by a local tailor that needed a good iron, a long scarf, and no hat – which in the 1930s was considered under-dressed . . . people felt rather sorry for his parents.[48]

That summer he formed relationships with a number of local women, probably more of which we'll never know about. Prominent among those we do know about, from surviving correspondence, was a gym teacher at St Felix's girls' school, Brenda Salkeld, and Eleanor Jaques, whose family had come to Southwold from Canada in 1921

and lived, for a while, next door to the Blairs. There were compli-
cations with both. Brenda, a vicar's daughter, seems to have been
an early adopter of Julia's anti-sex sash. Eleanor, easier-going, was
involved with, and later engaged to, Dennis Collings, the son of the
Blairs' family doctor.

Blair was generally regarded by the young men of the town,
and some husbands he is alleged to have cuckolded, as a sexual
raider. His Etonian airs did not endear him. On one occasion, as
D. J. Taylor discovered from interviews with aged residents, he was
chased across the Southwold commons by a rival on motorbike with
homicidal intent, for unwelcome attentions to his fiancée. Eleanor's
boyfriend, Dennis Collings, apparently did not know what Eric, his
supposed best friend, was up to when he was out of town. 'Horning
in', Americans call it. He finally got his way with Eleanor in summer
1932, al fresco, wild scents in his nostrils, as he always preferred:

> I cannot remember when I have ever enjoyed any expeditions so
> much as I did those with you. Especially that day in the wood
> along past Blythborough Lodge – you remember, where the deep
> beds of moss were. I shall always remember that & your nice
> white body in the dark green moss.[49]

Snapshots of Eleanor's nice white body resurface in *Keep the
Aspidistra Flying* and *Nineteen Eighty-Four*'s woody love scenes.
He apparently enjoyed her body in the mossy bank while Dennis
was away at Cambridge (studying anthropology), having left his
'girl' in his best friend's care. Dangerous. After summer passed,
in October 1932, Eric wrote to Eleanor, 'I hope you will let me make
love to you again some time, but if you don't it doesn't matter, I shall
always be grateful to you for your kindness to me.' In November he
wrote: 'When we were together, you didn't say whether you were
going to let me be your lover again. Of course you can't if Dennis
is in S'wold, but otherwise? You mustn't if you don't want to, but I

hope you will.' Did she? Who knows? But she did marry Collings in 1934.

Brenda Salkeld, the gym mistress, Orwell must have seen often stripped for calisthenics. He doubtless recalled the McGill postcard and fantasized about her getting her physical jerks under him. It never happened. She tantalized him for years but never gave in, despite eloquent wooing by letter and in person, two proposals of marriage and, yet again, what looks like a near rape in the fields. As Bowker records:

> He was not good at managing his relationships with women. One Sunday in July [1931] he invited Brenda for a fishing expedition-cum-picnic. On this occasion she must have permitted a little canoodling, and he must then have gone much too far for her – the abrupt move, perhaps, or his usual blunt proposition. When she rebuffed him he told her that if she did not want to make love to him it was better they part. Outraged at this she stormed off back to her lodgings.

Unlike Jacintha or Eleanor, Brenda – who worked out daily in the school gym – was quite capable of looking after her pearl beyond price. She was not, apparently, mollified by his letter of apology the next day in which he said, 'it hurts me not to have you altogether.' Brenda later concluded that he did not like women, but had an irresistible physical need to 'possess' them. 'Cock-tease' (one of his favourite blunt terms) that she was, Orwell admired Brenda's spirit and invited her to come with him to the Kent hop fields in the summer of 1932. She declined the manifest offer of rutting in ditches. They remained friends. There was an odd postscript. In 1939, Orwell now married, met her again and, extraordinarily, wrote her a love letter, on his birthday in 1940, evidently with a *ménage à trois* or an affair in mind. He got his wife's permission to do so.

There was a string of women who slept with Orwell once but preferred not to do it again. Eleanor is the first recorded. Sonia was the last – she, rather unwillingly, surrendered to him a single time before marriage, but not after, when sex was beyond him. One-timers seemed (like Eleanor and Sonia) willing to carry on 'liking' him. Those who did, as Jacintha puts it, 'go the whole way' found him, apparently, a graceless lover.

The years he had been away (1922–7) had been socially tumultuous. He had missed the General Strike – the nearest Britain had come to revolution since the seventeenth century. Its repercussions were still shaking the country. His contemporaries at Eton, Children of Sun, the Brideshead generation, golden youth, were meanwhile rising like rockets. And Eric Blair? Those who saw him were shocked at how prematurely aged he looked. Time was wasting him. He was understandably nervous about revealing the decision he had made about his 'career', and put off for weeks telling his father that he could no longer wear the uniform of the 'evil despotism' Richard Blair had proudly worn for thirty years. Now captain (the highest rank he ever achieved) of the Southwold golf club (his name is still commemorated on its walls), Richard Blair did not regard himself as an evil despot, retd. He was, however, a double-dyed snob and above all else anxious to maintain appearances. Peter Davison turned up a recollection from a 'high-class tailor' in Southwold who – as a tradesman – was routinely cut dead in the street by 2nd Lt Blair (retd): 'Old man Blair was terribly autocratic. If anyone got in his way at the golf course they'd get it in no uncertain terms! He felt his weight very much; he was full of his own importance.' Not having a son 'doing terribly well in Burma, thank you for inquiring' would not augment Old Man Blair's self-importance at the nineteenth hole.

Disclosure was awkward. Blair told his mother first. During the ructions that followed he went on to inform his parents, and Avril (who didn't count), that he was resolved to become a 'writer'. Had he

Orwell and the
Blair family
dog Hector in
Southwold. Cat
unknown.

stated a resolution to shave his head, borrow a bed sheet and become
a Buddhist priest they would doubtless, at this stage, have been less
shocked – and less worried about 'how it would look' in Southwold.
Orwell did not write directly about his family's reaction, but there
are bruising scenes in the most autobiographical of his novels, *Keep
the Aspidistra Flying*, when Gordon announces his career change
from a 'safe job' to what? A writer?

Eric was cut out of his father's will. It did not worry him for the
moment. He had earned around £3,000 in Burma and had managed
to save a nest egg. After he embarked on his new career, a gifted
young poet and potter, Ruth Pitter, who had rather taken to him

on first meeting him at a party, when he was an eighteen-year-old, helped him to find lodgings in London. In his garret Orwell wrote obsessively. And clumsily, Ruth recalled. She was a few years older, sophisticated, and getting known and liked in the London literary and artistic worlds. She and her girlfriends good-naturedly guffawed at samples he showed them of his work in progress (always an ill-advised thing for young writers to do). He was not 'there' yet. He may have tried it on with Ruth, but through life she seems to have preferred girlfriends. And the Orwell she had admired five years earlier no longer had the peach-bloom freshness he had at eighteen. But, with an effort, he could still photograph well, evoking his military bearing and Etonian hauteur. The fact that he liked to cut his own hair with kitchen scissors detracts a trifle.[50]

A Cambridge Education (Second Hand. Southwold College)

The word 'writer' (never 'author' – the distinction is important) did not clearly convey what was vaguely, and importantly, taking shape in Orwell's mind. His career moves were invariably intuitive and impulsive. What he had in mind, while keeping his Burmese novel simmering in pre-publication fluidity, was to embark on an ambitious social anthropological project, modelled on the inspirational fieldwork of Bronisław Malinowski, the pioneer ethnographer, and the work his disciples were doing in the academic powerhouse of British social anthropology – Cambridge University.

Orwell was, if not a sexual predator, always on the lookout for anything going. Sleeping with his best friend's fiancée while said best friend was away from 'S'wold' was, however you look at it, a bit low. More admirable was his plundering Dennis's mind for the up-to-date theory and practice in Malinowskian anthropology. Eric Blair was a masterly brain-picker. Collings was an interesting and, by the end of his life, distinguished man. In 1923, aged eighteen, he had set off on his own initiative for Portuguese East Africa to study tropical plants. Herbal anthropology (ethnobotany) was in its infancy; Collings was a pioneer in the field.[51] Eric had met Dennis before he left for Africa. Two years later he returned to Southwold. Around the same time, Eric returned from Burma and their friendship was renewed. In 1928 Collings went up to St John's College, Cambridge, to study anthropology. Following his graduation in 1932, he took up a post with the Museum of Cambridge, whose displays he reorganized over the three years he spent there. Among other things, he set up the Southwold Museum. He married Eleanor in 1934 and the two of them went off to Singapore, where he took charge of the Raffles Museum. Many times Eric must have been told how well his best friend was doing. During the long, dull years of Eric's Southwold residence, 1928–34, when Dennis was around (putting Eleanor temporarily off limits), the young men must have talked a lot about anthropology: what it was, who the current leaders of the discipline were. Eric never went to Cambridge, but Cambridge, via Dennis, came to him.[52]

Malinowski published his inspirational *Argonauts of the Western Pacific* in 1922. It wholly reformed Cambridge anthropology. He was 'in the air' in the 1920s, known well outside his academic field, and was further popularized by Aldous Huxley's *Brave New World* (1928). Huxley was a disciple.[53] Orwell read Huxley's novel when it first came out, and disagreed with its 'hedonism' – disagreement that would become polemically explicit in *Nineteen Eighty-Four*. Malinowski believed that the social anthropologist – the 'explorer' or 'argonaut' – must plunge into the society they wanted to know about; they must become what they wanted to understand, whatever the personal risk. This 'participant observation', as it was called, was a version of Joseph Conrad's 'in the destructive element immerse'. The aim was to discover 'the native's point of view' by 'going native'. As V. S. Pritchett memorably put it, Orwell went native in his own country.[54]

Orwell put his long, casual tutorial with Dennis Collings into practice. *Down and Out in Paris and London*, the work which came out of Orwell's immersion, begins with a ritual divestiture: and with it a change of identity. It is one of the most arresting moments in the book – Orwell is not merely changing clothes; he is losing caste. He goes to a rag-shop in London where he sells his middle-class (sadly rumpled) outfit. He gets a shilling and some dirty looking rags. He discovers a new self as he emerges in his new togs:

> My new clothes had put me instantly into a new world.
> Everyone's demeanour seemed to have changed abruptly.
> I helped a hawker pick up a barrow that he had upset. 'Thanks, mate,' he said with a grin. No one had called me mate before in my life . . . Clothes are powerful things.

He has gone native and made his first discovery. England is still a sumptuary society – clothes maketh class. Suddenly those ridiculous uniforms at Eton and in the Burmese mess make sense. Top hats = top people. Rags = ragamuffins.

In terms of its literary genesis, *Down and Out* shapes itself, sometimes close to plagiarism, along the lines of *People of the Abyss*. Jack London had been, since Eric's Eton days, a favourite author. In the summer of 1902 London had come to his namesake city to anatomize the country in its coronation year. He spent six weeks in 'darkest London', disguised as a stranded American sailor. Jack did not love the English: his aim was to reveal the old country's racial degeneration (something Max Nordau had recently popularized) and to argue that world leadership should pass to vital America. Vitality incarnate, of course, in Jack London. He spent nights in the 'spike' (workhouses for vagrant 'casuals') and in dosshouses. There is a striking description (which Orwell copied, almost word for word) about his divestiture from seaman's garb and re-emergence, in the rags he has purchased, as a down-and-outer: 'No sooner was I out on the streets than I was impressed by the difference in status effected by my clothes . . . The man in corduroy and dirty neckerchief no

longer addressed me as "sir" or "governor." It was "mate" now.' Orwell
and Jack London, 'mates' together. It is nice to see them eyeing each
other matily, in some timeless literary dimension.

Down and Out in Paris and London would be Orwell's first
book, published when he was verging on thirty, in January 1933.
It narrowly escaped literary abortion. Substantially written three
years before its publication, it drew on experience of four to five
years earlier. The title suggests a misleading sequence. Before going
to Paris, Orwell had made his preliminary 'recce' of the East End
London underworld: 'spikes', 'dosshouses', even 'clink'. He did it so
well that one wonders if in Burma, like Kipling's Kim, he had been
trained to go undercover. Dates help. The years 1927 (when Orwell
had his first overnight spike stay) to 1933 (when the book finally
appeared) were historically tumultuous. The jazz age – that post-war
saturnalia – ended in hours with the Wall Street Crash of October
1929. Worldwide unemployment followed. *Down and Out* pivots,
uneasily and accidentally, on that transitional historical moment in
the twentieth century, when the whole world went down and out.
The effect was to make the book, when it finally made it into print,
somewhat out of date chronologically (particularly the Paris section)
but, as a treatise on poverty and unemployment, more relevant.

Initially he foresaw reportage as the ideal form for what he had in
mind. But he could not raise serious magazine or newspaper interest
in articles about darkest London. The project enlarged in February
1928, when Orwell took off for Paris. He would stay there eighteen months, lodged most of the time in a cheap hotel in the Latin
Quarter. He spoke the language and could blend into his environment. He had a Limouzin aunt in Paris, an Esperantist of bohemian
character but chronically straitened means, who was fond of him and
helped as best she could. Whatever funds he himself had from his
years' service in Burma had melted away. Apart from the ten weeks
later chronicled, with fictional embellishments, in *Down and Out*,
and his fortnight in hospital (observing how the poor die), we know

virtually nothing of what Orwell did during his Parisian period, other than writing a lot, only a tiny fraction of which saw print, or has survived, and getting by tutoring in English and working in kitchens. He already had a keen and intrepid journalistic eye. The first piece of writing Orwell ever seriously published was in Paris, in French, in October 1928: 'La Censure en Angleterre' (Censorship in England). England was notably censorious at this period. In 1928, Radclyffe Hall's (feeble) lesbian novel *The Well of Loneliness* was prosecuted for obscenity, and the criminal edition burned. These years were the harsh regime of 'God's Policeman', 'Jix' (William Joynson-Hicks), home secretary, 1924–9. His Savonarola tendencies put English Literature back years. D. H. Lawrence's *Lady Chatterley's Lover* and James Joyce's *Ulysses* (and the worthless *Well of Loneliness*) could only be published, unexpurgated, in Paris. When eventually published in Britain, *Down and Out* suffered serious censorship at its publisher's insistence, particularly as regards the realism of its street language and sex scenes. Had Jix still been in office, the cuts and watering-down might have been even more severe.

America too was suffering a purgative wave of moralism, under Anthony Comstock's New York Society for the Suppression of Vice. The best literary energies in both English-speaking powerhouses were pushed overseas. 'Published in Paris' became a proud badge of literary freedom and quality. It was worn with pride by the 'lost generation' of American writers – Hemingway, Scott Fitzgerald, Henry Miller, Gertrude Stein and e e cummings. Another, less glamorous, attraction was that the weak post-war franc meant a little dollar went a long way.[55]

Culturally, 1928 Paris was at its interwar cosmopolitan zenith. As Eric Blair slummed it, George Gershwin immortalized the city with his symphonic poem *An American in Paris*. If Orwell heard Gershwin's paean it was as alien to him as the island's twanging melodies were to Caliban. Orwell, on the evidence of *Down and Out*, took not the slightest notice of the modernist artistic, musical, dance

and literary ferment going on around him. He may have distantly
glimpsed James Joyce once, he records. He would not read him (and
realize what he had missed) until five years later. His interest was
directed exclusively to how the Parisians lived, starved and died.
The Paris 'underneath' Paris. What was on top, he sneered in 'Inside
the Whale', was froth:

> During the boom years, when dollars were plentiful and the
> exchange-value of the franc was low, Paris was invaded by
> such a swarm of artists, writers, students, dilettanti, sight-seers,
> debauchees, and plain idlers as the world has probably never
> seen. In some quarters of the town the so-called artists must
> actually have outnumbered the working population.

Paris, after he had taken up residence in the 5th arrondissement, he
found to be peopled by the 'fantastically poor', eccentric, diverse and,
frankly, disgusting:

> There were the Rougiers, for instance, an old, ragged, dwarfish
> couple who plied an extraordinary trade. They used to sell
> postcards on the Boulevard St Michel. The curious thing was
> that the postcards were sold in sealed packets as pornographic
> ones, but were actually photographs of chateaux on the Loire;
> the buyers did not discover this till too late, and of course never
> complained . . . The filth of their room was such that one could
> smell it on the floor below. According to Madame F., neither of
> the Rougiers had taken off their clothes for four years.

Peter Davison is always at pains to remind us that Orwell is, when
he cares to turn it on, a comic writer. As here, in *Down and Out*, he
certainly is. But the observing Orwellian eye is cold and clear as ice.

The journey into even lower sub-Parisian depths began with a
happy disaster. Happy, that is, for Orwell's first book. He was robbed

of his money, as he records, by an Italian fellow lodger at his seedy hotel, the Coq d'Or (golden cock – a little Orwellian joke). In later life he disclosed, casually (to one of his other lovers), that the felonious Italian was actually a home-grown 'trollop' called Suzanne who was temporarily living with him (she would have been an interesting addition to his gallery of types).[56] Suzanne was 'beautiful and had a figure like a boy, [with] an Eton crop'. *Floreat Etona.* He had whored around in Paris, he later confided to an acquaintance. He may even have worked in a brothel, some hazard. It was not merely literary freedom that Paris offered. But he had to cut his literary cloth for his Southwold readership, his cautious publishers and prevailing English cultural timidity. Fig-leaved England was not yet ready for its Henry Miller. It was not pleasant to think of Richard enjoying a snifter in the 'club' and being asked 'how's that whoremonger of a son getting on, Richard? What a scamp, eh?'

After the theft Orwell was, in very short time, a 'down and out'. He did not, as he could have done, seek emergency help from his Parisian aunt Nellie, or his parents. He had lifelines. One telegram would have done it. But his ulterior motive was Malinowskian. To understand poverty, one had to be poor. The lifted wallet was less disaster than opportunity. He fell in with a series of low-lifes and came close to starvation, with his irrepressible, forever down-on-his-luck comrade Boris, a White Russian who had ridden with Cossacks, duelled and tasted the high life. He talked about it incessantly, as he picked bugs out of his bed and lice out of his underwear. Finally Blair (if that was what he was calling himself) found enough work to keep body and soul together as a restaurant *plongeur* (dishwasher); first at a good hotel, then a squalid restaurant. There are some appetite-killers of the kitchen-hand-spit-in-the-soup type in this section of the narrative. When the book was finally published, there were agonized letters of complaint to *The Times* by aggrieved Parisian hoteliers and restaurateurs about what this cursed 'Orwell' had done to their tourist trade.

Down and Out's Parisian narrative ends with a failed attempt at getting rich by smuggling cocaine and, finally, a mysterious offer of employment in England from 'B', which brings the narrator-hero back home. The 'B' business was a fiction devised to weld the two halves of the book together. Orwell, in real life, was of course free to return to England and middle-class amenities whenever someone loaned, or wired, him the travel money to do so. The cocaine and 'B' narrative is, to use Orwell's robust term, 'bollox'.

There was one event that is not chronicled in the book but which would resurface, fifteen years later, as one of his most authentic essays: 'How the Poor Die'. With his usual recklessness – hinting, as usual, at suicidal pathology – Blair had let his health run down catastrophically in Paris. He had chosen to come in February and live in a hotel that was dirty, cold and infectious. A year later, in February 1929, his lungs collapsed. He spat blood. He was dispatched to the hôpital Cochin, a pauper's hospital whose therapies were medieval ('cupping', even in the state he was in, fascinated Blair; he was spared leeches). Inevitably, it was the smell that struck him first:

> When we got into the ward I was aware of a strange feeling of familiarity whose origin I did not succeed in pinning down till later in the night. It was a long, rather low, ill-lit room, full of murmuring voices and with three rows of beds surprisingly close together. There was a foul smell, faecal and yet sweetish.

Inter urinas et faeces was, for Orwell, something accompanying both ends of life. We arrive and depart shit-smeared.

He who had come to see how the poor lived now saw, and smelled, how the poor died. It was an eerie forecast of how he himself would leave the world: in a hospital, beyond the power of medicine to save him. But at least he would be in UCL between clean sheets and in a private room. Bowker guesses, persuasively, that it was about this time, in places like this, or earlier, in some spike or dosshouse, that he contracted the TB which would carry him off all those years later.

He returned to Southwold (where else could he go?) almost simultaneously with the Wall Street Crash of October 1929 and the following worldwide 'slump'. Poverty is the theme of the Parisian half of his tale of two cities; unemployment is the theme of the London half. He became, for the best part of a year after his return, a 'tramp', ever more expert at the class impersonation this required. He had, as he had in Paris, friends and family. But he wanted raw material. And he wanted to feel it – in his empty belly, in unwashed clothes, in the daily humiliation heaped on tramps and beggars.

Hopping

'Kent, sir – everybody knows Kent – apples, cherries, hops and women.'

CHARLES DICKENS, *The Pickwick Papers* (1836–7)

In 1932 Orwell went, as a casual 'hopper', to the summer hop fields of Kent. He was following again in the footsteps of Jack London in *People of the Abyss*. London's description of the annual Cockney excursion was in his lofty, denunciatory, 'Downfall of Albion' style:

It is estimated that Kent alone requires eighty thousand of the street people to pick her hops. And out they come, obedient to the call, which is the call of their bellies and of the lingering dregs of adventure-lust still in them. Slum, stews, and ghetto pour them forth . . . and their withered crookedness, and their rottenness is a slimy desecration of the sweetness and purity of nature.

Forty years later, working-class Londoners, marginally less rotted, still went to the Kent fields as a kind of summer camping holiday – a Butlin's holiday camp *avant* Butlin's. There was, among the reading classes, steamy 'romance' about the hop-pickers. In one of Orwell's favourite books, Maugham's *Of Human Bondage*, the hero finds sexual fulfilment rutting in the fields.

The reality for Orwell was something else. Sex there was – but of no fulfilling variety. In his journal he gives a vivid picture of

> old Deafie, sitting on the grass with a newspaper in front of him. He lifted it aside, and we saw that he had his trousers undone and was exhibiting his penis to the women and children as they passed. I was surprised – such a decent old man, really; but there is hardly a tramp who has not some sexual abnormality.

This was too 'down' to be published in *Down and Out*.[57] In between his fieldwork, Orwell took on a number of local day jobs in Southwold – tutoring barely a notch or two above childminding. He liked children: he liked all animals, he once joked. The bona fide animal Hector, the Blair family dog, always got his best walks when Eric was home. The atmosphere at home was tense. He was contributing little if anything to the family kitty.

All the time his raw material was amassing, and promising, if only he could get it into shape and find takers. He persisted, expanding the French articles into a short book. Finally everything was stewed up together into a first draft of *Down and Out in Paris and London*. The manuscript (renamed 'A Scullion's Diary') was turned down by Jonathan Cape and, twice, with the faintest of praise, by T. S. Eliot at Faber & Faber. The book was too strong for the genteel London literary world, still bruised by Cape's prosecution, in 1928, for daring to publish *The Well of Loneliness*. *Down and Out*, like that burned book, had 'licentious' Parisian scenes. Brothel scenes (a rape, narrated by 'Charlie', is particularly brutal, even bowdlerized) and frank use of actual 'street' language (some asterisked 'f-wordage' got through) made potential takers nervous, as did possible libel suits. Throughout his life Orwell thought British publishers a 'gutless' crew.

In trips up to London he had made useful contacts in the
literary world: one in particular was the fellow Etonian 'socialist
baronet', Richard Rees, proprietor of *The Adelphi*. Orwell had been
getting occasional commissions to review in Rees's magazine. The
editors, John Middleton Murry and his successor, Max Plowman,
published 'The Spike', 'A Hanging', 'Hop Picking' and 'Poverty
Plain and Coloured'. In *Keep the Aspidistra Flying*, Orwell ungrate-
fully intimates that Rees ('Ravelston') did it as a favour – one
old Etonian scratching the back of another. In fact it was a sound
editorial choice to have encouraged this unknown writer, with
his uncomfortable subject matter, at Rees's proprietorial behest.
Plowman, with an echt working-class background and an inextin-
guishable hatred for the English ruling classes, had no objection,
even if he was being paid with a baronet's conscience money. The
Adelphi essays comprise a nugget of purest early Orwell.

Mabel

Mabel Fierz was a woman who did as much for Orwell's literary
prospects as Dennis Collings had done for his intellect. Collings was
Cambridge; she was, through and through, London Literary World.

In the face of that world's manifest lack of interest in it, Orwell
gave up on his down-and-out book, pinning his hopes on *Burmese
Days*. He left the manuscript of *Down and Out*, as a lost cause, with
Mabel. He had first come across her in the summer of 1930 on the
Southwold beach. She was married to a rich executive in the steel
business, and was of a certain age, cosmopolitan, 'mystically' socialist
(a 'crank', Orwell would have said) and sexually libertine (something
that mitigated any off-putting crankiness). She was also an *Adelphi*
contributor, and knew Richard Rees well. She was not the commonest
thing on Southwold beach. Orwell was painting when they met. (As
far as I know none of his artwork survives – it would be interesting
to see it.) Eric and Mabel went on to have an affair, in between

discussing things of the mind.[58] Her husband, Francis, was apparently complaisant. Wandering along the river it was Francis, apparently, who suggested the pen name 'Orwell'. A comment in a letter suggests that his first sexual enjoyment of Mabel was, for Orwell, that highest form of sexual bliss, copulation in the wild, in summer, with the scents of ripe nature in his nostrils and a woman under his loins. That kind of thing happened all too rarely. Mabel, unembarrassed, hit it off with Ida, another cosmopolitan woman. They played bridge together.

The Fierzes had a large house in Hampstead, and came to Southwold every summer for the air. When the affair cooled Orwell would, over the next few years, lodge with them and go to parties Mabel threw, often with interesting guests. She read the manuscript of *Down and Out* he had left with her, admired it and ignored Orwell's instruction to burn it (but keep the paper clips). He didn't mean it. Authors routinely give this order to the women they love as a test. Stephen King threw the first draft of *Carrie* (the novel that would 'make' him) into the rubbish bin, to be rescued by his loyal wife, Tabitha. Joyce threw the first draft of *A Portrait of the Artist as a Young Man* into the fire, to be rescued by his wife, Nora. And Mabel rescued *Down and Out in Paris and London*; the paper clips she may have thrown away. Mabel knew exactly whom to hassle. Eventually the manuscript found its way to the new, dynamically socialist publisher Victor Gollancz. A lover of the people, Gollancz lunched every working day in the Savoy Grill. But he had a vision of the books that would suit his list.[59]

To shield his family from possible embarrassment, and to keep his own identity, Eric Blair at this point became 'George Orwell' – a 'round English name', and a memorial to some good fishing he had had in its waters. Some of his journalism still came out under the name Eric Blair.

Down and Out in Paris and London was published in January 1933 and well reviewed. There was a pleasingly acute notice (anonymous) in the *TLS*:

It is vivid picture of an apparently mad world that Mr Orwell paints in his book, a world where unfortunate men are preyed upon by parasites, both insect and human, where a straight line of demarcation is drawn above which no man can hope to rise once he has fallen below its level. One lays down the book, wondering why men living in such conditions do not commit suicide; but Mr Orwell conveys the impression that they are too depressed and hopeless for such a final and definite effort as self-inflicted death.

Not too many 'parasites' crawling the walls in *The Times'* Printing House Square, one gathers.

Eric Blair at last had a book to his (other) name. Three helpers had got him going: Richard Rees, Dennis Collings and Mabel Fierz. Victor Gollancz could claim a second-row place in the little pro-Orwell scrum.

Paris and London

Down and Out in Paris and London is a tale of two cities. For the down and out, Orwell's Paris is more fun. Wine, baguette and *poules* are more palatable than a 'cup of tea and two slices of bread and marge' and Old Deafie's waggling penis. But, one notes, in Paris the narrator's closest companions were once as upper-class in origin as he, under his rags, still is. Boris was a former officer in the czarist army and Charlie a high-born Frenchman who had come down in the world. In London, the narrator's tramping companions were what he would call, in *Nineteen Eighty-Four*, 'proles': illiterates like the amiable Irishman Paddy, and Bozo the 'screever' (pavement artist, cripple and amateur astronomer). British law, unlike French, is less tolerant of down and outs. Since Elizabethan times they have been forced, by law and the police, to 'move on' (Dickens's phrase, in *Bleak House*). Legally they are always 'vagrants', not 'indigents', always 'tramping' nowhere. The 'spikes' allowed one night only. If it were England, Beckett's Vladimir and Estragon ('they do not move' is the last line in *Waiting for Godot*) would have been arrested or made to move. In France they can carry on waiting.[60]

Hardly a page of *Down and Out* is without a reference to money, usually low-denomination coinage. Lack of 'ready' combined with malnourishment was, Orwell believed, at the root of England's underclass problem. Without money you are chronically hungry: 'You discover that a man who has gone even a week on bread and margarine is not a man any longer, only a belly with a few accessory organs.' Orwell hints that after 1926, when, with the General Strike, Britain teetered on the brink of revolution, the authorities were not sorry to have an unmoneyed docile, above all *hungry*, working class. Starve the buggers into submission. 'You can't think when you're hungry' was a refrain with Orwell.

Orwell's Ambivalence About the Lower Classes

How terrible for Mrs Blair to have a son like that, he looks as though he never washes.

SOUTHWOLD RESIDENT, COMMISERATING WITH ERIC BLAIR'S MOTHER

Orwell's mixed fascination and disgust with the poor, the down and outs and the tramp population was crystallized in his first book. The tired Gallicism *nostalgie de la boue* (a yearning for mud – and worse) is routinely applied to his voluntary submersion into society's silt. It doesn't satisfactorily cover what he was doing. There was as much disgust as nostalgia. An Etonian in rags, he was, for one thing, always fastidious, however filthy the surroundings. He recalls, for example, starving in Paris: a bug falls from the ceiling into the milk that will keep him going. He throws the milk away with the bug. He would rather starve to death, and nearly does. He is sleeping in an English dosshouse and wakes to find a sailor's stinking feet in his face. But he sleeps there the next night. Foul smells are everywhere – only tobacco masks them. You could, you feel, contract bronchitis or worse from the miasma rising from the pages of Orwell's book.

And if in Burma he had discovered the imperial universality of Sambo's rattan cane, in the spike's washroom he discovered, for the working classes of England, the universality of the turd in Saint Cyp's 'plunge bath':

> The scene in the bathroom was extraordinarily repulsive. Fifty dirty, stark-naked men elbowing each other in a room twenty feet square, with only two bathtubs and two slimy roller towels between them all. I shall never forget the reek of dirty feet.

Nothing 'nostalgic' here. There is, to continue the theme, no more futile gesture by Jesus Christ than his washing the feet of his disciples, or kings (the last to do so in England was James II) and popes (they're still doing it) ritually washing, in honour of their saviour, the feet of the poor. They stink because they don't have the money not to. Kings and popes have a lot of money. Judas was right about that – silver matters.

At the end of *Down and Out* Orwell confesses that he has only scraped the 'fringe' of what it is to be poor and unemployed. It took Malinowski five years to fully 'participate' with his Trobriand islanders. Tourists stay longer in Paris than did Eric Blair. But few see as much. What comes through strongly in the envoi of *Down and Out* is not the depth of the research but Orwell's generosity of spirit and the rank simplicity of his proposed solution. The poor, he insists, are not parasites, not 'scroungers', not layabouts, not 'degenerate' (*pace* Jack London) – they are, most of them, victims of a society that will not give them the meagre wherewithal to be 'decent' and hard-working. A few pounds, a worthwhile job of work and some 'hope', and you will not have to worry about their smelly feet. Jesus can throw away his towel.

For the rest of his life Orwell would carry with him the
testimonial aura of the tramp. It made a point. Some saw it as a
kind of sanctity. Some, like Stephen Spender, saw it as 'phoney',
and giggled. Others, like Malcolm Muggeridge, saw it as class-
clownishness:

> I made Orwell's acquaintance in the flesh through Anthony
> Powell . . . It was arranged the three of us should lunch together
> in, I think, a restaurant in Fleet Street, and that was my first
> sight of Orwell. I had a certain stereotype of an Etonian in
> my mind, so Orwell's appearance came as a complete surprise.
> He was dressed in a sort of proletarian fancy dress; an ancient
> battered sports jacket and corduroy trousers, not actually tied up
> with string as in old comic drawings, but of the kind that could
> still be bought in those days in working-class districts and in
> seaside towns where fishermen live.[61]

Young ladies of Orwell's acquaintance, it is recorded by Crick, hoped
he was not using their loofah when, dying for a bath, he came back
from one of his expeditions into the underworld.

Hard Times, 1930–34

You can no more be cultured without money than you can join
the cavalry club.
Keep the Aspidistra Flying

Down and Out in Paris and London got good reviews, but its author
would have been back in the workhouse on the royalties. Even a
rave in the *TLS* did not put money in your pocket (it's a recurrent
joke in *Aspidistra*). And *Burmese Days* was, meanwhile, ageing in the
womb. It would eventually, after much reworking, come out first in
the u.s., as a 'sex-shocker', in October 1934. Even more reworking

would bring it to belated birth in the UK in June 1935, ten years after the events it depicted. A significant lag.

George Orwell has more lost years than William Shakespeare and 1930–34 are among the most lost. He was restless, unhappy, broke, largely unpublished, unknown and, as regards posterity, an invisible man. As Crick sourly puts it, he was cooped up for most of the time in 'a small rented house in an out-of-the-way seaside town, the home of his 73-year-old father and his 55-year-old mother'. Avril, now well into her twenties, was working in a tea shop. His family gave him bed and board. Recalling his *plongeur* skills, he is recorded as helping his mother with the washing-up. Nothing else of what went on in the house is recorded. There must have been rows. He fished, during long, empty hours of the day. A favourite spot was the pond at Walberswick, alongside one of East Anglia's many old water mills, commemorated by Constable. It teemed with eels, tench, gudgeon, carp and other piscine lovers of deep, still water.

There were sporadic reviewing commissions, mainly from Rees, but nothing that would make his name. And he suspected Rees was just doing another down-on-his-luck Etonian a favour. It was not until 1934 that Orwell made enough from his writing to live on. Not well – but enough to keep the wolf from the door and escape Southwold. Peter Davison's schedule of his earnings from 1928 to 1933 makes pitiful reading. He had given up £600 p.a. in the IPS for what? Out of these years would emerge his most spiteful novel and his most self-flagellating novels: *A Clergyman's Daughter* and *Keep the Aspidistra Flying*.

Teacher

Teaching is harder work than it looks.

A Clergyman's Daughter

Orwell was, hindsight makes clear, in a condition of 'latency',
like the moth in its pupa. But that is not what it looked like to
those close to him, who saw him as a layabout. On a visit to his
elder sister, Marjorie, in Leeds, his no-nonsense brother-in-law,
Humphrey (who had never warmed much to the 'stinker' Eric),
told him to stir his stumps. To make what he meant clear he gave
Orwell ten shillings a week to work on his (Humphrey's) allotment.
That ten-bob note ('half-bar', his down-and-out pals would have
called it) tilling the soil must have scorched. Humphrey recalled,
years later, that he had thought Eric lazy and self-pitying – and
not all that useful with a spade. He was wrong, of course. Eric was
preparing himself – although for what was not clear even to him.
While waiting to find out he took up a series of casual jobs that
were beneath him intellectually. He wanted nothing permanent.
No commitment.

Private schools were not inspected by any authority until the
1950s. Anyone, even a 1930s Wackford Squeers, interested in making
some money on the side could set up a school and run it as they
wanted. Derek Eunson (a Scottish surname, ominously), whose day
job was as an engineer at the local HMV (His Master's Voice) factory,
had set up an establishment in Hayes, outer London, called,
grandly, 'Hawthorns High School'. Its sole purpose was to make the
proprietor some pin money. Mr Eunson kept children as a less wily
man might have kept bantams. The Hawthorns had fourteen boys
and two teachers. Eunson himself was beneath even the modest
academic requirement for classroom work beyond the janitorial.
Neither of the 'staff' was professionally qualified. The salary was as
little as Eunson could get away with. Eric Blair was appointed 'head

master' and, doubtless, instructed to wear his Eton tie on parents' days. His service has been thought to warrant a plaque. His predecessor, Crick records, had been sent down for six years for sexual abuse of his pupils. The length of the sentence suggests a gross offence. It is extraordinary that the school, with half its teaching force locked up for arrant buggery, was not closed down.

What slender evidence there is suggests that Mr Blair did his work off-handedly, but not at all badly. According to the local Hayes historian Mike Paterson:

> Orwell was known as being strict in the classroom (not a word of English was allowed in French lessons), yet kindly and enthusiastic at extra-curricular activities. He frequently took the lads on nature rambles, showing them how to capture marsh gas in jars, that sort of thing; he also wrote and directed the school play – *Charles II* – which was performed in St Mary's Church nearby.[62]

The nearby church, St Mary's, which was 'high', interested Blair. He underwent, at this period, what looks like a spiritual conversion. He had befriended the curate, the Revd Ernest Parker – the only educated person in the vicinity of the Hawthorns. Blair assisted Parker with Sunday communion and visits to the dying. He subscribed to the *Church Times*. He took up radically anti-Catholic positions. He may, perhaps, have thought some holiness would endear him to the indomitably Blair-resistant Brenda Salkeld, the clergyman's daughter. Attendance at the church furnished material for the novel of that name. But he was at risk of becoming what he liked to call a 'creeping Jesus'. What was actually taking shape in his mind, alongside the novel, was a complex idea about the historical importance of Anglican religion, namely that you could revere the institution without believing in its doctrines (the conclusion Dorothy arrives at in *A Clergyman's Daughter*). There was a place for the church in Orwell's 'England, your England'. It is incarnate in John

Major's favourite image from Orwell: 'the old maids biking to Holy Communion through the mists of the autumn morning'. Or in what is agreed to be his best poem, read, by his request, at his funeral, before his interment in a church graveyard. It begins: 'A happy vicar I might have been / Two hundred years ago / To preach upon eternal doom / And watch my walnuts grow.'

Orwell's new sense of religion is spelled out in the contract Dorothy Hare, who has lost her faith, makes with the church in his next novel. It is a beautifully written passage that would have found a happy home in a late essay, or, indeed, a secularist sermon:

> It seemed to her that even though you no longer believe, it is better to go to church than not; better to follow in the ancient ways, than to drift in rootless freedom. She knew very well that she would never again be able to utter a prayer and mean it; but she knew also that for the rest of her life she must continue with the observances to which she had been bred. Just this much remained to her of the faith that had once, like the bones in a living frame, held all her life together.

It is similar to his compromised eulogy, worked out in *The Lion and Unicorn*, about 'England'. It's rotten, but it's all we have, and better than any alternative going.

There may have been some presence of God in St Mary's communion services but Hayes was, Orwell said, 'one of the most God-forsaken places I have ever struck'. He loathed it. Rescue came unexpectedly. In July 1933 Eunson went broke, sold up and summarily discharged his 'staff'. A headmaster from nearby Uxbridge, on the lookout for some cheap pre-owned desks, decided to include the Hawthorns' pre-owned French teacher in the package for his own institution, Frays College. The 'college' was named after the nearby river (not a grand stream, but good enough for Orwell to fish in, and one reason he accepted the offer). The proprietor, John Bennett, ran a more thriving and ambitious institution than the Hawthorns. It had some 200 pupils, boys and girls, 'day' and boarder, five to eighteen years old. The salary was £70 p.a. plus bed and board – 'coolie rates'. 'Mr Blair' was liked, despite his constitutional aloofness. He did what he was paid wretchedly to do, teaching French that his pupils would never seriously use, working, when he could, on what really mattered to him. Reportedly the clattering of the typewriter could be heard, all night long, from his ill-heated room. Uxbridge had nothing to tempt him out. His life seems to have been monastically sex-starved at this stage.

His teaching career was terminated by one of his typically suicidal impulses. He had earned enough to buy a second-hand motorbike. There was a kind of death-or-glory romance associated with these machines, on roads which the highway code, and speed restriction, had yet to civilize. A year or two later T. E. Lawrence would wipe himself out on his Brough Superior, a machine capable of the 'ton'. On a spin back home, in December 1933, Orwell took the road without leathers or warm clothes. Gordon Bowker pictures, vividly, what followed:

> Perhaps to impress Brenda or Eleanor, he drove his bike all the way to Southwold one weekend without an overcoat or any decent protection against the cold except his long Eton College scarf. Refusing advice to wrap up more, he then drove back to Uxbridge.

He was caught in a freezing rainstorm; his fourth bout of pneumonia followed. He was taken to Uxbridge Cottage Hospital, where his life was feared for. He hallucinated that he was back in a spike, and someone was trying to steal his money. He did not die, but was ordered to take at least half a year's total convalescence if he wanted to live longer than six months. It was farewell to Uxbridge and back to Southwold. George Orwell's teaching career was over. Two good things had come out of it. He had finally managed to lick *Burmese Days* into a shape that was acceptable to the finicky Gollancz. And he had worked out what his next major piece of writing should be.

Convalescence, he determined, would be a working sabbatical. His farewell to 'god-forsaken' Hayes was proclaimed in a poem, published in *The Adelphi*, 'On a Ruined Farm near His Master's Voice Gramophone Factory'. It's a work in the 'pylon style' popularized by Stephen Spender: 'The acid smoke has soured the fields, / And browned the few and windworn flowers; / But there, where steel and concrete soar / In dizzy, geometric towers –' and so it goes. Hateful: but it was the unstoppable future. A world in which, as he would later say, 'children grow up with intimate knowledge of magnetos and in complete ignorance of the Bible'.

There had been changes in the Blair family fortunes which meant having a sick Eric hanging about the house was less of a burden. Ida had received a legacy – the last of the Limouzin wealth. With it the Blairs bought a handsome new home, Montague House, in Southwold's High Street (as I write it is advertised as 'Grade II listed', with a £5,000 pcm rental; the Blairs picked it up for £100). Avril and Ida had sufficient start-up money left over for their longed-for Copper Kettle/Bridge club venture in the centre of town. One of his relatives suggested that Orwell might work there – he'd washed up quite happily at the Crillon in Paris, hadn't he?

A Clergyman's Daughter

> It is a classic case of an author misjudging his talent
> and his material.
> STANSKY AND ABRAHAMS

Orwell's Southwold convalescence would last from January until October. He was soon well enough to write and dashed off his next novel in six months. *A Clergyman's Daughter* is a bitter book. Being cooped up (even in Montague House's more spacious dimensions) was bound to brew bile in someone as raw-nerved as Blair/Orwell in 1932. The bile level was elevated by the fact that Eleanor, now Mrs Collings, was in Singapore and Brenda in Ireland.

A Clergyman's Daughter is the story of Dorothy Hare, whose life is one of servitude to her widowed, autocratic, snobbish, clergyman father, as negligent of his flock as he is careless of his daughter in a barely fictionalized, wholly hateful Knype Hill/Southwold which deserves no better than the Revd Hare for the care of its mean souls. The first half of the novel covers one hot day in August. Dorothy is less daughter and more skivvy, secretary, church janitor and domestic factotum. She works a seventeen-hour day and a seven-day week. The novel could well be called 'The Clergyman's Slave'. The Revd Hare has not the slightest interest in religion as such. He seethes with resentment that, as the distant twig of an aristocratic family, he has descended to *this* – the life of a country parson. It is not a vocation: it is an intolerable humiliation for the 'younger son of the younger son of a baronet'. He does not care that his congregation has shrunk to a wizened core, that the belfry is about to collapse, or that Dorothy can only provide the 'dainty' food he demands (*deserves*, by God) by starving herself. He fobs off Dorothy's request for money for overdue tradesmen's bills. He is a horrible father.

Dorothy has been traumatized by the horrific sex she witnessed, aged nine, between her parents. Her mother was mercifully carried off from further marital molestation in the 1921 flu epidemic. Dorothy has taken a nun's vow of chastity. She has a terror of 'that kind of thing'. It will soon not be a problem. She is verging on 28, the age at which, as Jane Austen grimly recorded, a woman loses her 'bloom'. There is already a hint of crow's feet around the eye; a grey hair or two. Dorothy mortifies her flesh with pinpricks, hunger and a morning cold bath. She is pursued by the Knype Hill lecher, Mr Warburton, another horrible man – middle-aged, wealthy and an inveterate groper and pincher.

Montague House.

After near-rape by Warburton, Dorothy loses her mind. She has been boiling pot after pot of smelly glue for the costumes in the annual children's play. It may have contributed to narcosis, together with the richly scented wine Warburton hopefully gave her too much of. More likely Orwell was recalling Agatha Christie's sensational 'amnesia' in which, after an obscure shock to do with her husband's infidelity, she went missing for eleven days in 1926. Dorothy comes to consciousness eight days later, dressed in rags, in a shabby London street, unaware of how she got there (nor will the reader ever know). She is still *virgo intacta*, we gather. She gradually recalls who she is and discovers the gutter press has headlined her as the naughty vicar's daughter who has done a bunk with the local Lothario. Warburton had left town at the same time as her (a loose link in the plot). The scandal has been fanned by the Knype Hill gossip-monger Mrs Semprill. 'It did not take much to get you "talked about" in Knype Hill.' Orwell himself had been the subject of prurient 'talking about' by curtain-twitchers in Southwold. He was probably a topic of conversation in the Copper Kettle.

Dorothy joins forces with three down-and-out Cockneys off for their summer break in the hop fields of Kent. It is almost a holiday and a liberation, but degrading for a clergyman's daughter. Back in London, after the crop is picked, penniless again, she is arrested for vagrancy after ten hallucinatory nights in Trafalgar Square, narrated in a fractured style in homage to Joyce's 'Nighttown' section in *Ulysses*, which, thanks to Mabel Fierz's smuggling, Orwell was currently reading. Though not Orwell's métier, it is not at all badly done.

Dorothy is rescued from many fates worse than death (still 'intact' under her rags) by a distant aristocratic relative, worried not about her but about the family name. She is buried away in a teaching position, under a pseudonym, in Hayes ('Southbridge'). It is hateful work and a hateful town. The malign, illiterate proprietor of the school, Mrs Creevy, is in it for the money alone: 'Her oft-repeated phrase, "It's the fees I'm after", was a motto that might be – indeed, ought to be – written over the doors of every private school in England.' (Including, one supposes, St Cyprian's in Eastbourne. Not until 1957 did the government trouble itself to inspect these catchpenny establishments or monitor what damage they were doing to the nation's children.) The school is filthy. The girls are rendered more stupid than nature made them by the educational pigswill that is served up to them. Dorothy's attempt to introduce general knowledge, 'interest' and Shakespeare provokes a parental uprising. She takes to beating the children. 'Nearly all teachers come to it in the end.' Here, as in the colonies, the cane rules.

Eventually Mr Warburton rides in to rescue her. The Knype Hill/Southwold scandal has been extinguished and the gossip-monger, Mrs Semprill, convicted of libel. Dorothy (whose pre-served virginity is the most miraculous hymenal survival since Mary's) resumes her domestic duties for a slightly reformed father. Scrambling his own eggs had been a trial. Dorothy refuses Warburton's honest proposal of marriage. She would rather wither than be slobbered over by a smelly man. She no longer believes in

God, but finds comfort in the church. She will never marry, but will be one of Orwell's spinsters cycling through the autumn mists to communion.

Hovering over the narrative is the image of Knype Hill/ Southwold as a huge glue-pot. Once there, you're stuck. The novel ends with the lines: 'It was beginning to get dark, but, too busy to stop and light the lamp, she worked on, pasting strip after strip of paper into place, with absorbed, with pious concentration, in the penetrating smell of the glue-pot.' Smells, always smells.

A Clergyman's Daughter was the fastest novel Orwell would ever put on paper. He sent it to his agent (appointed by Mabel Fierz) at the beginning of October 1934, already halfway out of the Montague House front door. In a sense, he threw it over his shoulder to settle some scores with Southwold, and made off to London.

Spite, Bollox and Remorse

I like to write when I feel spiteful. It is like having a good sneeze.
D. H. LAWRENCE, to Cynthia Asquith, 1913

I am so miserable struggling in the entrails of that dreadful book . . . loathing the sight of what I have done.
ORWELL, to Brenda Salkeld

Orwell suppressed *A Clergyman's Daughter* after its first printing during his lifetime and would have liked it to be gone for ever. 'I oughtn't to have published it,' he later said. The reason he gave was authorial disapproval. It was, as literature, 'bollox', 'tripe', 'a silly potboiler'. Orwell was never a friend to his own fiction. The truth is probably different. *A Clergyman's Daughter* is a cruel book. He was not, when himself, a cruel man. But those ten months in Southwold were a bad time for him; he was not himself. In order to feel the novel's cruelty one can set up a mind game.

Assume that George Orwell (known to some as Eric Blair) is reading out his new novel to a small group of invited listeners in the large drawing room in Montague House. It is the late summer of 1935. Tea has been served. Present are his father, mother and sister Avril. Also in the audience are Brenda Salkeld; the school owners, Messrs Eunson and Bennett; the Revd Ernest Parker; and, hovering at the door, the Southwold gossip-mongers – women with loose, malicious tongues. How would they all react to what Eric/George/ Mr Blair was reading out to them?

Avril and Ida's likely chagrin at the scornful description of their Copper Kettle/Ye Olde Tea Shoppe has been mentioned. Avril – her father's 'hand-maiden', aged, like Dorothy Hare, 27, on the edge of old-maidhood – would have had a particular pang. Was this how her brother saw her? As a no-longer nubile chattel caught for ever in the Southwold glue-pot?

Richard Blair would have wondered whether the domestic, snobbish, patriarch the Revd Hare (a rhyme in the surname?) was, in some sense, 'him'. He was, like Hare, boastful about his remotely aristocratic family: he was the great-great-grandson of an earl, and made no secret of it in his clubs. Eric, he might have observed, had always been put off by his removing his false teeth for breakfast. Dorothy too is disgusted by her father's gumminess when she brings him his morning hot shaving water (did Avril do that?). 'His voice always sounded muffled and senile until he put his false teeth in.'

Brenda – the clergyman's daughter – would have felt the narrative extremely painfully. For years Eric Blair had been pestering her for sex. He was aggressive in his demands. The novel alleges neurotic 'frigidity' on her part. Brenda would have thought it payback for not succumbing to Eric. This, for example, is how he describes Dorothy's antipathy:

> To be kissed or fondled by a man – to feel heavy male arms about her and thick male lips bearing down upon her own – was

terrifying and repulsive to her. Even in memory or imagination it made her wince. It was her especial secret, the especial, incurable disability that she carried through life.

Was this what Eric thought about Brenda and her 'man' aversions? That she was a covert lesbian? Brenda had refused the absurd offer to accompany him to the hop fields in 1932. What would have been left of her reputation, and her job at St Felix's school (a religious establishment), had she gone? ('Rector's Daughter's Wild Summer Romps in the Hop Fields! Exclusive!') In the person of his fictional clergyman's daughter, Eric put her in the hop fields anyway. A gym mistress, Brenda may, like Dorothy, have believed in the odd cold bath. Her relationship with her clergyman father we know nothing about. It may have been, as Orwell alleges, oppressive. The depiction of her in this novel is a violation: another tearing 'limb from limb', as Jacintha Buddicom called her treatment in *Nineteen Eighty-Four*.

The Hayes and Uxbridge school proprietors – honest men as far as one knows, and one of them, Bennett, educationally idealistic – would have regretted ever taking that Blair fellow on. And what had they done to be represented as the awful Creevy woman?

Poor Ernest Parker, the curate at St Mary's who had been so friendly to Mr Blair, would have gasped at his communion assistant's description, via Dorothy, of the Revd Hare's communicant, Miss Mayfill:

In her ancient, bloodless face her mouth was surprisingly large, loose, and wet. The underlip, pendulous with age, slobbered forward, exposing a strip of gum and a row of false teeth as yellow as the keys of an old piano. On the upper lip was a fringe of dark, dewy moustache.

In a letter to Eleanor, Eric had recalled sitting in Parker's church in Southwold 'behind a moribund hag who stinks of mothballs and gin and has to be more or less carried to and from the altar at communion'.

The Southwold curtain-twitching gossip, whoever the original of Mrs Semprill was, would have winced. Or perhaps she would merely have reloaded to keep up blackguarding that awful Blair man to harpies of Knype Hill/Southwold with even more venom. 'That nice Dennis Collings left our town a museum. And what did that awful young Blair leave Southwold? Knype Hill. He should be ashamed of himself.'

Perhaps, looking at that row of appalled faces, Eric would have been ashamed. There is so much sheer spite in this dashed-off novel that Orwell was quite right, once his anger subsided, to suppress it after its first publication. As he told his agent Leonard Moore in 1944, 'I oughtn't to have published it.'

On His Way

Written in months, during his Montague House incarceration, *A Clergyman's Daughter* was promptly accepted and published by Gollancz in March 1935, to be followed a couple of months later by his belated 'first' novel, *Burmese Days*. Both were well received. Some of the reviews of the Empire novel, particularly, glowed. Turning a nice phrase, the reviewer in the *Fortnightly* recommended it 'to all those who enjoy a lively hatred in fiction'. In *The Spectator*, V. S. Pritchett (already a confirmed admirer) hailed the 'cold talent' on display in *A Clergyman's Daughter*. They'd got his measure.[63]

Orwell was being taken notice of and picking up journalistic commissions. But he had not yet broken through to the first rank as a writer. He would never do so if he stayed in Montague House and the 'glue-pot'. One thing was clear to him: if he was ever to break through, he must get out of Southwold.

Keep the Aspidistra Flying

The money-stink, everywhere the money-stink.

Odo-Ro-No

Orwell got out of Southwold in the habitual way, with the help of friends. There are different accounts of how he got the job at Booklovers' Corner, which he had from October 1934 to August 1935. The helping hand was perhaps Richard Rees's, or Mabel Fierz's (who lived up the road from the bookshop), or shadowy aunt Nellie's (the Westropes, who owned the shop, were Esperantists). All of them were leaning politically towards the radical (Trotsky-tinged) Independent Labour Party – as, gradually, would Orwell himself.[64]

Hampstead was relief and release after ten months in the Southwold glue-pot. The job was not onerous. His preferred writing spells were three hours in the morning. His bookshop duties only occupied between 2 p.m. and 6.30 p.m. Business was quiet enough for him to read and browse 'alone with seven-thousand books'. Fresh air off the heath and the intellectual Hampstead atmosphere were both tonic, and made possible what Crick calls 'his great creative period'. The Booklovers' Corner job came with a rent-free room round the corner where he could write and entertain women (something that would have gone down badly at Montague House). He ran a number of girlfriends. He enjoyed literary parties at the Fierzes' and (more exclusively) at Rees's flat in Chelsea. Compared to Southwold, it was a different world. But he eventually came to hate the work the Westropes had generously put his way, and the awful literary taste of the shop's customers. Most of all he hated the sense that he was going nowhere.

It was in this mood that he conceived and wrote his next novel, a masochistic memoir. He had it completed when he gave up work at Booklovers' Corner in January 1936, to become a writer full-time.

Keep the Aspidistra Flying was written fast and fluently, in relative ease. The novel's hero, Gordon Comstock, by contrast finds himself unable to write because he's penniless, famished and too busy plotting how to throw the tea leaves from his illicit brew-ups down the loo without his landlady (ear to the door) hearing him break her rules. Orwell's portrait of himself as a prematurely withered, no longer young man (he was reading Joyce) is self-hating and self-pitying to a pathological degree, grossly falsifying the facts of his own life. Gordon is a 'short-arse', the product of a fourth-rate public school, with a family several notches duller than the Blairs. He is a loser. If Orwell was cruel to everyone within hitting range in *A Clergyman's Daughter*, *Keep the Aspidistra Flying* is cruel on himself – a tall, manly, Etonian author making his way rather promisingly in 1934 (when the novel is set).

Orwell's novel kicks off with an epigraph of bloody-minded blasphemy: 'Though I speak with the tongues of men and of angels, and have not money, I am become as a sounding brass, or a tinkling cymbal . . .'. This biblical travesty goes on, unamusingly, for half a page. There follow diatribes against the 'money-stink' on virtually every page.

Orwell's title has dated catastrophically. Aspidistras, and what they represent, are rarer in households today than Venus flytraps. The joke in the title about the Marxist anthem ('Though cowards flinch and traitors sneer, We'll keep the red flag flying here') makes it muddier for modern readers. The 'rather moth-eaten' hero is a victim of the damnable British class system cursed, as most of its victims lamentably aren't, by a clear sense of what that system is. The Comstocks are lower-middle class. Pooters with pretension. They do nothing, and nothing happens to them except slow generational decay. They have no more social will than jellyfish. Gordon has published a volume of poetry, which, because he didn't go to the right school or university, has sunk without trace. It is pointless for the likes of Gordon Comstock to submit his poems to the top magazines: 'He might as well have dropped his card at Buckingham Palace.' 'The sods! The bloody sods! "The Editor regrets!" Why be so bloody mealy-mouthed about it? Why not say outright, "We don't want your bloody poems. We only take poems from chaps we were at Cambridge with."' One knows the feeling. D. J. Taylor makes the sly point that Orwell was currently publishing his poems with a chap he was at Eton with – Richard Rees.

Orwell's protestations are unrealistic and flavoured with the bitterness of a man, closing in on middle age, who feels his career has gone nowhere. As Walter Bagehot said in *The English Constitution*, money alone, however many pots you have, won't get you into the top tier of English society: 'The experiment is tried every day, and every day it is proved that money alone – money *pur et simple* – will not buy "London Society".' Forget the Cavalry Club and Buckingham Palace if money is all you've got. The entrance fee is a lot higher. Money 'is kept down, and, so to say, cowed by the predominant authority of a different power'. That power, Bagehot believed, was 'aristocracy'. Modern sociology gives it a different name, the 'Power Elite'.[65]

Having given up a job as a copywriter, at which he might have risen to a fiver a week (the ceiling for the Comstocks of the world), Gordon scrapes a living as a counter-jumper in a Hampstead bookshop. Gordon takes the job as an opportunity to write the great poem he has in his head: 'London'. But the squalid conditions of pigging it, on the breadline, in fifteen-bob-a-week lodgings, make 'creativity' impossible. Artistically, he's a eunuch. Without money you can't think. The point is reiterated time and again in the novel.

Gordon has a loving girlfriend, Rosemary. They meet, glumly and sexlessly, in Lyons Corner Houses. Neither of their landladies will allow 'visits' and creaking bed springs. An attempt at love in the wild begins promisingly, then goes all wrong when it's discovered she's forgotten her diaphragm (Orwell loathed French letters). It gets worse. They are humiliated in a roadhouse restaurant by an uppity waiter who sees them for what they are, carless people of no importance and bad tippers.

Gordon can see through the sham of the British class system but lacks the will to break through it. Finally, in the spirit of Winston Smith loving Big Brother, he sells his writing talent to Big Business, in the shape of that most corrupt sideshow of capitalism, the advertising industry. 'Vicisti, Aspidistra.' He marries and sells out, taking up a job as a copywriter again, earning £4.10 a week, with the Queen of Sheba Toilet Requisites, Co. He's good at the job and comes up with a winner: 'pp' ('pedic perspiration', or foot odour), a variant on the never-fail 'bo' ('body odour', the acronym that sold soap for armpits and crotches).

Among the many points of interest in the novel is, as usual, the Orwellian obsession with smell. Gordon's invention of 'pp' satirizes the great hoax played (to huge commercial profit) on the u.s./uk populations, convincing them that they stank and that, for a small outlay, they could do something about it. Gordon's firm have decided that 'b.o. and halitosis were worked out' as anxiety generators: 'What was needed "was a really telling slogan; something in the class of 'Night-starvation' – something that would rankle in the public consciousness like a poisoned arrow."' 'pp' is the poisoned arrow. A monster ad campaign is mounted, centred on the bleak question:

'p.p.' what about you?

It is not exaggerated. The deodorant industry did not in Orwell's day, and does not today, mince words in its proclamations to the buying public about its quotidian stench. 'Body Odour' had been given wide currency by 'monster' advertising campaigns for Lifebuoy soap in the 1920s and after. The soap, scarlet in colour and reassuringly abrasive, worked on the simple policy of covering up a bodily odour with the powerful chemical scent of carbolic. It conveyed the comforting impression that science had solved the carnal problem. And you must use it daily. The term 'BO' had actually been invented in 1919 by the Odo-Ro-No firm, American deodorant pioneers. It was they who bluntly advocated the 'armhole odor test'. Listerine, around the same period, did the same for halitosis, with campaigns in the 1920s. The mouthwash had the added kick, as its advertisers pointed out, that you did not *know* you had bad breath, and 'even your best friends won't tell you.' Until, that is, you wonder where all your best friends have gone. The early deodorant industry was aimed at women, principally, but gradually became a man thing in the era of 1930s middle-class insecurity. What if you ponged at a job interview, or your boss picked up a whiff?

Orwell, who had suffered the smell of tramps' plates of meat in his down-and-out days ('I shall never forget the reek of dirty feet'), realized that the deodorant industry had yet to get round to what lay, seething, within the male sock and shoe. Oddly, the PP initiative wouldn't take off, in any very successful way, until the 1970s, when Johnson and Johnson came up with 'Odor-Eaters' – footwear insoles that gobbled up 'PP'. It would have caused Orwell grim mirth.

Keep the Aspidistra Flying was published in April 1936. Critics pronounced it interestingly disgusting. William Plomer wrote in *The Spectator* that Orwell 'spares us none of the horrors of sordid loneliness and a hypertrophied inferiority complex expressing itself in physical grubbiness and stupid debauchery'. Covertly gay, Plomer cannot have liked the crude depiction of 'nancies' in the novel, but he registered its raw power. So did Cyril Connolly, with whom Orwell was renewing an old friendship. Reading it, Connolly wrote in the *New Statesman*, one felt 'as if one was sitting in the dentist's chair with the drill whirring'. But dentists are necessary in a civilized society.[66] The same point was made, less wittily, by the *TLS*: 'If this book is persistently irritating, this is exactly what makes it worth reading.' On home ground, Richard Rees in *The Adelphi* observed that 'Mr Orwell is a good hater' (he may have been thinking of the Ravelston spitefulness).

The Road to Wigan Pier

The lower classes smell.

The Road to Wigan Pier

Gollancz, who was assembling a stable of congenial authors, accepted the latest novel without objection, other than possible libel (taking on Unilever with the BO stuff wasn't a pleasant prospect). He wasn't over-impressed with the novels, preferring the reportage of *Down and Out in Paris and London*, but he didn't want to lose Orwell and he had plans to use him, directly or as an adjunct to his great venture, the Left Book Club. The right books, Gollancz thought, could inform and revolutionize the masses.

On delivery of *Keep the Aspidistra Flying* in January 1936, Gollancz commissioned the kind of book he really wanted from Orwell: a trip to the slump-depressed industrial regions of the mining, manufacturing and dockland north, once but no longer 'the workshop of the world'. A generous £500 was promised. Orwell was armed with letters of introduction from Rees, the ILP and Gollancz's well-placed communist comrades. Travelling up by bus through the Black Country, he went on to visit the Lancashire coal mines, the Yorkshire textile region, the Sheffield foundries and the Liverpool docks. It was a modern-day Cobbett's ride – at the gallop. Orwell would spend only two months in the north, an area that was wholly foreign to him. They were the cruel months of February and March, and he was clad in what even one of his working-class informants unenviously called a 'threadbare' overcoat, 'shivering from head to foot'.

King Coal was the foundation on which the Industrial Revolution was founded (via Britannia's steam-propelled navy and coal-fired steel foundries) and still held the fraying Empire together. It was, as Orwell put it in a famous passage, as vital to England as air to the lungs. And you had to see it to know it:

It is only because miners sweat their guts out that superior persons can remain superior. You and I and the editor of the Times Lit. Supp., and the Nancy poets and the Archbishop of Canterbury and Comrade x, author of *Marxism for Infants* – all of us, really, owe the comparative decency of our lives to poor drudges underground, blackened to the eyes, with their throats full of coal dust, driving their shovels forward with arms and belly muscles of steel.

He did not have muscles of steel. After the trip to the coalface, which inspired the above rhapsody, he had to be 'half-carried' to the surface. Proving, one might say, his point. As does his magnificent prose. The book itself is structurally jumbled by its strong passions. It was framed originally as a diary, which might have worked as regards impact, but it was reframed as reportage. It opens, vividly and smellily, with a disgusted description of the lodgings over a tripe shop where the reporter spends his first night. It stinks 'like a ferret's cage'. (For the long trail of nauseating stink that runs through the book, see the appended smell narrative.)

It was a long-lasting complaint by Wigan folk that he overdid the squalor and stench. Crick's chapter 'The Crucial Year' (the strongest in his biography) separates fact from exaggerated fact with surgical precision. Orwell gothicized the general character of the working-class town with shuddering stress on such things as the brimming chamber pot under the breakfast table. Like the turd in the plunge bath, it's an Orwellian icon. But, once read, it sticks in the mind for ever.

The second section of *The Road to Wigan Pier* moves into social analysis. Orwell is less readable when he gets into statistics, but his main point is supported by them. It's immortalized in the folk-song:

It's the same the whole world over
Ain't it all a crying shame

It's the rich what gets the pleasure
It's the poor what gets the blame.

The world did not need a man of letters dispatched from literary
London to reveal that British miners were getting a raw deal. Or
that if, on an industrial scale, you cram a family into a small miner's
cottage on thirty bob a week it won't be the Ritz and there will be
trouble with hand-washing (Orwell lingers on the black smear in
the butter dish), sanitation and clean underwear. These facts were
known, but then wilfully forgotten by England's luckier classes on the
grounds that there was nothing one could do about it. But the power
with which Orwell writes rubs the nose of the complacent into the
social facts of working-class England, AD 1936. Mining and trawling
were the two most dangerous lines of work in interwar Britain: casu-
alties ran at wartime levels. Invisibly. The middle class, Orwell's class,
gave it not a thought – or suppressed any thought – as they warmed
their rumps at the roaring fire, or tucked into their breakfast kippers.

There is a large component of memoir in *The Road to Wigan
Pier*. The reminiscence about Burma is revealing. But the crux of
the book – what makes it stick in the craws of so many readers of
all classes – is the smell question, particularly Orwell's thesis about
what lies behind the British class system: 'It is summed up in four
frightful words which people nowadays are chary of uttering, but
which were bandied about quite freely in my childhood. The words
were: *The lower classes smell.*' The standard king-four-to-king-four
defence is that Orwell is not himself asserting that the lower classes
actually smell but that we have been fooled, by social conditioning,
into falsely thinking they do.

The fifty occurrences of the word 'smell' in the text don't quite
support this apologetic explanation. Later, for example, Orwell
asserts: 'I do not blame the working man because he stinks, but
stink he does.' He goes on, however, to argue that the working
man stinks not because of class but because of work, or – worse

still – worklessness. Orwell himself had stunk like the proverbial polecat when he was living in dosshouses and tramping the road. It's remediable. Indeed, albeit slowly, remedy is happening: 'The English are growing visibly cleaner, and we may hope that in a hundred years they will be almost as clean as the Japanese.' And, one may add, as fragrant as the Burman. Give the poor and unemployed a decent, well-paid job and the smell problem will be solved.

The manuscript was sent, oven-ready for publication, to Gollancz in December 1936. He was appalled at the gross departures from the party line, but he went ahead. When the proofs came back in March, *compañero* Orwell was in the trenches at Huesca, with more to fear than a cutting review.

The Great Unwashed

From his earliest days he grew to associate smell with oppression.
BERNARD CRICK

For Orwell, class was, above all else, a matter of smell. English society was arranged, hierarchically, from the toffee-nosed to the Great Unwashed, with the Lifebuoy-carbolic-washed middle classes squashed, uneasily, between underclass stink and aristocratic, Bond Street perfumer (or, for the male, Imperial Leather) fragrance. By their odour shall ye know them. I have wondered whether the phrase 'toffee-nosed' is a version of toff's nose or a metaphor for the snot-swollen hypertrophic-turbinate-plugged nose that can smell nothing. The OED would clear it up, but I like to preserve the uncertainly double meaning. The toffee nose has a posture: 'stuck up', it's called – the ostentatiously lifted English nose in the odoriferous presence of someone 'low'. Their smell offends (in previous times a 'pomander' would be placed on a necklace to relieve the nostrils in the presence of a lower being – or the nose stuffed with some sweet-smelling herb, such as rue).

Baked beans, postcard by Donald McGill.

It's too simple, of course. Working people's 'stink' is, for Orwell, who thought about it a lot, a more complex thing than the mere lack of the gleaming sanitary facilities their 'betters' have. There is another dimension. One of the things that attracted Orwell, moth-like, to the working class (Jack London's 'abyss') was the Great Unwashed's positive relish of their 'stink'. It was identity: not something to shed, but something aggressively to assert. That famous Donald McGill postcard which must have been in his private collection shows a family in gasmasks round the dinner table and the simple caption:

'Haricot Beans Again!' Or the even broader one depicted here. The expression on fatso's face is not one of shame. The fart that follows his working-class blow-out is as important a part of the ritual as cooking smells. Salivation to flatulation.[67]

For most of the twentieth century, the Bisto Kids were as well known in the UK as the Dead End Kids were to our U.S. counterparts. Look at their leggings in the ubiquitous advertisement. When, one wonders, was the Bisto Kids' underwear last changed? When was the last 'all over' bath? Could one imagine young Etonians sniffing as lasciviously with all that toffee up their snouts? The 'Eton collar', like the puritan ruff, is a badge of supererogatory cleanliness.

Alain Corbin suggests that the marked reluctance of the lower classes in nineteenth-century France to surrender their ostentatious stench, their stubborn adherence to the sweaty armpit, the public fart and garlic-powered halitosis, was political: a disinclination, that is, to lose their class authenticity 'in the wash'. The French, as Corbin further notes, associated compulsory baths, delousing and ventilation with prison and shunned them accordingly. They wanted, literally, to get up the nose of their oppressive 'betters'. Their motto, 'I smell, therefore I exist.' Or, as the English lower classes put it, 'Up Yours.'[68] That political defiance – the Great Unwashed's refusal to wash itself into non-existence – was of lifelong fascination to Orwell. No one has wondered about it in purer English prose.

Marriage

Eileen is one of the larger silences in Orwell studies.
D. J. TAYLOR

To track Orwell's route to marriage one needs to go back a couple of years. In March 1935 he was obliged to give up the Westrope room around the corner. He may have overdone Myfanwy's female visitor permission. Mabel, ever helpful, arranged for him to move into a large communal boarding house at 77 Parliament Hill, with her Hampstead friend Rosalind Henschel Obermeyer. Unknown to George – falsely priding himself on, at last, paying his way as a writer – Mabel, as recent biographers have discovered, kicked in half the rent to Rosalind. The Fierzes had a spare bedroom but Francis, tolerant as he was about Eric overnighting, did not want to eat breakfast every day of the week with his cuckolder dipping into the same Gentleman's Relish jar (Orwell's favourite confection).

Orwell's manifest ease with the Jewish intellectual community of Hampstead, who clearly liked him, argues conclusively against the accusations of anti-Semitism that dogged him in later life.[69] Obermeyer, amiably divorced from her husband, Charles, was studying under Cyril Burt at UCL's Psychology Department. It was a dynamic academic unit, devising the IQ theory that would, in a few years, underlie the 1944 Butler Education Act and change British school education for generations. What the department was doing would certainly have interested Orwell.[70] Charles Obermeyer was working on his major work, *Body, Soul and Society: A Critique of Modern Psychology* (1936). Rosalind Obermeyer ran one of the many Hampstead salons. Her house faced the heath. Orwell could work every morning in a room which, a fellow paying guest (never 'lodger') recalls, was 'filthy'. Mice serenely shared his tins of mouldy biscuits. But it was ventilated by the freshest air in London and commanded a fine view of London's open land.

He was now reviewing regularly for the *New English Weekly* as well as *The Adelphi*. And his books were toppling over themselves to get to press. 'It was only from 1934 onwards that I was able to live on what I earned from my writing,' he later recorded.[71] He was, aged 33, what he had 'known' he would be when he was five: a writer.

Obermeyer's other paying guests were women. Wanting male company, Orwell moved on in August 1935 to a shared flat in Kentish Town with a couple of young men – writers on their way, like himself. He would spend six months with them enjoying easy access to Hampstead's literary parties up the hill and Camden's rowdy Irish pubs down the hill. He was at ease in both environments. Everready Mabel had again helped him with the move. His flatmates ('junior republicans') wrote for some of the same journals as he did, but their company was, for Orwell, eventually unsettling. Rayner Heppenstall and Michael Sayers were a decade behind him in years and a generation ahead in literary terms. It did not help that he looked ten years older, even, than his age. They would no more have sported toothbrush moustaches than bowler hats. Sayers was Irish, red-haired, Jewish and wild – a student of Samuel Beckett, no less, and a contributor to Eliot's *Criterion*, a Faber nut Orwell would never crack. Sayers had written an intelligent review of *Down and Out* in *The Adelphi* (in the month they moved in together) and he was the first critic to apply the necessary word, in praise of 'the lucidity – so to speak, the *transparence* – of his prose'. That hallmark 'windowpane' quality had, at last, been noticed.

Heppenstall was a young man in a hurry from Yorkshire. Four years later, when Orwell was writing his Wellsian homage to *The History of Mr Polly*, *Coming Up for Air*, Rayner would be writing a pioneer *roman nouveau*: fiction of the future, not the Edwardian past. Orwell had met Heppenstall for the first time at a Fitzrovia party where he also met the twenty-year-old Dylan Thomas – the bard of Fitzrovia – whose poetry was talked about in advanced circles. The young 'apocalyptic' wasn't much to Orwell's taste. He himself was still writing verses in the Swiftian-Augustan style.

Sayers lived until 2010 and dredged up faded, but doubtless much retold, recollections for Bowker:

To Sayers and Heppenstall, Orwell seemed an odd fish with old-fashioned and low-brow literary tastes. While they preferred Yeats, Eliot and Pound, he preferred Housman and Kipling ('He used to rattle off Kipling like a barrel-organ,' Sayers told me, 'but he did it with great feeling.') And they were bewildered by his

liking for detective stories and fascination with boys' comics, like
The Gem and *The Magnet*, which he discussed endlessly.

The notion of going to Wigan(!) to look at half-naked coal miners
– which Orwell was proposing to do – must have seemed to his
flatmates well beyond odd fishery.

Orwell pub-crawled with Rayner Heppenstall. In later years the
younger man dined out on Orwell stories and liked to tell two in
particular. One was about dragging a drunken Orwell away from the
clutches of a tart in a Hampstead pub; the other was about himself
coming back late, drunk and noisy to the flat and being attacked
by a murderous-looking Orwell with a shooting stick, aimed like
a bayoneted rifle, at his guts. There was, Sayers recalled, something
'homo-erotic' about the arrangement at 50 Lawford Road. It echoed
Mabel's sage verdict about the shooting-stick assault – 'disappointed
homosexuality'. The observation has been much pondered and taken
very seriously by Bowker. No conclusion has been reached. None,
probably, ever will be about Orwell's sexuality.

But one thing was clear. Orwell was no longer up for this rack-
ety life with compartmentalized 'girl friends', one-off tarts, too much
booze and the abrasive company of youngsters irritatingly more in
touch with what was going on at the front line of literature than he
would ever be. It was wearing him out. When Cyril Connolly saw
him at this period, after years, he was appalled, Crick records, at
the 'ravaged grooves that ran down from cheek to chin'. He must,
Orwell felt, settle down. As with Gordon Comstock, it would be a
kind of selling out. But the alternative – a superannuated bohemian
like those sozzled 'subjects', hanging around M. P. Shiel, the mixed-
race science fiction 'King of Redonda', in his (Orwell's) favourite
Fitzrovia pub, the Wheatsheaf – was not to be thought of. (Shiel,
incidentally, was very high on Orwell's list of 'Good-Bad' authors.)

He came across the woman he would marry at a party of
Rosalind Obermeyer's in the early summer of 1935. Present was one

of the hostess's fellow postgraduates, also working under Burt. She
was a clever young woman, two years younger than Orwell, with
a 'cat's face' and a pensive expression, caught on the few surviving
photographs of her. Obermeyer recalls Orwell saying, as they washed
up (*plongeur* again) after the party, 'Eileen O'Shaughnessy is the girl
I want to marry.'[72] He courted her rather more carefully than he had
her predecessors. Horse riding is recorded. Both were, at the time,
'Hampstead intellectuals'. It is hard to believe that Eileen wouldn't
have shown him her poem, called '1984', published in 1934 for the
fiftieth anniversary of her Sunderland high school, it looked gloomily
at what the world would be like, fifty years hence. A techno-dystopia:

> No book disturbs the lucid line
> For sun-bronzed scholars tune their thought
> To Telepathic Station 9
> From which they know just what they ought:

Much has been made of the obvious coincidence.[73]

They hit it off and seem to have been lovers at an early stage.
When in autumn he proposed, she accepted. When asked by a
friend why, she replied, jauntily: 'You see, I told myself that when I
was thirty I would accept the first man who asked me to marry him.
Well . . . I shall be thirty next year.' The prospect, as Orwell jested,
of a wedding ring from Woolworth's 3*d* and 6*d* stores did not put
her off. They would, it was agreed, postpone the wedding until she
submitted her thesis the following June. Orwell was still carrying
on with at least one other woman. Anglo-Irish by background, and
the daughter of a well-off customs official, Eileen had been brought
up in Sheffield. The O'Shaughnessys were a high-achieving family.
Eileen's elder brother, Lawrence, would become a distinguished
medical scientist and practitioner (specializing, usefully for his future
brother-in-law, in TB). Eileen adored him. Lawrence's wife Gwen
was also a doctor.

Eileen was, when she met Orwell, living with her brother and Gwen in Greenwich. Eileen was a grammar-school girl who made it to Oxford to read English, and got an 'upper second', but not quite upper enough to go on to research. A couple of marks more (on such things does life depend) and she would quite likely have been a distinguished academic in later life, like at least three of her Oxford contemporaries, whom she probably knew.[74] After graduation Eileen had bounced around, doing a variety of jobs before, in September 1934, enrolling for a Master's degree in the psychology department at UCL, then under Cyril Burt, a world leader in his field. Stansky and Abrahams interviewed Burt, who recalled finding in Miss O'Shaughnessy 'more than professional aptitude' – prof-speak for alpha-quality mind. This was confirmed by her best friend and fellow student, Lydia Jackson. Miss Jackson, a Russian émigrée, did not have much time for Orwell, whom she saw as a suppressor of clever women. Particularly Eileen O'Shaughnessy.

Eileen and George: Marriage of Minds. No Children.

We get our groceries at wholesale prices.

EILEEN ORWELL

What was being done at UCL, at the level at which Eileen was working, merits digression. MSCs were doctoral level in the 1930s and Burt required his postgraduates to base their dissertations on strenuous fieldwork, supportive of his great project. It centred on separated twins whose IQs, despite entirely different 'nurture' and life histories, were exactly the same. The results were, as Burt massaged them, overwhelmingly clear. Intelligence was innate. You were born with it as a constant – like the colour of your eyes. And intellectual capacity could be found, variably, in every level of society. Burt's findings would revolutionize British school education for decades as the basis of the eleven-plus IQ test and the grammar school system, which dominated British education until the late 1960s.

Eileen was interested in this and in something else – children's 'imagination', as reflected in their school essays, writing and games (the subject would be developed, a generation later, by the Opies).[75] The link to what was forming in one of the honeycombed compartments of Orwell's mind – the essay on 'Boys' Weeklies' (published by Connolly in *Horizon*, 1940) – is clear. Take, for example, the following in that admired essay:

> If one glances very superficially at some of these stories it is possible to imagine that a democratic spirit has crept into the boys' weeklies, but when one looks more closely one sees that they merely reflect the bitter jealousies that exist within the white-collar class. Their real function is to allow the boy who goes to a cheap private school (*not* a Council school) to feel that his school is just as 'posh' in the sight of God as Winchester or Eton.

This is miles ahead of the sledgehammer satire, and contempt for private school pupils en masse, in the pre-Eileen *A Clergyman's Daughter*. Orwell (as he had been with Dennis Collings) was a master brain-picker. Eileen's input is similarly deducible. Orwell must have attentively discussed her research, as he had done Collings's anthropological scholarship. UCL, like Cambridge, came to him, extramurally.

Biography has been occasionally condescending about Orwell's first wife, with irritating time-wasting on whether the woman was 'pretty' or not. What is significant is that she had a mind better trained than his, in subjects that fructified his own thinking. Miss O'Shaughnessy did not leave her mind at the altar on 9 June 1936. With her Master's under her belt she would, her friends thought (had that damned Orwell not got in the way), have gone on to do great things in social psychology.

They married in the village church according to the forms of the Anglican service (despite what Orwell called its 'obscenities'). Eileen's family pastor officiated. The families were represented but Orwell was oddly worried they disapproved and might combine to prevent the ceremony from going forward. The omens were not entirely happy. As Eileen later recalled: 'on the wedding day Mrs Blair shook her head & said that I'd be a brave girl if I knew what I was in for, & Avril the sister said obviously I didn't know what I was in for or I shouldn't be there.'

These veterans of the 'living with Eric' experience knew what they were talking about. He was given a set of Blair family silver by way of wedding present. The newlyweds' home was not one where silver would be required on a daily basis. Two months earlier, Orwell had, sight unseen, acquired a cottage in Wallington, Hertfordshire, called 'The Stores' – a former, unthriving village shop and post office. The rent was 7/6*d.* a week. Cash was required to start up the shop (not the post office) again and to stock a smallholding at the back.

Comfortless Wallington. Orwell at gate?

He had Gollancz funds for that, although the money dribbled in, over two years, more slowly than he would have liked. Sales in the shop yielded 30/- in a good week: enough, after costs, to pay the rent. 'The Stores' sold fresh garden produce from the back of the cottage, and other wares were bought wholesale.

George Orwell the shopkeeper has inspired much scorn among Marxist critics. Could bourgeois be pettier? The scorn rather misses the point. As in his last sojourn in Jura, it was the stripped-down Tolstoyan peasant life Orwell was aiming at. Wallington was an embryonic 'animal farm'. And he could joke about the shop as readily as his critics. When he signed up for the POUM in Barcelona, it was as 'Eric Blair, grocer'. His stock was mainly vegetables, acquired from Baldock, and harvested seasonally from the back garden. Livestock provided eggs (chickens) and milk (goats).

As D. J. Taylor wonderingly describes it, Eileen might have been wise to listen to the Blair women:

> Even by the standards of the 30s [The Stores] was inconveniently remote – Baldock, the nearest town, was three miles away – and uncomfortably primitive, high on damp and low on modern amenities. 'They didn't even have an inside loo,' one friend recalled. 'You had to go to the bottom of the garden.'

The cottage was centuries old and leaky. It had no electricity or inside water supply. Calor gas cylinders provided heat, paraffin tilly lamps light. They smelled. Even worse, the outside 'lav' was not always functional. If, economically, you used cut-up newspaper, as did the working classes with their '*Mirrors*' and '*News of the Screws*', the drain to the cesspool clogged and 'backed up'. The only toilet paper that worked was the expensive scented 'Bronco' (it was, oddly, Princess Margaret's required paper when she descended on often unwilling hosts). It was tightropes over the cesspit again. Orwell stayed at Wallington (on and off) long enough to make The Stores more habitable, with 'mains', and to see the trees he planted grow. But it was always primitive. Bathing was catlicks, with kettles of hot water heated on the gas and, presumably, visits to public baths in Baldock.

Eileen had deliberately deleted the woman's 'obey' vow from the wedding ceremony. But obey she most certainly did. Only a few months from submitting her dissertation, she withdrew from UCL. Wedding preparations had been distracting. School visiting and attendance at UCL with her supervisor, Burt, was impossible with chickens to feed and goat udders to tug on. And Eric's boiled eggs to boil. The writer's wife was not quite the clergyman's daughter, but close. Lettice Cooper, who knew Eileen later, makes a rather bitter remark about her friend routinely washing up at midnight. Later submission of her thesis was perfectly possible, and would have led to more research and good things professionally. Perhaps George

Orwell, goat lover.

did not want that. Part of Eileen must surely have wanted it. Eileen accepted, instead, a hand-to-mouth existence, feeding animals, serving in a run-down shop, peeling home-grown 'spuds' for supper, boiling eggs (which made her sick, but were Orwell's staple food) and making long, cold, nocturnal trips to the bottom of the garden via the garden goats, Kate and Muriel, washing her hands at the garden tap on the way back. If, as George dearly wanted, she had got pregnant, it would have inserted some point into it all. But either she was barren or he was sterile. They never discovered which, and he was adamant about not being tested.

The act of love was, apparently, not entirely compensatory for the domestic hardship that came with it. Eileen went so far as to speculate that George had had too much sex before marriage, making his performance perfunctory. 'Urgent' was the word other partners used. Like his recommended prose style, it was always to the point. What actually went on in the long, lonely, post-marital nights at The Stores is unknown. The Orwells (she took his professional surname and called him 'George') were capable of putting on a brave face. Much has been built on Geoffrey Gorer's remark, when he visited, that 'the only year in which he ever saw Orwell really happy was in the first year of his marriage to Eileen and living at Wallington'. A Hertfordshire Derby and Joan. Lydia Jackson, who saw more of them, thought he took her 'very much for granted. Any man, I thought, ought to treasure such a wife.' And an anything but happy life was disclosed by the discovery in 2005 of a cache of Eileen's correspondence.[76] It was, evidently, a short honeymoon. For some reason, the elusive Esperantist aunt Nellie had come to stay in the tiny cottage for an indefinite period (her partner, Eugene Adam, had belatedly married her, then gone round the world, never to be heard of again). There must have been a morning queue for the outside loo. The Orwells named a third goat after her.

George, Eileen's letters reveal, made it clear that his work must never be interrupted – even by wedding bells. He 'complained bitterly when we'd been married a week that he'd only done two good days' work out of seven'. A disappointing kind of honeymoon. He was writing, over those two good days, one of the finest of his essays – on shooting the Burmese elephant. It was a major part of her dowry that Eileen had been to typing school and had worked as a secretary. Fair copies assisted his publication chances and yielded precious time to write.

Wallington, as the year moved on, got worse. 'I forgot to mention', Eileen wrote to her friend Nora, 'that he had his "bronchitis" for three weeks in July & that it rained every day for six weeks during the whole of which the kitchen was flooded & all the food went mouldy in a few hours.' In November, as the nights drew in, she wrote to Nora again, explaining her silence:

> I lost my habit of punctual correspondence during the first few weeks of marriage . . . because we quarrelled so continuously & really bitterly that I thought I'd save time & just write one letter to everyone when the murder or separation had been accomplished.

D. J. Taylor, who has given these letters thought, says that 'Eileen's characteristic amalgam of irony and jauntiness is very difficult to separate out, but the air of exasperation is undisguised.' One could put it more strongly. Eileen's close friend Lydia Jackson did: 'Eileen did all the work, prepared the meals, and served them and answered the shop bell when it rang.'

Eventually, it seems, the 'bitter' quarrelling died down and the Orwells settled on an open marriage. His door would always be more open than hers. He would be unfaithful (or 'faithful in his fashion'); she could (and apparently did) take occasional lovers. They would, whoever else was in their beds, be companionable and comradely, but not strict with each other's private lives. Love, within those rules, was just about possible. The mutual tolerance verged, at times, on the bizarre: his asking her permission, for example, to enjoy a 'young Arabian girl' when they were in Morocco;[77] or her going along with his outrageous suggestion, three years after marriage, that they set up a *ménage à trois* with the ever-elusive Brenda Salkeld, for whom he had a lifelong yearning.

The basic emptiness in the marriage was that children were expected but never came. It left Eileen dangling, emptily. She must have wondered what life would have held for her if she'd gone on and submitted her thesis at UCL rather than submitting to housework at Wallington. But there were rewards. He was evolving fast as a writer and thinker. She had influence over that evolution, particularly the political writing. Her family affiliation to the ILP was clearer cut and of longer standing. Her literary training was also influential. To compare Orwell's clumsy obituary essay on Kipling in 1936 with that published in *Horizon* six years later is to see how far he had come in literary criticism.

Geoffrey and Kathleen Tillotson, and Humphry House, the three greatest Dickensians of the middle and late twentieth century, were Eileen's contemporaries at Oxford, doing the same classes. Orwell went on to write what is rightly regarded as a classic essay on Dickens in 1940. This turn to literary and cultural studies (as in 'Boys' Weeklies') is latent from his schoolboy enthusiasms as a reader, but the discourse in the years after 1936 is sharpened and, frankly, better. A string of literary critical works distinguishes his 'great phase' (as Crick calls it) – long pieces on Raffles and Henry Miller and a mass of book reviews. Their literary-critical sophistication owes something, surely, to his silent partner and night-time chats with her under the light of the tilly lamp in Wallington.

Orwell's blood-curdled 'last words' as he lay shot through the throat, mortally as he thought, fighting in Spain, were, 'Tell Eileen I love her.'[78] One believes him. He had good reason to love her.

Catalonia: Blood and Excrement

> I don't quite know in what year I first knew for certain that the
> present war was coming. After 1936, of course, the thing was obvious
> to anyone except an idiot.
> 'My Country Right or Left' (1940)

> I believe a writer can only remain honest if he feels free
> from party labels.
> 'Autobiographical Note' (1942)

Every man, according to Orwell, has a Quixote inside him. His
going, five months after marriage, to fight in Spain is Orwell the
'Don', the knight of the rueful countenance, lance *en levée*. It was not
duty; it was a quest. What, though, did he think he could achieve?
A cool look, in early 1937, would have confirmed the struggle was on
the way to being won and lost, with Franco bombarding Madrid
with German shells, corroding the besieged capital inwardly with
his fifth column, and 'non intervention' starving the Republicans of
any long-term chance of defeating the Fascists. Why would a sickly,
prematurely middle-aged man, with no more military expertise
than he could recall from cadet drills with ancient muskets at Eton,
throw himself into the cauldron? Other literary men (particularly the
'pansy' contingent Orwell calumniated) went into second-echelon
ambulance or media work, very seldom where the bullets were
flying.[79] Henry Miller, whom Orwell admired and praised publicly
for his *je-m'en-foutisme*, told him frankly, on a stopover in Paris on his
way to the Spanish front, that he was an 'idiot'. Fuck that for a game
of soldiers. Orwell never quite respected Miller thereafter. Orwell's
last recorded words before leaving for Barcelona in December 1936
(aided on his way with a £50 'sub' from Victor Gollancz, another £50
overdraft and what the pawnbroker gave him for the family silver)
were more hopeful: 'This Fascism. Somebody's got to stop it.'

Orwell's vague account of how he got to Spain – not sure whether he wanted to be a journalist or 'fight' (and under which factional flag – Communist, Trade Union or Anarchist?) – is blurry. Blurry too is his assertion that he accidentally became a POUM rifleman (without, for a disconcertingly long time, any rifle to put on his shoulder). One must suspect that he knew from the start where he was going, as a salmon knows it must swim upriver. POUM (Partido Obrero de Unificación Marxista) was Trotsky-sympathizing, loosely aligned with the local anarchist forces, but not over-strong on *unificación*.

The anarchists were passionately regional. Orwell's war memoir would be called *Homage to Catalonia*, not 'Homage to Spain'. They were different things. Catalonia had always had differences with Madrid. POUM had 'fraternal' links with the British ILP, to which Orwell was loosely loyal in these years. The ILP was recruiting UK volunteers for the POUM in November 1936. It would take only hale, unmarried men, of whom it sent out a vanguard of 25 on 8 January 1937. Orwell, neither hale nor unmarried, had made his own way a fortnight earlier. The ILP intended to send out a larger contingent, but in January the British Government announced it would prosecute anyone going to fight in Spain (journalists were permitted). Britain, as always, was skittish about its nationals fighting under foreign flags.

It was murky, but Orwell got there. As do the salmon. It is feasible that Eileen, more dedicated to the ILP than he was, and with stronger links within it, was a driving force in her husband's ill-advised Spanish quixotism. Having corrected the proofs of *The Road to Wigan Pier*, she left to join George as soon as British, French and Spanish bureaucracy permitted. Mrs Quixote made it to Barcelona in February. While the Orwells were away it was arranged that Nellie would take care of The Stores house, garden and animal stock. Doubtless she crooned to the goats in Esperanto as she milked them. 'Estu singardaj bonaj kaprinoj' (was it, when Nellie was there, Esperanto over the teacups? It would be quaint to think so). The

shop was closed, its till never to ring again. It was killed by vans
delivering fresher produce, cheaper, and at the door of Wallington
customers.

Eileen would, she said, serve Franco as his personal manicurist
if only it got her to Spain. As later events proved, there was a useful
touch of Mata Hari in her personality. She got herself a post in
the Barcelona office of the ILP. Her sister-in-law Gwen came out a
little later, bringing supplies and medical expertise for POUM in her
surgeon husband's limousine. In March Eileen wangled a visit to the
Huesca Front during an actual exchange of fire. 'I have never enjoyed
anything more,' she said. One deduces the O'Shaughnessys were ILP/
POUM body and soul.

POUM along with the Trade Unionist party, before 80,000 of
their young men were sucked to the Aragon front, were a dom-
inating presence in Barcelona in 1936. The Spanish people's (not
the Spanish state's) resistance against Franco's invasion, village by
village, fighting to the death town by town, had been inflammatory.
Barcelona's was a truly 'proletarian' resistance, enthused Trotsky. His
praise (despite his later disowning POUM) was a death warrant. The
founder of POUM, Andreu Nin, had once been Trotsky's secretary.
Moscow would eliminate Trotsky and POUM in their own good
time. In Barcelona the people had opted for revolution, rejecting
any restoration of the Republican status quo ante with all its feudal
nonsense. When Orwell arrived, the largest anarchist experiment
in history was being run. His euphoric description of Barcelona in
December 1936 bears repeating:

> It was the first time that I had ever been in a town where the
> working class was in the saddle. Practically every building of any
> size had been seized by the workers and was draped with red
> flags or with the red and black flag of the Anarchists; every wall
> was scrawled with the hammer and sickle and with the initials
> of the revolutionary parties; every church had been gutted and

its images burnt. . . . Every shop and café had an inscription
saying it had been collectivized; even the bootblacks had been
collectivized and their boxes painted red and black. Waiters and
shop-walkers looked you in the face and treated you as an equal
. . . In outward appearance it was a town in which the wealthy
classes had practically ceased to exist.

Behind the scenes the anarchists were less publicly 'ceasing the
existence' of factory owners and any high-bourgeois Barcelonans
beyond re-education. Bloodily. The Ritz became a hospital, grand
hotels workers' kitchens. Prostitutes were 'liberated' into a more
comradely relationship with their clients; marriage was abolished in
favour of unbinding partnership. In some places money was abolished,
to be replaced by barter. How many silk stockings the famed ladies
of Las Ramblas charged for their services is unrecorded. It was social
quixotism run mad. Orwell's enduring fame is as a dystopian writer.
Barcelona in January 1937 is a rare glimpse of the Orwellian utopia.
His land of milk and honey. And blood. And absurdity. It was an
enduring dream. Even when forced to flee Spain, socialist murderers
at his heels, in June 1937, he could write to Connolly, 'I have seen
wonderful things and at last really believe in Socialism, which I never
did before.' One recalls Anne Frank's 'In spite of everything I still
believe that people are really good at heart.' One should doubt both
of them.

POUM was an army without ranks, uniform or pay differentials.
Or, more importantly, the weaponry of modern war or any skill
in using it. They had no serviceable heavy artillery, no tanks and
only one aeroplane, permanently grounded. A symbol. There was
a chronic shortage of bayonets, which meant hand-to-hand trench
fighting had to be done, disadvantageously, with dagger or cosh. What
armament came to the Republican side went to the Communist
Republicans, Moscow's clients. But morale, POUM believed, could
conquer all. The rifle Orwell eventually ended up with was a

forty-year-old, ill-maintained Mauser. There were persistent problems with calibres and rusted rifling. A lot of the ammunition was 're-cartridged', and unreliable. The first shot Orwell ever heard fired in anger was a dud. You were as likely to be killed by your rifle backfiring in your face as by a Fascist bullet. Assuming, that is, your homemade POUM hand grenade hadn't killed you first. 'Drill' and 'musketry' skills ('commands'?) were regarded as bourgeois. The truth was that you could no more run a modern army on anarchist principles than you could a brothel.

POUM was organized in 'militias' – military communes. They were called 'centuras' – eighty men (despite the name) and company strength. There was no internal structure of unit (squad/platoon/company). Orwell's centura was in the Lenin Division, housed in the Lenin Barracks. It was a former stables, a grand building, still smelling of oats and horse piss – smells to Orwell's taste. His comrades' anarchic defecations and urinations wherever there was a quiet corner, less so. It was, he concluded sadly, an army of 'eager children'. Orwell was lucky in that the leader of his centura was an adult called Georges Kopp – Belgian (perhaps), vastly corpulent, rootlessly cosmopolitan, an inveterate liar, charming and an unscrupulous womanizer. Kopp claimed to be an old warhorse. In fact he had no military background at all. He was a world-class bluffer.

Orwell picked up sufficient Catalan and Spanish with the ease with which he picked up any language. He was promoted, first to corporal and, by the end, after the rank had been restored, to lieutenant. After interminable delay his centura was sent upline to the Aragon front to be met by (for the first time in Orwell's life) the smell of war: 'a smell of excrement and decaying food'. Oddly, given the bloodiness, winter cold, lice, scampering rats and palpable, long-term damage to his lungs, Orwell found active service to be something of a tonic. As Eileen observed, with her usual wry sting in the tail: 'The Spanish government feeds George on bread without butter and "rather rough food" and has arranged that he doesn't sleep at all, so he has no anxieties.'[80] About his wife, for example. He even put up with having to shave and brush his teeth in wine. All for two-pence (10 pesetas) a day. Pneumonia was, as ever, his real enemy. But even that seemed to be keeping its distance. The half-dozen full-life biographers have done a thorough job in chronicling Orwell's brief military career. He himself is typically dismissive: 'No aeroplane ever dropped a bomb anywhere near me, I do not think a shell exploded within 50 yards of me, and I was only in hand-to-hand fighting once (once is once too often I may say).'

The government-controlled high command had fears about POUM. Its manpower was placed in quiet sectors with no responsib-ility but to be there with a vague '¡No pasarán!' command. Besieged Madrid was the fulcrum. There was, history has revealed, an ulterior motive. Away from Barcelona, in distant trenches, the shock troops of anarchy were out of play. Castilian Madrid has never trusted Catalonia, with its separate language and culture and its breakaway tendencies. Certainly not with large numbers of armed, chauvinistic, anarchists walking 'their' streets thinking of independence.

Orwell had two spells at the front. It was mainly 'waiting' in entrenched positions. In winter the excrement-flavoured mud froze, in spring it melted, in early summer it stank. So feeble was their weaponry, and so thin was the defensive line extended, that a troop of boy scouts with airguns could have overrun them, Orwell thought. There was some trench fighting and night patrols for the domination of no-man's-land. Orwell may have killed a Nationalist 'bastard' or two with a lucky grenade. He was frightening to friend and foe, comrades testified, when his blood was up. He did not, he piously records, snipe a Fascist he spied crapping (assuming his aim and decrepit Mauser were up to a shot across 300 yards).

There was a spell of leave in Barcelona, in late April/early May. It was dispiriting. The great anarchist experiment was being meth-odically rolled back in the absence of the centuras: waiters were taking tips again, prostitutes plying for trade for money, not soap, limousines cruising like sharks to luxurious places. The Ritz was ritzy again. Army ranks had been restored – even in the anarchist brigades. Militias were broken up. Auguries were bad for POUM. The idea of a 'popular front', 'all together comrades!', was the order of the day. In Orwell's jaundiced view, a combination of POUM and Moscow had 'about as much vitality, and about as much right to exist, as a pig with two heads or some other Barnum and Bailey monstrosity'.[81] Behind the scenes a Stalinist purge was being mounted. Lists were being drawn up; the Orwells' names were on them. Moscow had infiltrated a spy (aptly named David Crook) into POUM. His reports identified the Orwells as 'rabidly Trotskyist'.[82] Crook also reported (accurately) that Eileen was Kopp's secret lover. That fact would be useful when Kopp and the unwitting cuckold were interrogated. ('She betrayed you, Eric . . .').

Orwell had been making tentative moves to get transferred to besieged Madrid with the International Brigades. It came to nothing. He was lucky it did – the brigades were in the habit of covertly shooting nuisances. The writer John Cornford, whom Orwell admired, transferred himself from POUM to the IB and was, rumour had it, shot in the back, 'in action'. Luckier still, Orwell's active service came to an end days after he returned to the front for the second time. His 1.9-m (6 ft 3 in.) frame never fitted trenches dug for diminutive Catalans, any more than, in death, his abnormally long coffin fitted his grave. He was reckless about exposing his head above the parapet. A sharp-eyed Nationalist sniper, with a much better rifle than Orwell's, took a pot shot and got him in the throat. 'The sand bags in front of me receded into immense distance,' Orwell recalled. He felt a mild resentment at losing a life he suddenly realized he had rather enjoyed. It was assumed, as he himself assumed, that he was a goner. But he survived by a lucky millimetre, and by the actions of a comrade, Harry Milton, who staunched the flow of blood with his bare hands.

Orwell was invalided back to Barcelona – and more danger. The purge of anarchism and POUM was now in full ruthless sway. These were the ironically termed 'May Days'. POUM had been declared an illegal organization. They were neo-Fascist pests to be exterminated. The 'necessary murders' (Auden's phrase, which always niggled Orwell) were cheered on by Harry Pollitt and his hacks of 'international socialism'. There were reports of IB hardliners on the rampage killing more Trotskyists than Fascists, assuming the former to be the more fascistic. Paranoia ruled. By now Orwell had his discharge papers – necessary lest he be proscribed as a deserter and shot out of hand. The doctors certified him officially 'useless'. It was a Blighty wound – but could he get back to Blighty? Eileen proved herself resourceful in throwing the police off his tracks. But the May Days, London friends would later testify, took years off her. She chain-smoked her way to an early grave, after Spain. George used his down-and-out skills to melt into the Barcelona streets. By now he looked Catalan and could sound like one.

The POUM founder and leader, Andreu Nin, was arrested and tortured. One version of events suggests that he was flayed alive to make him confess to ulterior Fascist motives. Kopp was arrested, interrogated, tortured and starved. He survived (he survived everything), and was discharged in December, 45 kg (7 stone) lighter. Orwell, skinny as Rocinante and badly wounded, would have gone in days. Kopp may well have named names. If you did you were more useful alive than dead for propaganda purposes. Eileen took risks to see her lover, Kopp, in prison, for what she assumed was the last time. It wasn't, it would transpire. He bobbed back up like a cork. Captain Georges Kopp lived on to fight in the Second World War, serve with the Resistance in France and spend his last days in England to die a peaceful death – by now married to one of Orwell's cousins.

Not all POUM veterans were as lucky as Kopp and the Orwells. In the ranks, George and Georges had befriended a young Glaswegian comrade in their centura, Bob Smillie. He was the namesake grandson of the Clyde working-class hero Robert Smillie, a miners' leader.

Bob had given up his university studies to fight in Spain. He was arrested and, it is plausibly suspected, kicked to death by the 'comrades' he'd given up everything to fight alongside. He reportedly refused to sign incriminating confessions and betrayals. The details, acquired by fellow prisoner Kopp from stolen files (and later passed on to Orwell), are sickening. After his socialist comrades had done with him his intestines were hanging outside his ruptured stomach. The boots had been aimed there because he was suffering from acute appendicitis, and the pain was therefore more acute. Bob Smillie's 'evil and meaningless death' was, for Orwell, the last straw. The Orwells escaped, duping, dodging and bribing their way back across the French frontier as well-off tourists. Orwell carried a volume of Wordsworth's poems as part of their disguise. It was the narrowest of escapes, but they made it. Thus ended what Robert Colls calls the 'Orwellian small footnote to the history of the Spanish Civil War'.[83]

Pariah

Gollancz is of course part of the Communism-racket.

ORWELL, to Rayner Heppenstall (July 1937)

When he returned to England, there was a concerted attempt by 'fellow socialists' to render George Orwell a non-author. Not with an ice pick in the back of the neck but by covert denunciation, ostracism and the peculiarly effective mechanisms of English 'soft censorship'. He would encounter it again, with *Animal Farm*.

A degree of Orwellian eccentricity – 'crankiness' – had been tolerated. Socialism was a big tent. It became 'heretical' with *The Road to Wigan Pier*, when he threw back the accusation that it was the communists, not George Orwell, who were 'cranky'. After some nervous toe-dipping (Orwell was obstinately unwilling to 'revise'), Gollancz had taken the plunge and published the book in the Left Book Club. It sold in the orange club livery like hot cakes, as the subscribers' half-crown offering for March 1937; 45,000 flew out, hot off the press. This despite Gollancz prefacing the volume ('his' volume) with 'just a hint' (in fact 5,000 words of mealy-mouthed blather) as to how 'his' members should read the book. They must bear in mind, members were solemnly warned, that Mr Orwell was not one of them but a 'member of the middle class'. LBC's membership was, in point of fact, not overwhelmingly from the horny-handed sons of toil smudging the pages of their treasured volumes with sooty fingers. Schoolteachers predominated. How does Orwell's tirade against 'Socialists' go in *The Road to Wigan Pier*? 'One sometimes gets the impression that the mere words "Socialism" and "Communism" draw towards them with magnetic force every fruit-juice drinker, nudist, sandal-wearer, sex-maniac, Quaker, "Nature Cure" quack, pacifist, and feminist in England.' LBC subscribers' could be added to the list of the faithfully gathered and sandalled under the Gollancz-LBC banner. And imprint.

Nor was Orwell in possession of quite enough 'middle-class' loot to tuck in with the publisher at his daily lunches at the Savoy Grill, meditating how revolution could be achieved without destroying the omelette Arnold Bennett. Orwell, as Peter Davison records, earned a grand (if that's the word) total of £246 in 1935. 'Mr Orwell' was still a victim of his 'public school' background, lamented Gollancz (himself St Paul's, Oxford, family wealth from the wholesale jewel business). The foci of Gollancz's 'hints' are, inevitably, Orwell's comments on working-class 'smell' and the 'odd' allegation of socialist crankiness. It is curious too, adds Gollancz, that he refers to 'Russian commissars as "half-gramophones, half-gangsters".' How on earth could he have come to that conclusion?

Harry Pollitt, General Secretary of the Communist Party of Great Britain (odd they kept the 'Great'), reviewed the book in the *Daily Worker*. No 'hints' for Harry (as Gollancz addressed him in letters about *Homage to Catalonia*; his author was 'Dear Orwell'). It was hobnails all the way:

Here is George Orwell, a disillusioned little middle-class boy who, seeing through imperialism, decided to discover what Socialism has to offer . . . a late imperialist policeman . . . I gather that the chief thing that worries Mr Orwell is the 'smell' of the working class.

Readers were urged to picture Mr Orwell in full IPS uniform – topi helmet, jingling spurs and all, rather than bundled in rags, against the freezing cold, dodging bullets in the Spanish trenches. And, of course, stinking to high heaven.

Pollitt regarded the 1936 Moscow Trials, the highpoint of Stalin's psychotic purge, as 'a new triumph in the history of progress'. Had the Orwells, whose names were inscribed as 'rabid Trotskyists' on Party lists after the May Day purge, been brought to trial in Barcelona and shot, that would have been another triumph to be notched up in the *Daily Worker*.

Harold Laski, one of the LSE's 'sleek' professoriate, reviewed *The Road to Wigan Pier* with suave savagery and total dishonesty. Laski (with Gollancz and John Strachey) was one of the three paid 'selectors' of books on the LBC list. He was in de-selection mood. The author of *The Road to Wigan Pier*, its co-publisher concluded, was the kind of socialist who is 'not prepared to pay the price of socialism'. A bullet through the throat was too small a price. Laski himself was born into a family of rich cotton merchants (enriched by Indian exploitation). He lived, well above the level of his LSE salary, in a mansion in Kensington and enjoyed his feted trips to Moscow. He too had cheered on the Moscow show trials as not purge but purification. He is credited with the moral equation: 'Basically I did not observe much difference between the general character of a trial in Russia and in this country.' He was personally reassured, in a private conversation with Stalin, no less, that, when the Soviet Union took over Western Europe, Laski's 'British Socialism' would be allowed to keep its own time-honoured privileges. Kensington, not Siberia.

Laski, apparently, believed Stalin. Both Laski and Gollancz went on to suffer severe nervous breakdowns during the Second World War, under the pressure of doublethinking their way through the Russo-German pact. The price of orthodox socialism was indeed high.

In his essay on 'Politics and the English Language', Orwell hauls Laski over the coals as a virtuoso of the gramophonic-megaphonic style. The example he cites is one of the few passages of Laski that are still read. And this, of course, is the crux. Despite the anathemas, which continue to the present day, Orwell enjoys a mass readership, still growing ever more massively. Orwell's inextinguishability puts his socialist critics in a quandary. The masses, with their perpetual Orwellian infatuation, are either congenitally stupid (so many 'Boxers') or wholly incorrigible – class enemies to their own class. Whither socialism with incorrigible masses? Ideally, to borrow Bertolt Brecht's joke, the people should be dismissed and a new people appointed. There is no mechanism in the LSE for doing that. Stalin had one.

Soft Suppression

> Was it really 700 . . . it struck me that it may have been a typist's error.
>
> ORWELL, on getting the first sales returns for *Homage to Catalonia*

On New Year's Day 1938 (holidays seem to have been little celebrated at Wallington) Eileen wrote in a letter that George was 'just finishing the book about it [*Homage to Catalonia*] and always having to speak about it'. If the English literary establishment had had its way, he would have been speaking to himself. The book was rejected, sight unseen, by Gollancz and Laski. Associated articles (one entitled 'Spilling the Spanish Beans') were turned down by the *New Statesman*, the country's leading socialist opinion-former. Beans were not to be spilled. Orwell came to loathe the very sight of the

Statesman's editor, Kingsley Martin. He would move tables so as not to see him lunching at the same restaurant. If socialism had a bad smell, Martin, parlour Bolshy, was that smell incarnate.

The book was taken on by Fred Warburg, a long-time ILP supporter, through the good offices of ILP stalwart Fenner Brockway. It was brought out in a small edition, in April 1938, and sold, in three years, fewer than a thousand copies – a fiftieth of what *The Road to Wigan Pier* had sold. It was literary anoxia. Warburg would later do well by Orwell – but not with *Homage to Catalonia*. A pamphlet he wrote on 'Socialism and War' was submitted to the Woolfs' Hogarth Press. Bloomsbury, it transpired, did not want George Orwell either. The typescript is lost. If, as has been claimed, Orwell raised political writing to an art, that art would have to find an outlet in the (few) organs of higher journalism whose doors were open to him. Pre-eminently those connected to his pals from school days – Cyril Connolly, his backer Peter Watson and David Astor. Etonians all.

Childish Socialism

> Dickens had the most childish view of politics.
> 'Notes on the Way' (1940)

> Orwell thinks that commonsense is socialism.
> TERRY EAGLETON (2003)

The word that attaches itself magnetically to Orwell's political thought is 'naive'. He belongs to that English socialist amateurism, immortalized by William Morris's bluff outburst: 'To speak quite frankly I do not know what Marx's theory of value is, and I'm damned if I want to know.' But he was still, Morris maintained, a communist – in his fashion.

It encourages condescension. Richard Hoggart, for example, saw himself (with justice) as the heir to Orwell's 'honest Joe' credentials after his star performance in the November 1960 *Lady Chatterley* trial. He (Hoggart) had worked on a building site for a while, in emulation of what Orwell had done in the London spikes and Kent hop fields. But, Hoggart laments, Orwell 'never quite lost the habit of seeing the working classes through the cosy fug of an Edwardian music hall'. There are many fugs in Orwell's descriptions of working-class life. Few are cosy, one would object.

Orwell, concluded Stephen Spender in an obituary article, was 'an *Innocent*, a kind of English Candide of the twentieth century'. He should, one infers, have stuck, like Voltaire's hero, to his garden in Wallington. He was better with spuds and chickens than with the Marxist theory of value. Morris, on his part, was better with wallpaper. Spender's 'Innocent' is foolish but has been much echoed. Orwell gave hostages to such condescension with remarks such as that about the awful May Days purge and massacre: 'Throughout the fighting I never made the correct "analysis" of the situation that was so glibly made by journalists hundreds of miles away.' He did not, those with analytic minds believed, have the necessary intellectual equipment, any more than did Morris or Dickens. Strange that people still read the three of them.

A book (*Inside the Myth*) was published in 1984 (meaningfully) to 'de-mythologize' Orwell. The 'Honest George' hoax, the editor proclaimed, must be 'patiently deconstructed'. In the volume one finds a choric complaint from what he would have called 'Bolshy Professors' that Orwell simply did not understand the war he fought in. This by Robert Stradling, for example:

His innocence [that word again] of Marxism-Leninism affected his judgment of all parties of the Spanish War, and since he was unaware of modern socialist dialectic and its tropes he was unable to examine them via a critical comparison with empirical reality.

By that stern criterion, 99.99 per cent of combatants on every side in every war do not understand what they are prepared to die for. And what is the 'empirical reality' of war? As Orwell put it, 'Bullets hurt, corpses stink, men under fire are often so frightened that they wet their trousers.' Trope that.

Breakdown and Recovery

The difficulty about Spain is that it still dominates our lives
in a most unreasonable manner.
EILEEN ORWELL (New Year 1938)

It is a mistake to think that Spain was politically enlightening for George Orwell. On his return he suffered what would now be called PTSD. Every bush was a Fascist bear. The fascistic virus was entrenched, he firmly believed, in the working class (in their for-hire Muscovite Union leaders). 'International Socialism' was another name for it. And, of course, fascism with aristocratic gloss was always there in the English upper classes, those wrong members in charge of the great English family.

The war was coming. Orwell foresaw it as a contest between British Fascism and German Fascism, with Russian Fascism waiting on the sidelines to see which victorious fascism to stab in the back. He would, he bleakly jested, complete his next novel in a concentration camp. Given the skills he had picked up in his down-and-out years, he might have survived better than most. Put bluntly, Orwell was temporarily maddened by Spain. And he felt 'duped'. The wool had been pulled over his eyes. He joined the ILP in 1938, he said, because never again would he 'be led up the garden path in the name of capitalist democracy'. It was ill conceived. The ILP was melting away and had become marshmallow pacifist and vague in its aims. Its *raison d'être* was that it was neither Communist nor Labour. Orwell's membership lasted only a couple of years.

On her side, Eileen was in emotional turmoil about Georges and George. In a New Year's Day 1938 letter, she wrote:

> It was always understood that I wasn't what they call in love with Georges – our association progressed in little leaps, each leap immediately preceding some attack or operation in which he would almost inevitably be killed, but the last time I saw him he was in jail waiting, as we were both confident, to be shot, and I simply couldn't explain to him again as a kind of farewell that he could never be a rival to George.[84]

When, if ever, Orwell knew all the details of her adulteries is not clear.

A breakdown in health, for both Orwells, was imminent. It was not long coming. No sooner had he got *Homage* off to Warburg than he was spitting buckets of blood. Eileen got her omnicompetent ('something of a fascist', she called him ironically) brother to examine him. And, more important, to take him in hand. It was not easy. A difficult patient, George regarded hospitals (ever since his Parisian experiences and before that the Saint Cyp's 'san') as charnel houses. His nostrils could snuff the 'sweetish faecal' smell even in the best-regulated lazarets. His resistance, and pathological indifference ('it always turns out to be not serious,' he told Connolly airily), were, for once, overridden. 'The condition', ominously, was diagnosed as 'tubercular'. As was usual, the truth wasn't fully disclosed to the patient. It was revealed, apparently, to the carer, Eileen.

Lawrence took him under his personal care at a sanatorium, Preston Hall in Aylesford, Kent. It was what in Switzerland would be called a *Kurort* – a place to get well, gradually and expensively. His magic mountain. One firm prescription was no work whatsoever. Lawrence paid for Orwell's private room – a 'cell', he doubtless thought. Privacy doubtless enabled him to smoke his 'foul black shag' roll-ups without disturbing more valetudinarian tuberculars.

Orwell had been placed into convalescent paralysis. Manacled. Between the publication of *Homage to Catalonia* (April 1938) and *Coming Up for Air* (June 1939), his literary cv is vacant. He could still think, however. And, in the Preston Hall longueur, memories from his early life came flooding back. It was less a cell, from this aspect, than Proust's cork-lined room. An apolitical novel, set in his Henley childhood past, was 'seething' (Eileen's term) in his mind: 'The title I thought of is "Coming Up for Air"', he confided. It was an appropriate title for a man close himself to terminal suffocation – although he was thinking of the way in which carp come to the surface, in hot weather, and gulp.[85] He had got in some fishing at Preston Hall after the annual close season ended on 15 June.

By spring he was as much on the mend as he would ever be. Eileen's close friend Lydia Jackson visited him alone. A walk in the estate grounds in the company of an attractive woman had its usual aphrodisiac effect. There occurred the 'Orwellian pounce' and what Bowker gallantly calls a 'moment of dalliance' and the *News of the World* that Sunday would have called 'intimacy'. If not cured, he was himself again. It led to one of the more discomfiting escapades one knows about, as disclosed by Jackson in her memoirs. He pursued her for months afterwards, pressing for a furtive, full-blown affair. She presents herself as having merely submitted that once in the grounds out of charity. She was appalled by the idea of betraying Eileen, her best friend. Eileen was also, Lydia hinted, put off by the smell of sickness he carried about with him.[86] Eileen was tolerant of such lapses: the only time we know her to have been badly upset was when he had a long-term 'serious' relationship with a secretary in his later *Tribune* years. But in fact, with mutual tolerance, it was – at this period anyway – an oddly happy marriage. He was the demanding genius; she was the willing helpmeet. But one can fantasize about Lawrence and Gwen huffing and puffing a bit about how their sibling was being treated.

Morocco: Eileen's Story

There are beautiful arches with vile smells coming out of them and adorable children covered in ringworm and flies.
EILEEN ORWELL on Marrakesh

Their slender flanks and pointed breasts . . . the odour of spices that clung to their satiny skins.
ORWELL, nostalgic for the smell of Arab girls, recorded conversationally by Christopher Hollis

The massed O'Shaughnessy pressure meant that Orwell was, for once, biddable. After five and a half months' supervised convalescence at Preston Hall, Lawrence insisted that he convalesce in a warm, dry climate. It should have been the South of France, but that was expensive. Neither Orwell had worked gainfully for months and the Côte d'Azur was beyond their means. He was bitter. He felt he had been lied to (he had been, about the seriousness of his condition) and forcibly prevented from working. As Eileen said, 'He is in debt for the first time in his life & has wasted practically a year out of the very few in which he can expect to function.' The clock was already ticking on him. A British winter in Wallington would undo all the good Preston Hall had done.

Eton pitched in to help him. The novelist L. H. Myers, well known in his day, was an admirer and schoolfellow. It is worth repeating that, having learned about Orwell's plight, Myers dispatched £300 anonymously via a discreet intermediary, Max Plowman (an *Adelphi* editor). Orwell, years later, would offer honourably to repay it, when he discovered who his benefactor was. But Myers had by then committed suicide. The gesture almost makes one eager to read Myers's best-known work (an Indian narrative), *The Root and the Flower*. Orwell's aura of 'sanctity' often inspired disinterested generosity in others. It's an odd feature of his life.[87]

French Morocco was chosen. It was cheap and Orwell may have been curious about French imperialism. It was, of course, in Spanish Morocco that the Civil War began. If a book was in mind, all that survives is a harsh essay, published in an obscure magazine. Even by his standards, Orwell's eye is cold:

> Sore-eyed children cluster everywhere in unbelievable numbers, like clouds of flies. Down the centre of the street there is generally running a little river of urine. In the bazaar huge families of Jews, all dressed in the long black robe and little black skull-cap, are working in dark fly-infested booths that look like caves.

Eileen later said: 'Of course we were silly to come but I found it impossible to refuse.' They cruised via liner to Marrakesh, since any feasible rail journey would have taken them through Spain. So cheap were prices they could afford a villa and garden large enough for livestock on the outskirts of town. Backyard goats and chickens again figured in their family life. Marrakesh was sufficiently emetic not to distract Orwell from writing. The city was, if anything, even more revolting to Eileen than to him:

> Marrakech crawls with disease of every kind, the ringworm group, the tuberculosis group, the dysentery group; & if you lunch in a restaurant the flies only show themselves as flies as distinct from black masses when they hurry out for a moment to taste a corpse on its way to the cemetery.[88]

Heretical to say so but, from the small samples one has, Eileen often strikes one as the more vivacious writer of the two.

They were refreshed by a trip to the Atlas Mountains. As in Burma, only in the distant back country could one find anything nobly pre-colonial. Orwell particularly admired the noble savagery of the Berbers and made an odd request that Eileen allow him to sample 'a young arab girl'. Eileen's permission for this relief adultery was as inexplicable as his asking permission for it. One assumes it was because, for some reason, conjugal relations had ceased between them. There may have been more than one young Arab girl. The unreliable Harold Acton (a fellow Etonian) describes, in his *More Memoirs of an Aesthete* (2009), a lubricious conversation: 'This cadaverous ascetic . . . admitted that he had seldom tasted such bliss as with certain Moroccan girls.' Cadaverous relic is hard.

Morocco was less recovery than stay of execution. Orwell lost the weight he had gained at Preston Hall in the first month and there was a bloody relapse. As Eileen told a friend, over the first month he 'coughed all day & particularly all night so that we didn't get thirty minutes' consecutive rest until November'. Towards the end of the stay he was, she said, about where he was when he had started. By that point, as she stoically put it, 'Now that we're hardened to the general frightfulness of the country we're quite enjoying it & Eric is writing a book that pleases both of us very much.' That she was sharing in the writing of the book is revealing. He liked reading aloud to her and, of course, she typed the fair copies.[89]

They returned, in March 1939, with a virtually complete *Coming Up for Air*, to an England numb with false relief at Chamberlain's 'piece of paper' assurance of peace in their time.

Real Air

The very first thing I remember is the smell of sainfoin chaff.
GEORGE BOWLING, in *Coming Up for Air*

If Orwell's last book had been quixotic, *Coming Up for Air* is the squire Panza's tale. In a virtuoso act of ventriloquism, Orwell took on the voice, stream of consciousness and personality of George Bowling, a shrewd, tubby, middle-aged (but still lecherous, when he has cash in his pocket to buy sex) insurance salesman. George is recently possessed of a set of gleaming false teeth and a lifelong down-to-earth view of a world going to hell. He is also possessed, at times unconvincingly, of an engagingly Orwellian cast of thought. For example: 'It's queer, I thought, as I ate a bit of roll, how dull murders are nowadays.' Orwell wrote one of his more famous essays on the same, De Quinceyan subject, seven years later. Orwellian, too, is Bowling's prescient vision of what is just a year or two away: 1984, to put the obviously resonant date to it, is prophesied. It is not the war, but the 'after-war' that will bring the real disaster:

The coloured shirts, the barbed wire, the rubber truncheons. The secret cells where the electric light burns night and day, and the detectives watching you while you sleep. And the processions and the posters with enormous faces, and the crowds of a million people all cheering for the Leader till they deafen themselves into thinking that they really worship him, and all the time, underneath, they hate him so that they want to puke. It's all going to happen.

Having come into a seventeen-quid windfall, Bowling resolves, rather than buying himself a woman and some razzle as he normally does, to revisit that foreign country, his childhood past in Lower Binfield – a place where the sun always shone and the fish always bit. Patently Henley-on-Thames. He doesn't tell his nag of a wife Hilda. (There are no good wives in Orwell's fiction; in his life there were two.) George's trip back to Edwardian Binfield is inspired by a rare whiff, in motorized London where the latest fast food is synthetic fishburger, of a carthorse's droppings. Dung brings back the 'real air' of his childhood.

The narrative is strung along George's remembered life story. He was born the son of a high-street seed merchant, doomed to extinction by competition from larger firms than his. There are echoes throughout of Orwell's favourite novel, H. G. Wells's *The*

History of Mr Polly. In that wonderful novel, it will be remembered, the hero, at peace at last, is pictured fishing serenely alongside the Thames. For Orwell, that would be Paradise Regained. Bowling left the smell of the big schoolroom and its smell of ink and dust and boots aged fifteen. He was a clever lad, but no one encouraged him to do anything worthwhile with his cleverness. He goes to work as a counter assistant in a Sainsbury's-like food shop (the kind of establishment which was destroying small shops like Orwell's in Wallington). It's a 'good' job. Come the 'War' he is swept up and – such is the fearsome casualty rate – promoted to the commissioned rank of 'temporary gentleman'. Not a good job. A 'Blighty' wound, and his knowledge of 'food supplies' (in other words, how to slice bacon), puts him in charge of 'Twelve Mile Dump', a supplies store that has no supplies. It does, however, have a vast quantity of 'Good-Bad' novels hanging around which constitute George Bowling's higher education.

On demobilization he is a gentleman no more, and drifts into what he does best – fooling customers into buying 'insurance' in a world about to be destroyed. He is, in 1939, a five-pound-a-week man, with the prospect of retiring a seven-pound-a-week man on a petty pension from Pearl Insurance. 'And properly speaking that's the end of my story' – except that, with seventeen quid burning a hole in his pocket, he wants to recover his *temps perdus.*

Coming Up for Air is the most aromatic of Orwell's novels. There are passages that fairly caress the nostrils, as, for example (he's thinking of the epic heatwave of 1911):

> It was a hot July that year. How we sweated in the shop, and how the cheese and the ground coffee smelt! And then the cool of the evening outside, the smell of night-stocks and pipe-tobacco in the lane behind the allotments, the soft dust underfoot, and the nightjars hawking after the cockchafers.

But at the heart of the novel is fishing – the 'angling' celebrated by Izaak Walton. Visitors noticed a fishing rod and tackle at the foot of Orwell's bed when he was dying. It was the only luxury (it cost a whopping eight quid) we know him to have bought himself. The rod was purchased on General Election Day, 1945. Clement Attlee, the winner, reminded him, Orwell said, of a dead fish which was still slimy. He did not cheer much at the result. Coarse fishing had irresistible attractions and profound meaning for Orwell. Angling, even more than football (whose massed supporters he feared might be proto-fascistic), is the people's true sport. It is individualistic and non-competitive. It promotes rumination, not hot blood. It connects the angler with the rhythms of nature. And its artful skills have been built up over years and passed down, generation to generation. PETA (People for the Ethical Treatment of Animals – a title that would have made Orwell's skin crawl) insist that angling is as sadistic as badger baiting. 'Fish', they say, 'suffer horribly at the hands of anglers.' They are right, but no political party dares bring in a 'ban' such as that which did away with John Peel's ('in his coat so gay') successors. Angling matters too much to the working classes. One might as well abolish beer and skittles.

For Orwell there was also the peculiar attraction that fishing is an extremely smelly sport – but one whose smells attract and uplift, like the 'real air' of Binfield. Toff fishing, for salmon and trout, with cunning artificial flies, thigh-boots, landing nets, protected rivers and – at its toffiest – ghillies, is relatively scentless. Coarse fishing has a rich menu for the nose. For example, the primitive bread-paste bait (no roach or gudgeon can resist it), moistened with spittle for those at the bent-pin entry level, then kneaded into a ball in a handkerchief with thumb and index finger. You smell it, and by the end of the day your hands smell of it and it of your hands. There is the dangerous toxic taste of the lead weights, which you bite onto the catgut. The loamy smell of earthworms and ranker smell of maggots ('gentles'), still wriggling as the hook goes through them (no PETA cares a damn about them). Overhanging it all are the ambient smells of the river, which change during the day with the course of the weather and season. Orwell notes the increase in the aroma of wild peppermint as the day's sport comes to a twilight end.

In my youth (I was as 'mad' about freshwater fishing as Orwell and Bowling are),[90] I was aware of the different smells the caught fish had. Eels, for example, which wriggle furiously until their heads are cut off – and even then squirm a bit – had a deep, slimy smell that stuck on your hands like glue, drying and flaking off like piscine dandruff by the end of the day. Dace, the most beautifully darting of freshwater fish, were so fragrant you could eat them raw, as the Japanese do their favourite fish. The smell of fish is notoriously erotic for the *renifleur*-inclined, and there is a vague sexual gratification that one doesn't like to dwell on too much. It is exclusively a male sport. The sensory ensemble of freshwater fishing is much more subtle than that of sea-fishing, which for Orwell, like all true anglers, is second best.

Orwell was 'mad' about fishing from childhood to adolescence, and fond of it, thereafter, through life. It is, Bowling says in a fine rhapsody, the 'soul' of English civilization. Fishing under a willow tree, by a quiet pool (when there were still such things),

> belongs to the time before the war, before the radio, before aeroplanes, before Hitler. There's a kind of peacefulness even in the names of English coarse fish. Roach, rudd, dace, bleak, barbel, bream, gudgeon, pike, chub, carp, tench. They're solid kind of names. The people who made them up hadn't heard of machine-guns, they didn't live in terror of the sack or spend their time eating aspirins, going to the pictures, and wondering how to keep out of the concentration camp.

Bowling, newly kitted out, aims to revisit a secret pool he came across as a boy in Binfield, where he saw a vast pike. He finds the

pool a stinking rubbish dump. At the end of the novel he goes back
to the real world of fishburgers, motor cars, the shrewish Hilda
and, in a year or two, bet on it, the concentration camp. But he's a
clever kind of fellow. Who knows? George Bowling may dodge the
Gestapo bullet.

Unreal Air

To Jack Common, the friend who was looking after Wallington
while they were in Morocco, Orwell wrote: 'I don't know whether or
not you will be fitting on your gas mask by the time this gets to you.'
In the run-up to war it was assumed that the bomber would always

Gas mask,
as issued by
the Ministry of
Home Security,
c. 1939/40.

get through and airborne fleets would rain down on Britain not just explosives (for which an air-raid shelter campaign was launched), but poison gas.

Remarkably, some 40 million of the protective devices were issued, nationwide, in 1938–9. I'm one of the few Britons living who actually wore a government-issued gas mask in the fond expectation that it might, perhaps, save my little life. In the first years of the war the gas-mask case was the nation's ubiquitous unisex handbag. By the end of the war (when the Germans, anyway, would have dropped nerve gas, against which masks were no protection) the gas mask, swinging in its canvas bag by the side, was history. The bags were, oddly, much valued by anglers. The gas masks themselves were nauseating. The smell of the protective chemicals, and new rubber, was itself enough to produce a faint. For lungs like Orwell's, mustard gas would have been preferable.

There is an oddly surreal event narrated in *Coming Up for Air*. A bomb is accidentally dropped by the RAF on Binfield. There is panic – the war has started! George sees what looks like a stampede of Gadarene swine:

> At the other end of the market-place the High Street rises a little. And down this little hill a herd of pigs was galloping, a sort of huge flood of pig-faces. The next moment, of course, I saw what it was. It wasn't pigs at all, it was only the schoolchildren in their gas-masks.

Pigs were always Farmer Orwell's least-loved animals. Gas-masked pigs were something out of Hieronymus Bosch.

War

1939 was Orwell's worst year.

D. J. TAYLOR

Coming Up for Air was published by Gollancz. He was no longer a Stalinist and was keen to re-establish a relationship with Orwell. The novel was well received but, since the war it solemnly warned against actually broke out three months after publication, it was *après coup*. The nation had put away its fishing rods.

For the early months of the war Orwell found himself surplus to his country's requirements. He was medically graded 'C' – 'useless', as the Spanish medics had said a couple of years earlier. He was too broken and too old to serve in any military capacity. And his political record had black marks (for example, 'Trotskyist'), which blocked his serving in 'intelligence', as did fellow Etonians like David Astor, A. J. Ayer and Orwell's new friend Malcolm Muggeridge. George Orwell could not be trusted. In the phoney war interval, he dug further into *Coming Up for Air*'s vein of English nostalgia and childhood, with two classic essays: on boys' comics and Dickens.

He and Eileen moved to London on weekdays: she to work in the government censorship department ('inconceivably dull'). He landed a regular reviewing position with the eccentric Lady Rhonda's *Time and Tide* and churned out for the magazine's meagre readership low-grade pap on literature and film. Similarly dull. Avril and her mother found catering work in London. It was Wallington at weekends. Eileen found it (after the exhausting wartime blackout journey) dirtier than London and no break. She put up with a life of grime, an outside lavatory and midnight washing-up for George. A poignant letter, written a few days before her death, recorded her loyally stifled distaste at the life he insisted on for the two of them.

As the country girded itself for another world war, Orwell became, briefly, excited about the LDV (Local Defence Volunteers) militia. It could use even old crocks like him. It brought back inflammatory recollections of Barcelona, 1936. Anthony Eden's LDV radio appeal got a quarter of a million volunteers (including Eric Blair) in 24 hours, and another million in a month. There was a rally at Lord's Cricket Ground, which Orwell attended. The LDV sparked the last flare-up of Orwell's anarchist romanticism. He foresaw revolutionary things for a people's army armed to the teeth (Orwell had sadly few remaining – and his musketry was a bit rusty). The 'volunteers' could be the shock-troops of radical reform. He had friends of the same extreme political opinion. They conspired enthusiastically among themselves at the LDV training camp at Osterley Park in west London. Its owner had allowed Tom Wintringham to set up a school for would-be fighters in the early summer of 1940. An old-school Marxist and CPGB veteran blooded in Spain, Wintringham had gone off the Stalinist rails. Orwell saw him as a fellow 'revolutionary patriot'. Strict doctrinal differences could be buried during total war.[91] Wintringham was particularly keen on the guerrilla and street-fighting skills that had been effective with the International Brigade in Spain. Hulton's *Picture Post* (then a radical picture paper) popularized the LDV.

Churchill, when he took over as prime minister in May 1940, was wary, recalling the Irish stab in the back of 1916. There must be no enemies within. The LDV force was neutered into the 'Home Guard' – 'Dad's Army'. There was no risk of the Captain Mainwarings of England leading any uprising. Wintringham's operation was closed down in September 1941. The LDV teeth were drawn, to be replaced by the toothless gums of the Home Guard. Orwell was, by then, well disillusioned. He had been promoted to sergeant in the St John's Wood Home Guard unit but it took the authorities three months even to get him a uniform to stitch his three stripes onto. And he had to sit through interminable lectures by 'wretched old blimps'.

He did his bit for a year or so, with growing boredom, and resigned in late 1943. He had more than enough of a medical excuse, and the Wehrmacht was not, after all, on its way.

His brother-in-law Lawrence had volunteered for the RAMC on the outbreak of war. He was a world leader in his surgical field and 36 years old. The Expeditionary Force in France had little need of thoracic/pulmonary specialisms at the front lines where, serving as a medic, Major O'Shaughnessy was blown to bits by a Stuka bomb (it is thought) during the chaotic Dunkirk evacuations in May 1940. Dunkirk was the lowest point of the war for Britain. Given the 'little boats' chaos, no telegram could be sent to Lawrence's next of kin. His body was irrecoverable. Orwell vainly searched trains arriving at London stations, in the hope he might have survived, and was told to keep out of the way. It was a gallant death and merited an obituary in *The Times*. The loss shattered Eileen, whose love for her always-dependable brother, from various hints, had been stronger and simpler than her love for George, or for out-and-out rogues like Georges Kopp. If she desperately needed him, Eileen said, Laurence would always come. George perhaps not: 'for him his work comes first'.

Gwen went to practise in Newcastle. Eileen complains, in one of her surviving letters, about the grim business of disposing of the O'Shaughnessy family house in Greenwich, the nearest thing she had ever had to a permanent home. She and Orwell lived like gypsies in wartime London at half a dozen addresses – some very seedy (a flat in St John's Wood was the original for Victory Mansions, broken lift and all). For him it was solidarity with Londoners. For her it was Mrs Mopp and her bucket. So distraught was she that, as she ironically told a friend, air raids were positively restful interruptions from the drudgery of being Mrs Orwell. Eileen was now suffering unidentified gynaecological problems, whose more serious details she kept from her husband – and possibly herself. The couple realized that the children they wanted would never come. They dealt with pointlessness in different ways. She chain-smoked; he was promiscuous.

Eileen's secretarial skills were useful to the war effort. Typists were desperately needed for wartime bureaucracy and she had transferred to the Ministry of Food, where she formed a close friendship with Lettice Cooper.[92] The two of them came up with scripts for the BBC's *The Kitchen Front* (nice title) on how to create appetizing meals out of the ration-book allowances. Cunning variations on the famed Woolton Pie, scrag end and baconless bubble and squeak were jauntily recommended. Cooper (later an accomplished novelist, one of whose characters, in *Black Bethlehem*, is a tender portrait of Eileen) recalled her friend coming into work relaying, daily, how *Animal Farm* was coming along. There was, Cooper recalled, always housework for her friend. From Eileen's confidences about his sexual waywardness, George, Cooper bleakly concluded, 'was not the kind of person who likes being married all the time'. What was actually going on in the marriage will (probably) forever be unknown.

There was an episode, during the war, which a clearly embarrassed Bernard Crick felt obliged to describe. Orwell had befriended the poet-critic William Empson, whose cubicle was near his in the wartime BBC offices (Empson is the too-clever-for-his-own-good Newspeak linguistician Ampleforth in *Nineteen Eighty-Four*). Orwell often socialized with Empson and his partner Hetta. They were all hard drinkers. One evening in high summer, writes Crick:

> The merest acquaintance from BBC days who had only come across Orwell before as a rather quiet and melancholy figure in the background of BBC pubs, met him again at the Empsons', sitting on his own in a corner, drinking fairly heavily. When neither was able to get a taxi, Orwell insisted, very much against her inclination, as she was young and was nervous of him, on walking her home and then trying, while crossing [Hampstead] Heath, to make love to her far too persistently, somewhat

violently even. To keep him off she promised to meet him again when next she was in London, but on not keeping the unlikely rendezvous, she received a violent letter of formal reproach.

One knows so little about this side of things that no downright moral assumptions can be made. Except perhaps that after he knew, or even feared, that he was tubercularly infectious, it was grossly irresponsible. His line, if it came up, was that he had been infected but the 'lesions' were dead and 'non-progressive'. But he coughed a lot. And it was known that coughed airborne saliva and spitting spread TB.

Marital relations, given Eileen's health problems, may have ceased. Moral codes relaxed in wartime on the 'tomorrow we die' principle – as even I, then a child, remember personally (used condoms on the pavement on the way to school). Eileen, as George routinely confided to women he fancied, may have taken lovers herself. It is doubtful, however, that she lured them to Hampstead Heath and pounced on them or that her health conditions (cancer was grimly feared towards the end of her life) were catching.

How the couple managed the decision to get Gwen to arrange the private adoption of an illegitimate child, from South Shields, in 1944 is unclear. Corners must have been cut, strings pulled. The June 1943 Adoption Act had tightened up regulations, following newspaper reports of the abuse of children orphaned, evacuated or displaced by bombing. Illegitimacy rates had shot up, as they inevitably do in wartime. Social services, answerable to councils, would not routinely have acceded to adoption by two chronically ill, elderly applicants with no fixed home address other than a primitive cottage without hot running water, well beyond the council follow-up inspection range. The agency would have been right to oppose the arrangement. Nonetheless, after a month's approval process, Mr and Mrs Orwell took parental possession of one-month-old Richard Horatio Blair in summer 1944. Avril no longer had parents to care for (Ida had died

Eileen and Richard.

in March 1943, Richard four years earlier). Her services to the family would be again called on – first to help out Eileen (who gave up her job for motherhood) and eventually to become young Richard's full-time adoptive mother. She did it very well. But like all Avril's good services, they were largely unnoticed.

How Eileen actually died has never been clear. She went, discreetly (so as not to worry George), for an operation – a hysterectomy. It was arranged for the end of March 1945 in Newcastle, where Gwen could take care of her. There seems, strangely, to have been some ill-advised cost-cutting. Pre-NHS prices were high. She downplayed the forthcoming operation as a routine thing. It was in fact major surgery. She had a heart attack under anaesthetic and died on the table. She was six months short of forty. J. J. Ross assumes that she was allergic to chloroform. The inquest cleared the surgical team. As bad luck would have it, George was with the invasion force in Paris and Germany, reporting on the war for *The Observer*. He was in no physical condition to be in the field and was hospitalized himself. It was all muddle and telegrams. He kept his grief and, possibly, his guilt to himself. He should, of course, have been with her. The 'victory' he observed in the overrun ruined cities of Germany was no solace. The shocking debris convinced him that 'civilization' was at an end. For ever. Only the Fascist boot on the face would last.

Among the few revealing pieces of evidence left us to form any picture of Mrs George Orwell (the name she adopted and died under) in the last years of the marriage are her last letters. They record candidly how much she had hated 'nightmare' London, what with the morally righteous (as Orwell saw it) squalor, the chronic shortage of cash, the forever unsettled residences, the lack of anything that could be called 'home-life'.[93] Wallington was no refuge: just another dirty sink, unwashed saucepans, clothes washed in buckets, chickens to feed, eggs to boil and, for the last two years, nappies to change without hot running water or decent sanitation. Yet Eileen Orwell thought it a sacrifice worth making and made it. George was always hardest on himself and made those around him guilty about how easy they had it by comparison. Eileen left everything to him, 'including a house inherited from her mother'. Possessions, particularly houses, meant little to him. But the loss of her was material. Eileen's typing had become essential to him. He was fast, but inaccurate, on the keyboard. Having to type the manuscript of *Nineteen Eighty-Four* a few years later was something that hastened his death. Some commentators say it actually killed him. Had Eileen been up there, in Jura, making, as she had always done, the 'fair copy', he might have lived a few more years and written the two novels he felt he had in him when he died.[94]

The Astor Connection

It is a land where the bus conductors are good-tempered
and the policemen carry no revolvers.
'My Country Right or Left' (1940)

In his fallow months after the outbreak of war, unwanted as he was
for the 'effort', Orwell had had time to put his thoughts in order.
Eileen told a friend, tartly, that George had 'written a little book
explaining how to be a Socialist though Tory'.[95] The sarcasm is one
of many fleeting hints that her political views were more consistently
radical than his. And her wit razor-sharp.

The little book was *The Lion and the Unicorn*. It was published,
in February 1941, by Warburg under the new 'Searchlight' imprint,
of which Orwell was an editor. Searchlights, as the Blitz began,
were raking the skies by night. Publication coincided with the
Blitz, and has the famous opening line, 'As I write, highly civilized
human beings are flying overhead, trying to kill me.' They failed.
But German bombers did manage to destroy Warburg's paper stock,
which put *The Lion and the Unicorn* out of print, after healthy early
sales, in 1942. Score one for the Heinkel.

Civilian bombing meant, Orwell said, that 'blimpishness' –
'keep the home fires burning' patriotism – was no longer viable.
Ask not for whom the Luftwaffe bomb falls. It falls for thee, Civvy
Street. The Orwells would, a little later in the war, be bombed out
themselves. The Luftwaffe almost destroyed the only manuscript
copy of the work in progress, *Animal Farm*, having done their worst
on printed copies of *The Lion and the Unicorn*. Luckily the Orwells
were out of the house when the V1 fell. They usually weren't: Orwell
insisted on spending weekdays and, more dangerously, nights in
London, even though he had a safe home in the country. It was,
like the king and queen in Buckingham Palace, an act of solidarity
with the East Enders (the docks were primary targets) who had no

shelter by night other than the underground station (they smelled, Orwell observed).

The less self-sacrificing Cyril Connolly took himself, and his magazine, to Cornwall (along with Sonia Brownell, or 'Buttocks Brownell' as she was nicknamed, a woman in whom Orwell was always interested). Cyril enjoyed the lobsters, his co-editor Stephen Spender recalled. *Horizon* was, meanwhile, doing very well by Orwell, publishing his best, most thoughtful meditations. Its six-figure circulation was the highest ever recorded by a literary magazine. Orwell helped raise it.[96]

Un-blimpish patriotism was, Orwell believed, possible. It was a duty, in fact, with invasion imminent. There was, he concluded as the bombs rained down and the AA barrage made every night Guy Fawkes Night, enough of old England left (the England he had celebrated in *Coming Up for Air*) to be worth dying for. The Tory political oligarchs (those 'wrong people' at the head of the great English family), the soft-faced profiteers, the sandal-wearing vegetarians, the half-megaphone/half-microphone commissars ranting in the LSE, and the Stalinist Trade Unionists could be dealt with later. The title, 'The Lion and the Unicorn', harks back to the heraldic inscription: 'Ich dien' – 'I serve'. Bolshy George Orwell would, at last, bend the knee. The book contains his most tenderly Anglophiliac iconography: the old spinsters, so revered by John Major, cycling through the autumn mist to early communion, the warm beer, the greener grass, the knobbly faces, the bad teeth (all that oversweetened tea, the national tipple), English 'gentleness' (the man ahead of you in the orderly bus queue will not be carrying a knife) – above all, the English 'air'. His first 'sniff' of it, on his return from Burma, convinced him this was where he had to be. It was Bowling's 'real air' – the good smell of England.

The book caught the attention of David Astor. Orwell's scathing attack on the 'moneyed classes' bounced off him. Astor was, of course, one of the most obscenely moneyed men in

England. The Astors' original wealth – now generations 'clean' – had come from the American fur trade. But, of course, Orwell's family money (although it was now all gone) had come, substantially, from the slave trade, the opium trade and 'blood timber'. The Blairs and the Limouzins were not morally superior, just financially unluckier, than the Astors. Losers in the great capitalistic, social-Darwinistic struggle. The British Astors owned *The Observer* Sunday newspaper. Cyril Connolly suggested that David, who took a close interest in its columns, might use Orwell, as he (Connolly) was using him, as a free-ranging essayist, on his and Peter Watson's magazine, *Horizon*. The four of them had all been at Eton – 'that festering centre of snobbishness' as Orwell called it in *The Lion and the Unicorn*. No matter.[97] Connolly arranged an introduction and Orwell and Astor met at a tea shop near the BBC. They hit it off and struck up what was the strongest friendship in both their later lives. Orwell's 'war' was, by 1942, getting better; Astor was having a very good war indeed. A captain in the Marines, the epitome of sangfroid and daring, he survived the disastrous Dieppe raid. He went to a London party a few hours later and was reportedly good company, if a trifle subdued.[98] He slummed it in Orwell's flat and Orwell, presumably, visited the Astors' establishment, Cliveden in Berkshire.

Astor was later seconded to SOE, the secret service, organizing, among much else, underground resistance to the Nazis in Europe. Long after Orwell's death, Astor was asked if he had somehow involved Orwell in 'intelligence' work.[99] He said no, but suspicions remain. He was, for example, suspiciously keen about bending regulations to get Orwell into front-line war reporting missions – work for which he was about as medically unfit as to join Captain Astor in the Royal Marines. Malcolm Muggeridge, also up to his armpits in the intelligence war, begins to figure centrally in Orwell's life. The wittiest man of his time, Mug wrote diaries that contain the most acrid vignettes of the knight of the mournful countenance.

Astor gave Orwell a freehold on *The Observer*'s columns. At last he had the power of Fleet Street behind his prose. And, more lastingly, he had the power to raise political journalism to what he thought it should be – an influential prose art. His influence on *The Observer* itself was formative. As the historian of the paper Richard Cockett notes, Orwell was 'the man who more than any other . . . helped to shape the new *Observer*'. It is one of his most lasting, yet least visible, achievements. After the war, in 1948, Astor took direct editorial authority of the paper. *The Observer* organized liberal opinion in Britain into a powerful extra-parliamentary, contra-establishment force. The paper, despite its patrician ownership (a little doublethink never hurt any newspaper), adopted the Orwellian line that the Tory governing 'elite' were so many 'holes in the air'. Anti-imperialism was the paper's constant mission. It climaxed with the Suez debacle, in 1956. *The Observer* mobilized the nation's revulsion, which, with the toppling of Eden and Macmillan's follow-up 'winds of change', led to the winding up of the British Empire. It cost the paper, temporarily, half its massive circulation – a price worth paying. And it was Orwell's proudest moment. He was not, alas, there to enjoy what he had helped bring about.[100]

Despite the force he exercised within it, Orwell did not take up the offered salaried post on Astor's paper. Independence – what he called the 'as I please' factor – was too dear to him. But being taken notice of was something he found he liked. He went on to accept (Astor may have been instrumental) the position of literary editor on the socialist weekly *Tribune* in November 1943. It meant a cut in salary to £500. But with a Labour government preparing for power, and eventually in office, the paper had lines of influence feeding directly into the most reformist government Britain has ever had – the 'nationalizing', welfare-state creating, Attlee administration. Party spokespeople and cabinet members, such as Stafford Cripps and Aneurin Bevan, used *Tribune* as an extra-mural platform and were directly involved in the paper's management. Orwell attended editors' conferences – kitchen cabinets. He was no longer a voice in the wilderness. He was also well enough known and respected to attract eminent contributors for the pittance *Tribune* coughed up. Sometimes not even that.

Astor was a more generous paymaster for the fortnightly literary reviews Orwell continued to write for *The Observer* – they are generally agreed to be among his best literary commentary. He now had many voices: the Orwell of *Horizon*, or the more arid *Polemic*, is very different from the chatty Orwell of his 'London Letters' for the American *Partisan Review*. And for *Tribune* he wrote *autour de mon chapeau* columns under the 'As I Please' rubric, which are among his nimblest work. A notable 'As I Please' is his diatribe against the 'fascistic' behaviour of British football fans when Moscow Dinamo came to play in the winter of 1945. They beat Britain's best, provoking an ugly reaction from supporters who could not bear the way Muscovite factory workers with unpronounceable names could run rings around the likes of Tommy Lawton and Stanley Matthews. As Orwell said, prophetically:

> The significant thing is not the behaviour of the players but the attitude of the spectators: and, behind the spectators, of the nations who work themselves into furies over these absurd contests, and seriously believe – at any rate for short periods – that running, jumping and kicking a ball are tests of national virtue.

Fascism in the football stands. Orwell said it first.

The Empson Connection

He stank.

WILLIAM EMPSON

The British wartime government was very clever in recruiting the country's cleverest oddballs – most notably Alan Turing – to help win the war. Chess masters, classicists with the dustiest scholarly expertise and crossword virtuosi did their bit and more. Had Lewis Carroll been alive he would quite likely have been summoned to Bletchley Park, Turing's Wonderland.

Although many clever ex-Etonians served, the government found no wartime use for George Orwell. That was a mistake. Where 'propaganda' was concerned, the necessary guarding of truth by lies, his mind would have been Turing-class. There were, presumably, too many black marks against his name – all that Trotsky/ILP baggage. Eventually something sufficiently riskless to the state was found for him in the BBC's Indian section of the Overseas Service, as a talks assistant. The BBC did not impress him as an institution. 'Half lunatic asylum, half girl's school', he called it in his wartime diary. In conversation it was 'half whorehouse'. Auntie returned the compliment in 2011 by turning down 'flat' the offer of a bronze statue of George Orwell in the forecourt of the newly refurbished HQ, on the grounds that he was 'too left wing'.[101]

Orwell joined the BBC in August 1941 and resigned in September 1943. The salary for an assistant talks producer was generous – just about what he had been earning as an assistant superintendent in Burma. As Peter Davison neatly observes, George Orwell was always best paid when he was a servant of the Raj. The hours, given the time difference, were gruelling. It was a wonder, his closest friends thought, that he found time to turn out so much extra-mural journalism (something that niggled the BBC authorities, not least because it was so good). He was also writing a 'fairy story', which

would eventually fight its way over a publishing obstacle race to
emerge, delayed by years, as *Animal Farm*. For most of his two
years at the BBC his desk was on the converted second floor of
Peter Robinson's department store in Oxford Street. In peacetime
it specialized in school uniforms. His St Cyprian's outfit may
have been purchased there. His desk would be grimly portrayed as
Winston Smith's in Minitrue: the memory hole by his side, for the
necessary perversions of historical fact. It was a private joke that
Orwell, *The Observer*'s premier columnist, made Winston a *Times*
('paper of record') journalist. Orwell hated the toxins Northcliffe
had injected into Fleet Street. The BBC canteen was on the ground
floor, immortalized in *Nineteen Eighty-Four*, with its sugarless tea
and pink-tinged lumps swimming in grease, 'with a sour metallic
smell'. To the disgust of his snootier colleagues, Orwell slurped his
tea defiantly from the saucer, Wigan-style, and puffed his black
shag 'roll-ups'. All unlucky enough to be in smelling range agreed
that the fumes were uniquely 'foul'. George Orwell was, when he
wanted to be, very 'bolshy'.

He was, of course, well up on Burma (currently under savage
Japanese occupation), but apart from being born there he had no
first-hand knowledge of the larger subcontinent or its languages.
There were two burning concerns. India was seething with revolt
(both Gandhian-peaceful and mutinously militant). Hard-to-spare
military forces were needed for internal policing as well as to fend
off Japanese invasion. India, like Ireland in the First World War,
was a thorn in Britain's thigh.

Orwell had stated his considered view on how to defuse the
Indian powder keg in *The Lion and the Unicorn*:

> What we must offer India is not 'freedom', which, I have said
> earlier, is impossible, but alliance, partnership – in a word,
> equality. But we must also tell the Indians that they are free to
> secede, if they want to. Without that there can be no equality of

partnership, and our claim to be defending the coloured peoples against Fascism will never be believed.

It went on in the same colonially patronizing ('coloured peoples'?), doublethinking vein for several pages. Britain had won India by the sword. It would hold on to the vast country by the sheathed sword – a defence pact, with all the defence armaments (and canes?) in one partner's hands. As Crick notes, Orwell skilfully sidestepped the hottest Indian topic (independence) in the talks he was responsible for, playing the cultural, topical interest cards instead. His diaries, which have survived, record someone with a keen ability to see through propaganda to geopolitical fact. But his BBC years would have been mere time-serving, were it not for one thing: the man in the adjoining cubicle.

That man, William Empson, was the cleverest literary critic of the century. A poet himself, Empson was fascinated by polysemy in verse. The ways, that is, in which 'ordinary language' – words and lines – could 'compress' so much diverse meaning into themselves and explode on the page. He had begun his investigation as a brilliant Cambridge postgraduate under I. A. Richards. Richards was the co-inventor, with C. K. Ogden, of 'Basic English' – language boiled down to its 'kernel' state. Empson's doctoral thesis, published in 1930 as the monograph *Seven Types of Ambiguity*, revolutionized the reading and teaching of English verse. For his part, Orwell was fascinated by linguistic simplification of the Basic English kind. He conceded that the ambiguity (which he called 'coincidence') that Empson so relished was, doubtless, a very good thing in poetry. But 'disambiguation' – 'straight talk' – was what was necessary in political discourse. Who wanted a prime minister adept in seven kinds of ambiguity?

Orwell had spent a lot of time in the company of fervent Esperantists, for whom language had the compression of the oxo cube. The Esperanto evangelist aunt Nellie was a constant, shadowy presence on the outskirts of his life. The packing and unpacking of language was of primary interest to both men, doing their routine office work in Oxford Street, and in the pub (famously the 'glue-pot', the George – so nicknamed because once you went in, you never came out). The BBC was, in these years, positively clogged with poets: Dylan Thomas, Roy Campbell (hated by Orwell for having fought for Franco), Louis MacNeice, Stephen Spender and W. R. Rodgers. Orwell was physically closest to Empson. Too close for comfort, as it happened. Orwell 'stank', Empson said. His 'foul' black shag roll-ups were a prophylactic. Both men chain-smoked. On his side, Orwell was close enough to observe Empson's 'hairiness' – his hallmark moustache and other face-fungus.[102]

There was the by now routine Orwellian sexual foolery. Empson had been dumped in this lowly place in the BBC for the same reason as Orwell. There were black marks against his name. His partner, later his wife, Hetta Crouse, was beautiful, an equal in intelligence, a journalist, and more radical politically than 'Bill'. Orwell fell head over heels for the woman. He would, he said, divorce (ailing) Eileen and marry Hetta if, on her part, she gave up Empson. Apparently he meant it, as earlier he had meant his mad proposal to set up a *ménage à trois* with Brenda Salkeld. Hetta (soon to be Mrs Empson and the mother of children, not all her husband's) declined, although she was flattered by his being 'crazy' about her, and spread the fact about. It must have got back to Eileen. Empson was amused. Although a believer in Leninist free love before and during marriage, Hetta would not sleep with Orwell.[103] She 'didn't like him enough', she said. It was the smell, Empson grimly implied. Hetta and Eileen had jointly bemoaned the problem of George's disgusting body odour. And he didn't smoke while copulating. At least Bill had that protection.

Through the collectively generated nicotine fug and after-hours beer, there developed a disputatious conversation between these two supremely clever men on the English language and 'honest' usage. Two variant positions were crystallized. Empson's considered position emerged, sadly too late for Orwell, in his 1951 monograph, *The Structure of Complex Words*. Poetry – language at its highest pitch – is, Empson argued, not 'diction' (a separate dialect), but supercharged 'ordinary language'. Cambridge 'Ordinary Language Philosophers', notably Wittgenstein, pursued a parallel line. Orwell's position, not congruent but compatible, was that the language of journalism and of political discourse had its own necessary rules. He wrote relatively little about verse but his aesthetic theory is stated succinctly in a radio essay, later printed in *The Listener*, 'The Meaning of a Poem'. The poem in question is Gerard Manley Hopkins's 'Felix Randal' (1870s). Orwell loved the sonnet. He recited it, by heart, to comrades in the trenches in Spain. It's easy to see why he loved it. The dying man, to whom the poet priest will give final unction, is a village farrier, a man whose life is among horses, in a blacksmith's forge. Orwell loved equine smells and smithy smells (the only smell he had liked in Wigan was that of burning red coal).

But for Orwell, a poem can have only one meaning – 'emotional', he called it. Unsurprisingly the poet he writes about most, Kipling, attracts him because the meanings of the barrack-room ballads are plain as plain can be. There is no mystery about what 'The White Man's Burden' means. It means the white man's burden. Whatever the elegant 'pattern of words' that Hopkins dazzles us with, for Orwell it is the single core meaning that one has to extract. Empson's position is as different as can be. And Hopkins, as it happens, is one of his prime examples in *Seven Types of Ambiguity*. In the poet's most famous poem, 'The Windhover' (1877), the hovering falcon 'buckles' its wings to fall, like a stone, on its prey. For Empson, 'buckle' can legitimately suggest a belt buckle (the wings 'locked' together), something akin to a bicycle wheel being buckled ('crumpled' or 'broken'), or Christ's wounded arms clasping together as he is taken down from the Cross. There is no 'essential' meaning: only meanings. Where Orwell was concerned, language should say what it means. For Empson, the more meanings generated the richer, and all are valid. It was a fascinating conflict between the journalist and the poet, each with his own linguistic imperative. Above all Orwell sees 'plain' language as vital for the politician, and the political journalist. It is widely called his 'windowpane' thesis. For Empson, language at its highest, poetic level of expression is a stained-glass window. And the stains matter.

The relationship between Orwell and Empson is laid out in the conversations between Winston Smith (journalist) and Ampleforth (poet), and Orwell's appendix on 'Newspeak' in *Nineteen Eighty-Four* ('that dreadful book', Empson called it in *The Structure of Complex Words*, meaning praise). Ampleforth, 'a mild, ineffectual, dreamy creature . . . with very hairy ears and a surprising talent for juggling with rhymes and metres', occupies an adjoining cubicle to Winston's. Ampleforth 'was engaged in producing garbled versions – definitive texts, they were called – of poems which had become ideologically offensive, but which for one reason or another were to be retained in the anthologies'. 'Hairy Ears' is a low blow. The two men have desultory conversations in the abysmal canteen. They meet for the last time in the Miniluv, awaiting their respective Rooms 101. 'Ampleforth!', Winston exclaims. What, he wonders, has brought *him* to the place where there is no darkness?

'We were producing a definitive edition of the poems of Kipling. I allowed the word "God" to remain at the end of a line. I could not help it!' he added almost indignantly, raising his face to look at Winston. 'It was impossible to change the line. The rhyme was "rod". Do you realize that there are only twelve rhymes to "rod" in the entire language?'

Alongside Ampleforth and Winston in the Minitrue office and canteen is the odious goblin Syme, inspired by Joseph Goebbels. As a lexicographer, Syme's role is to impoverish language so that with the perfection of 'Newspeak', thoughtcrime is no longer possible. 'The whole climate of thought will be different,' Syme tells Winston: 'In fact there will be no thought, as we understand it now. Orthodoxy means not thinking – not needing to think. Orthodoxy is unconsciousness.'

Winston and Ampleforth are, in their different ways, fervent believers in Oldspeak. Syme is the new-speaking future. He does not live to see the completion of the eleventh edition of his Newspeak dictionary, or the universal linguistic lobotomy it will bring about. Too clever for his own good, he is vaporized shortly after his lecture to Winston.

Orwell resigned from the BBC in September 1943. Empson stayed on, to become an old China hand. Hetta, Mrs William Empson, slept with lots of other men. But never George Orwell.

Windowpane Language

> The louder people yap about the proletariat the more
> they despise its language.
> 'Propaganda and Demotic Speech' (1944)

Ask what is the best Orwell essay and you will start an argument. Shot elephants, hanged men, Billy Bunter and Raffles will be invoked. Ask what is Orwell's most influential essay and there will be no argument.

'Politics and the English Language' was first published by *Horizon* in April 1946. The date is significant. Orwell was nauseated by what politics had done to language over the war years. It wasn't merely an 'English' problem. Günter Grass would begin his literary career from the ground-zero point that Nazism had so soiled the German language that an honest writer must scrub it clean and start all over again. In Russia, Vasily Grossman was a journalist and novelist judged so dangerous that the NKVD even confiscated his typewriter ribbons. Post-war language, for all these writers, was a bombsite. What D. H. Lawrence called 'hygienisation' was required. All this was 1946 and very post-war. Orwell's essay, and its five-rule catechism, have since become, via the 'national curriculum', universal 'best practice' in British education. Children are fed the 'rules' as their unluckier wartime predecessors were fed cod-liver oil (I remember the daily dose well). Astor, when he was in charge of *The Observer*, decreed that every newly appointed journalist to the paper should be given a copy of 'Politics and the English Language'.

Despite its universal prescriptions, Orwell's 'windowpane' thesis has been deplored. Denis Donoghue, a critic with a very fine ear, concludes, sorrowfully, 'The shoddiest part of Orwell was his determination to link plain English to freedom and truth-telling.'[104] In a merrier vein (although he took Orwell very seriously), Raymond Williams offers mock applause for Orwell's 'successful impersonation of the plain man who bumps into experience in an unmediated way, and is simply telling the truth about it'.[105] The plain man's plain man. A fake, through and through, Williams concluded. Objections to Orwell's 'reductionist' view of English language are numerous and eloquent. Scorn is poured on his 'good prose = windowpane' analogy.[106] Did the foolish man not realize that the complexities of life and politics cannot be boiled down into baby talk? To which Orwell might have answered that simple prose is not where one starts, but where one ends. As is clear thought. Few make it.

The notion that Orwell, contra-Orwell, was advocating his own kind of Newspeak is grotesque. He and Empson had worked out their positions. On his side Orwell revered the stark richness of the 'ordinary' English language. His example of best English is from Ecclesiastes, the King James version: 'I returned and saw under the sun, that the race is not to the swift, nor the battle to the strong.' What could be plainer? What could be more complex? Historically, Orwell's argument is in a long tradition of stylistic polemic. It goes back to the great Senecan/Ciceronian style battles of the seventeenth century. Simplicity versus *copia* was the central issue. Donne is an arch-exponent of the Senecan style, as in: 'never send to know for whom the bell tolls/ It tolls for thee.' Twelve monosyllables. Not a Latinism among them. Compare it with the Ciceronian floridity of Sir Thomas Browne: 'When I take a full view and circle of myself without this reasonable moderator, and equal piece of justice, death, I do conceive myself the miserablest person extant.' Both are fine English prose, but chalk and cheese (Browne would have put it more colourfully). Orwell is Senecan to the core. His model, as he proclaims in another late essay, is Swift. 'Johnson said once to me,' recalls Boswell, 'speaking of the simplicity of Swift's style, "The rogue never hazards a metaphor".' Johnson would have said the same about that other rogue, Orwell.

So what was Orwell doing? He was not ordaining that 'reduction', but language appropriate to situation. One wishes that, as with Empson, he had sat at a desk alongside Bertolt Brecht. On his desk Brecht had a child's toy donkey with a placard around its neck that read, 'I too must understand.' Over his desk was a ceiling joist, on which Brecht had written 'Truth is Concrete'. In the windowpane of his study Orwell, had he been as witty as Brecht (which he wasn't), might have scrawled, 'Prose is transparent.' Enough said.

Smell: Conclusions

Bookstink

In the years between 1943 and 1946 Orwell came to some conclusions about how nasal hyperaesthesia like his interacted with the creative mind. His conclusions are spelled out in three works: 'Politics vs. Literature – An Examination of *Gulliver's Travels*' (1946); 'Benefit of Clergy: Some Notes on Salvador Dali' (1944); and, pre-eminently, *Animal Farm* (1945).

Dalí

For a man as cultivated as he, Orwell wrote very little on pictorial art. Excepting a piece on Donald McGill, his one extended cogitation on the subject is his essay on *The Secret Life of Salvador Dali*, a book not generally available in Britain in 1944 and which some bookshops would have been nervous about stocking. Orwell notes, fascinatedly, such Dalí-esque outrages on decency as:

> When he is about five he gets hold of a wounded bat which he puts into a tin pail. Next morning he finds that the bat is almost dead and is covered with ants which are devouring it. He puts it in his mouth, ants and all, and bites it almost in half.

This, one recalls, is the Orwell who once, when a wasp was attracted by the jam on his plate (afternoon tea was an important ritual for Orwell), cut the insect in two and then watched with cold fascination as the front half of the wasp kept guzzling, and jam was excreted in a steady stream at its severed waist-pipe. (Orwell ruminatively munched his toast at the time, one surmises, for more orthodox excretion.) It was, he thought, an apt metaphor for the British ruling classes who, as Lenin said, would sell you the rope to hang themselves with.

As the twig is bent, so the tree is shaped. Very bent in the Spaniard's case. Sexual perversity and necrophilia are constants in his artistic and personal career. There is, Orwell notes:

> a well-marked excretory motif as well. In his painting, *Le Jeu Lugubre*, he says, 'the drawers bespattered with excrement were painted with such minute and realistic complacency that the whole little Surrealist group was anguished by the question: Is he coprophagic or not?'

One might as well ask if the Pope is Catholic. Orwell concludes, magisterially:

> It is a book that stinks. If it were possible for a book to give a physical stink off its pages, this one would – a thought that might please Dali, who before wooing his future wife for the first time rubbed himself all over with an ointment made of goat's dung boiled up in fish glue.

Dalí's obsession with extreme smell is beyond the needs of even surrealism. But it fascinates. Particularly someone, like Orwell, who was never averse to having a fleck or two of goat dung on his shoes and was a passionate, hands-on angler. Was he too a coprophage?

Swift

Swift's morbid obsession with smell reaches its mad crisis point in the fourth book of *Gulliver's Travels*. There has been a long build-up – the hero's swooning away at the unperfumed 'natural smell' of the vast armpits of the Brobdingnagian ladies, for example – an image Dalí would have relished. In Houyhnhnmland the humanoid Yahoo population lives in stink 'somewhat between a weasel and a fox, but much more disagreeable' (Orwell must have admired the fine discrimination of animal scent Swift makes). Gulliver, loathe them as he does, cannot separate himself biologically from his own species. His kinship is proven whenever he excretes, urinates or farts (as the adult does, on average, fourteen times a day). In hating the Yahoo, Gulliver hates Gulliver. He finds refuge from himself in the company of the calm, 'rational' horses (Swift, whose irony is wholly unstable at this stage of the fable, is thought to be attacking Deism, for its objectionably bloodless religiosity). Horse dung is tolerable. The Houyhnhnm pelts give off a sweet smell, as does their breath.

When he is rescued by the kindly Portuguese captain, Gulliver recoils at the Yahoo stench of the man, and can only make the voyage back to his home country (Yahooland) towed behind the ship in a lifeboat. Smell has alienated him from his own kind and from himself. There is no refuge in teeming Yahoo-reeking London:

> During the first year, I could not endure my wife or children in my presence; the very smell of them was intolerable; much less could I suffer them to eat in the same room ... The first money I laid out was to buy two young stone-horses, which I keep in a good stable; and next to them, the groom is my greatest favourite, for I feel my spirits revived by the smell he contracts in the stable.

The Swiftian depiction of the human condition is diseased, Orwell grants. But it's a disease he (Orwell) understands. Better than most, probably.

Were his own years' long retreats to Wallington and his flight to Jura the equivalent to Gulliver's retreat to his sweet-smelling stable? Orwell's conclusion about fellow-suffering Swift contrives to be both severe and fraternal:

> Swift is a diseased writer. He remains permanently in a depressed mood which in most people is only intermittent, rather as though someone suffering from jaundice or the after-effects of influenza should have the energy to write books. But we all know that mood, and something in us responds to the expression of it.

Orwell was blessed, or cursed, to 'know it' better than most of Yahoo-kind.

Animal Farm

> The only hope is to have a home with a few animals
> in some place not worth a bomb.
>
> ORWELL, after Hiroshima and Nagasaki

> I like animals.
>
> GEORGE ORWELL

One can easily overlook a consistent feature in Orwell's life – his desire to be a smallholding farmer of an old-fashioned, pre-agroindustry kind. It had its surreal aspects: keeping chickens out the back in a wartime London flat, for example (feeding them at daybreak was a chore Eileen hated); or going to Marrakesh to recover from TB and believing that a couple of goats in the yard would help.

Orwell's instinctive desire for the company and, clearly, the smell of farmyard animals is as pronounced an element in his makeup as his love of coarse fishing. He found in livestock, as in angling, upliftingly natural smells. It was, to adapt a Lawrence slogan, on the side of life. Human smells, so antisocial in 'company', could merge naturally with those of the land and livestock. Washing facilities were never good anywhere Orwell lived (in Wallington and Jura particularly) with animals outside. He smelled along with them. It somewhat redeemed the Yahoo in him, like Gulliver in his stable. Anyone who has gone into a stable, or cow byre, in the still of a warm summer night will know the strange comfort they offer. His sexual violence, triggered uncontrollably by the smells of nature (preferably heath, woodland or riverside in spring or high summer), was probably part of the same psycho-pathology. Bowker notes the vein of sadism in Orwell shooting animals and, sometimes dramatically, disembowelling them.[107] He was not the kind of angler who sportingly threw his catch back.

To put it at its simplest, old-fashioned farms – a foundation of the England Orwell loved and was prepared to die for – are smelly places: sweat, animal breath and excrement. But it is an ensemble sweet to the nose. And the excrement returns to the earth as fertilizer to make the most wholesome of smells – wild flowers and cornfields.

Animal Farm began, like the first book of *Gulliver's Travels*, as a tract with a political intent. Fables, like pamphlets and even 'fairy stories' (Orwell's initial subtitle), can have political potency out of all proportion to their number of words or their verbal complexity. Farmer Jones's Manor Farm is an Orwellian Lilliput satirizing the absurd optimisms of the Russian Revolution of 1917 and their prompt corruption by a new, more ruthless power elite. The farm was once owned by aristocrats – lords of the manor. Before the 'Rebellion' (the other R-word is avoided) it is the property of a gentleman farmer – in fact a drunken, philistine brute.

The clever pigs make the political analysis that the animals slave, and are 'harvested', for the benefit of their owner. What right has he to exploit them, their labour, and their very flesh? The pigs mastermind a successful uprising. The animals take over the farm. Power then has its universal effect. Having ruthlessly secured their leadership, the pigs install a totalitarian state, complete with canine police, thought control, liquidation and purge. They reserve for themselves creature comfort and owners' privileges. They are probably putting their piglets down for Eton. For the lower animals, life is, if anything, harder than it was under Jones:

> But if there were hardships to be borne, they were partly offset by the fact that life nowadays had a greater dignity than it had had before. There were more songs, more speeches, more processions. Napoleon had commanded that once a week there should be held something called a Spontaneous Demonstration, the object of which was to celebrate the struggles and triumphs of Animal Farm.

In the fable's controversial conclusion the pigs – now owners of a highly profitable enterprise (for them and the dogs) – make peace with their 'fellow' human farmers. The animals look, in perplexity, through the windows of the farmhouse: 'The creatures outside looked from pig to man, and from man to pig, and from pig to man again; but already it was impossible to say which was which.' But the pigs' farm, of course, is infinitely worse than Mr Jones's. It will never be overthrown. The future? A pig's trotter, stamping on the animals' faces for ever.

Like all the best parables (Christ's par excellence) *Animal Farm* is enigmatic. Is Orwell thinking only about Stalinist Russia and the collective farming debacle? Or is it a statement about human society everywhere and at all times? Socialists, particularly, object to Orwell's depiction of the working classes as irredeemably 'lower' animals. Their 'betters' are humans or porcine humanoids. Orwell, said Empson, his closest friend as he was composing *Animal Farm*, would give comfort to 'evil stinking Tories'. The pig class. Within Orwell's animal kingdom there is no equality and no potential for class aspiration among the lower orders: the sheep will always bray slogans mindlessly, the chickens will always run round in circles clucking senselessly, the horses (principally Boxer) will always work brainlessly. Only the pigs have higher mentality and a capacity to change, but into what? So many Joneses. Is the subtext that Trotsky and his followers (depicted as the assassinated Snowball) would have done better by the Russian people than Stalin? Via the ILP, the only party he ever belonged to, Orwell had a soft spot for Trotsky – although Emmanuel Goldstein, in *Nineteen Eighty-Four*, is not a friendly depiction.[108]

What is clear is that, as usual, Orwell was out of step with the times – and, perhaps, with himself. The core elements had formed embryonically in his mind after Barcelona. It was in 1936, he said, that he became a political animal. It is plausibly suggested Eileen may have had a co-authorial influence. The suspicion is that Mrs Orwell was always less wavering in her Trotskyist-ILP doctrine.

Lettice Cooper, who shared a wartime office with her, recalled Eileen describing every morning how George tested the previous day's writing on her after she got home from work. It would be nice to think that Eileen left her mark. For most of her life, as Mrs George Orwell, she was invisible.

A draft was finished in the summer of 1944 and submitted (at his request) to Victor Gollancz, who was still sufficiently a Stalinist to reject it by return of post. Other publishers were reluctant, post-Stalingrad, to launch something so virulently anti-Soviet. The British loved 'Uncle Joe'. He was, as Churchill put it, tearing the guts out of the Nazi empire while the Allies were dickering about a second front. T. S. Eliot, at Faber, praised the limpid prose but felt in his usual oblique way that, since the pigs were the most intelligent beasts, they should indeed run things. What the farm needed was more benign piggery. It rhymes with Whiggery. Five American publishers were uninterested. Too English. Where were the McCormick combine harvesters? And a 'fairy story'? Please. In the home market Orwell had run, yet again, into the peculiar soft censorship that had stifled *Homage to Catalonia* in the womb. As he had then, he fell back on Fred Warburg: he was never Orwell's first choice, but always his most enterprising publisher. He saw a lot of money in the book.

Animal Farm had to await the end of the hot war and the onset of the cold war (a term Orwell invented). It was finally published in August 1945, as the bells were ringing for vj day. Once it was on the market money flooded in. So much so that within a few months Orwell had to incorporate himself to protect his income from the then punitive rates of British tax. George Orwell was now a limited company. That, too, was a fable. He put Richard down for Eton. If he was on a sinking ship he might as well go down first class.[109]

Animal Farm was not merely a fable: it was destined to become a pre-emptive weapon in the Cold War and the Tory Party arsenal, something Orwell never intended. The book had positively sinister admirers. It was serialized by the CIA in *Der Monat*, its German newspaper in occupied Germany. J. Edgar Hoover himself was solicited for an endorsement. Over the following years, *Animal Farm* was disseminated behind the Iron Curtain as black propaganda. Successfully.

In her study of the CIA's Cold War culture war, Frances Stonor Saunders describes how the CIA covertly acquired the subsidiary rights from Sonia Orwell.[110] Rather touchingly, what softened her up was the meeting the cunning Americans arranged with her idol, Clark Gable. The film of the book was produced in England and released in 1954, the ending radically changed to predict the eventual overthrow of swine-human totalitarianism by the unquenchable forces of Western democracy. It was nonsensically non-Orwellian, ranking with Nahum Tate's happy ending of *King Lear*.

Farmer

> A good deal of rain.
>
> ORWELL, in his Jura diary

Orwell's last years were, in two ways, his most fulfilled. He was a sage. He was listened to. David Astor had been primarily responsible for spring-boarding him to his eminence as a political commentator. And, alongside this new eminence, he managed to be what he seems most to have more humbly wanted to be.

In previous years it amused him to describe himself, on supererogatory forms, as 'Eric Blair: grocer'. He could as justifiably, in his last years, have described himself as 'George Orwell: farmer'. This came about through Astor, who owned a chunk of a Hebridean island, Jura. He suggested his friend holiday there. Good fishing, he was told. Another Etonian, Robin Fletcher (Jura's 'Laird'), had a run-down property, Barnhill, at the remote end of the island. Barnhill would, once licked into shape, be a real farm with fields, cows, pigs, a horse (for Orwell the iconic agrarian thing) and poultry.

Orwell leased it at a peppercorn rate, and prepared to invest in it. He was, for the first time in his life, in good shape financially: in the thousand-a-year class. The ever-increasing revenue from *Animal Farm* enabled him to resign from *Tribune* and begin his own animal farm. Wallington, its modest precursor, was wound up.

Since Orwell 'knew' nuclear war was coming, Jura would be one of the best bomb and fall-out shelters in the UK, principally for little Richard. Barnhill was, however, no sanatorium for a man with collapsing lungs. There was no electricity, mains water or paved road. And civilization (shops, doctors, telephones) was twenty miles away. Although the Gulf Stream keeps the Hebrides warmer than London, summers are damp and cool. He recruited the ever-available Avril to keep the house straight and look after Richard. The canteen work she had done during the war had come to an end. To do the heavy work on the farm there was a local man, Bill Dunn, a war veteran, who would eventually marry Avril in 1951. Richard Rees, a friend to the end, gave the Dunns (and their adoptive Richard) enough money to set up their own farm.

The End

> The tragedy of Orwell's life was that when at last he achieved fame and success he was a dying man and knew it. He had fame and was too ill to leave his room, money and nothing to spend it on.
> CYRIL CONNOLLY (1961)

Orwell was in a four-horse race. He had to get Barnhill in shape; write the 'dystopian' novel Warburg was champing for; find a wife; and get those three things done before the final collapse of his lungs. He now, at last, accepted that he was tubercular.[III] He was still smoking heavily. Five-year-old Richard found one of his 'disgusting old pipes' and stuffed it with one of the many mountains of his father's dog-ends. Then the little fellow coolly asked for a light: 'What amazed me was that nobody seemed to notice what I was doing! The result was inevitable, I turned green and gave up smoking until I got to the senior school twelve years later.'[112] It was one of the three things Richard remembers from his Jura years. Would that his father had also given up smoking.

The widowed Orwell was lonely and frantically asked any eligible woman who came his way to marry him. If they came up to Jura on spec, they were not lured. The house was at the end of an eight-mile dirt track. Orwell had no reliable van, only an unreliable motorbike and pillion. The west coast of Scotland has the highest rainfall in Britain. His pied-à-terre in Islington – during some of the worst winters in history – was freezing and leaked. His lungs needed warm, dry air and his body total rest. The fact that he was infectiously tubercular (he carefully avoided breathing on Richard and had him x-rayed) was no attraction in the marriage market.

Astor bent regulations to get supplies of the new American 'wonder drug', streptomycin. Orwell proved allergic – a cruel irony. Emergency visits to Scottish hospitals were followed by an extended sanatorium stay, failed surgical intervention and finally the private room at UCL that he would never leave alive. With an income now rising to the level of wealth, he could afford to die (12 guineas a week) in more comfort than he had ever lived.

Final Arrangements

The reasons why I married him are not clear.
SONIA BROWNELL, later Orwell

His last weeks sped into a gallop to the grave. He finished, with huge labour, *Nineteen Eighty-Four* in March 1949. It was published three months later. In September he was admitted to UCL hospital. Sonia agreed to marry him and did so, in hospital, him prone in bed, her standing in front of the hospital chaplain, on 13 October. He made his will three days before he died, in the same bed, on 21 January 1950. Its terms made Sonia the sole beneficiary and co-executor with his first patron, Richard Rees, of his literary estate. His son, Richard, was made the beneficiary of a less generous insurance policy. His ever-neglected sister, Avril, who would be Richard's carer (as she had been over the last few years), was apparently left nothing directly.

Two funerals (one in London) and interment in the churchyard of All Saints, Sutton Courtenay, Berkshire – farming country – followed. He was, for the first time, in his last few months, admitted into *Who's Who*.

Nineteen Eighty-Four

If we ask what it is he stands for, what he is the figure of, the answer is: the virtue of not being, of fronting the world with nothing more than one's simple, direct, undeceived intelligence.

LIONEL TRILLING (1949)

Nineteen Eighty-Four will be a curio in 1984.

New Left Review (1979)

Nineteen Eighty-Four was first conceived 'some time between mid-1940 and the end of 1943', when it looked quite likely that Britain would lose the war. Orwell's first outlines of his new novel, then provisionally entitled 'The Last Man in Europe', emerge in his notebook between January 1944 and the summer of 1946, when victory was followed by crippling austerity in Britain. By the last date, some fifty pages were written. The year 1946 saw the first fully fledged 'English Socialist' ('Ingsoc') government in the UK, under Clement Attlee. The first complete draft was written up by summer 1947, with the inception of the Cold War, which would last until 1989. The novel was finished by October 1947 and extensively revised and typed up in May–November 1948. This labour, it is plausibly suggested, accelerated Orwell's final decline and death. He sacrificed years of life for the completion of the book. Knowing that, he admitted, cast a pessimistic cloud over the narrative.

The manuscript was sent to Orwell's publishers in December 1948. The first edition went on sale in the u.s., initially, as a cut-price Book of the Month Club volume, in June 1949; a few days later it was brought out in the UK as a 10-shilling hardback. Orwell died in January 1950. After five years of socialist government, Winston Churchill became Conservative prime minister in October 1951. Big Brother had arrived.

As I write, the English teachers' unions have prescribed *Nineteen Eighty-Four* in the same way that, in my school days, the New Testament was prescribed to the pupils of the country. And, in its day, Mao's little red book in China. Orwell's book needs no exegesis from me. But from the point of view of 'nasocriticism', it is worth noting that it depicts a world in which all wholesome smell is a thing of the past. The only fragrant relics of times when such smells were around are Julia's hair, the whiff of good coffee and wine which the perplexed Winston and Julia encounter in O'Brien's luxurious quarters, the antique redolence of Mr Charrington's junk shop whose oil lamps give off 'an unclean but friendly smell' (a typically nice discrimination) and, most ecstatically, the idyllic, one-off lovemaking in the 'Golden Country' among a host of bluebells, with their 'faint sickly smell' (another nice discrimination). Otherwise it is Parsons's sweat (worse still his shit, as they wait for Room 101), boiled cabbage (Orwell's pet culinary hate for its persistence), 'tinny' tea and coffee, Victory fags, rot-gut Victory Gin and stews with unspeakable matter, masquerading as meat. The stenches of totalitarian oppression.

There is not a single animal in *Nineteen Eighty-Four*. Unless, that is, you count the rat, debating whether to start with Winston's cheeks or eyeballs. Its rodent smell will never, after he has been re-educated, leave Winston's nostrils. And the working class ('proles') smell, if anything, worse than they did in the Brookers' lodging house in Wigan.

'Cause of Death: Suicide?'

The death certificate was unequivocal: Orwell died in the middle of the night, with no nurse around, of an unexpected haemorrhage of one of his lungs. One could argue a different cause of death: suicide. He would rather die a young(ish) man than grow old.

Orwell's growing-up years coincided with world cataclysm – 'the War', as it was called for decades afterwards, as if humankind had known no other conflict. His school assemblies were darkened by lists of former pupils, gloriously 'fallen'. You soon will join them, was the daily subliminal message. You will die, many of you, virgins as regards everything enjoyable in life, never having lived. *Pro gloria et patria*. The old, be consoled, will live on to mourn you and build monuments on which your name will be scratched. The 'sediment' of that ceaseless, juvenile carnage Orwell diagnosed as burning 'hatred'. Not hatred for King and Country ('Old England' was still lovable for its Englishness) or the Empire (disgusting 'racket' though that was) but the 'old'. The survivors. Orwell waxed eloquently on the subject (now himself, at 1933, no longer young) in *The Road to Wigan Pier*:

> But those years, during and just after the war, were a queer time to be at school, for England was nearer revolution than she has been since or had been for a century earlier . . . it was a revolt of youth against age, resulting directly from the war . . . the war had been conducted mainly by old men and had been conducted with supreme incompetence . . . At that time there was, among the young, a curious cult of hatred of 'old men'.

The old cut a very poor figure in Orwell's fiction. It is, as Yeats would say, 'no country for old men'. He hated, viscerally, senility and the physical ugliness of age that came with the remorselessly passing years. One can imagine him sharing Swift's morbid but fascinated disgust at the Struldbruggs – those ever-decaying, ever-living corpses.

There are many reasons for not wanting to be old. The mirror is one. Swift's picture of age is grisly and unforgettably accurate:

> At ninety, they lose their teeth and hair; they have at that age no distinction of taste, but eat and drink whatever they can get, without relish or appetite. The diseases they were subject to still continue, without increasing or diminishing. In talking, they forget the common appellation of things, and the names of persons, even of those who are their nearest friends and relations. For the same reason, they never can amuse themselves with reading, because their memory will not serve to carry them from the beginning of a sentence to the end; and by this defect, they are deprived of the only entertainment whereof they might otherwise be capable.

In *Nineteen Eighty-Four* the horror of the street prostitute Winston uses is not that she stinks (bad enough), or that she is mindless (no 'hope' in this particular prole), but, 'When I saw her in the light she was quite an old woman, fifty years old at least. But I went ahead and did it just the same.'

Orwell's favourite poet was A. E. Housman. It was a high point in his life that he met him, at Cambridge, in 1927. And it's a safe guess that one of his (and everyone's) favourite Housman poems was 'To an Athlete Dying Young': 'Now you will not swell the rout / Of lads that wore their honours out, / Runners whom renown outran / And the name died before the man.' Orwell, it is safe to say, loathed the idea of himself getting old, losing what remained of his teeth, his fine head of hair and, horror of horrors, his mind, like the Struldbruggs. He must have observed that Struldbruggian decline in his eighty-year-old father. This leads to a plausible speculation. Orwell deliberately took life-threatening risks with his health. In Paris his failure to look after himself led to his ending up in the awful paupers' ward with one of his recurrent (but wholly preventable) bouts of pneumonia. It is plausibly suggested that this is where his TB was contracted. A little care of himself would have prevented that. Virtually everything he did in life was bad for his lungs and his lifespan. Not least, of course, the chain-smoking – even in hospital. He put off treatments for his pulmonary condition, denying it was real. He did not have to raise his head above the trench parapet in Aragon and get shot in the throat. He did not have to take a long, unnecessary, motorbike ride in freezing, sleety December, clad only in a sweater and an Eton scarf. That image is glorious. The pneumonia (his most serious bout) that followed is not. He did not have to go to Burma, a white man's grave for someone with his weakness. It ruined his health, he said airily. It brought his death that much closer. Jura was a fulfilment of a lifelong dream, but in winter, miles from even a general practitioner, it was ill-advised, verging on madness. Or suicidal. Orwell's life was one long game of Russian roulette. In January 1950, when he was 46, the bullet was in the chamber.

A few years earlier, in his 1942 essay 'How the Poor Die', he had intimated his revulsion at living beyond youth, and his horror of living beyond middle age:

> One wants to live, of course, indeed one only stays alive by virtue of the fear of death, but I think now, as I thought then, that it's better to die violently and not too old . . . 'Natural' death, almost by definition, means something slow, smelly and painful. Even at that, it makes a difference if you can achieve it in your own home and not in a public institution.

The word 'smelly' resonates here as it does through everything he wrote. The odour of mortality. Write on the unofficial death certificate, 'suicide'.

APPENDIX I
Blair/Orwell's Smoking Diary

He nearly killed me with his black tobacco.

PADDY DONOVAN, Orwell's comrade in the Aragon trenches

The above title should have a parenthesis 'with apologies to Simon Gray'. It was Gray who, in one of the great comic works of the last half-century, identified the essence of his being in the cigarettes he dragged on. I smoke, therefore I am.

Cyril Connolly recalls visiting Eric Blair in his room at Eton, reposing coolly among 'a litter of cigarette ash'. Doubtless there was an overflowing ashtray in the hospital room where he died. In the notes for novels he might, if he lived, write alongside his bed in UCH was one provisionally called 'Smoking Room Story'. It could be the story of George Orwell's life.

It is not recorded when Orwell had his first drag. Like one's first lover's kiss, he himself would have known. It was when he was very young, in Henley, one guesses. And furtive – a 'behind the cycle sheds' kind of thing. By the time he got to Eton, he had what would be a lifelong 'habit'. His taste, and the kind of cigarette he favoured, changed over the years. When hard up, he went for the working-class standby, 'Wild ["Willy"] Woodbines' (a year's use, he calculated, could be had for £40). The name 'Wild Woodbine' contained a literary allusion, and Orwell must have been one of the few of the puffers who recognized and relished it: 'I know a bank where the wild thyme blows, Where ox-lips and the nodding violet grows; Quite over-canopied with luscious woodbine, With sweet musk-roses and with eglantine' (*A Midsummer Night's Dream*). In his down-and-out period, in Paris and London, he developed a taste for harsher, 'foul-smelling' roll-ups. He would be loyal to Gallic 'black shag' tobacco for life. It fascinated the children he taught, in his school-teaching year, that he had learned in Paris how to roll a cigarette single-handed.

As foul as his roll-ups was the stench of the places Orwell visited in this down-and-out phase of his life. The following, for example, is from 'The Spike':

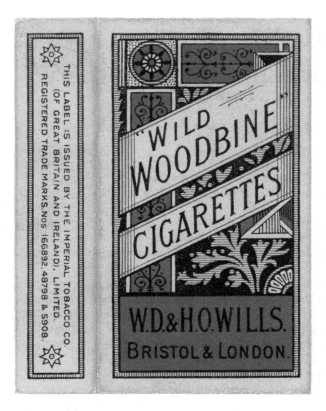

Willy Woodbines.

In the morning they told us we must work till eleven, and set
us to scrubbing out one of the dormitories . . . The dormitory
was a room of fifty beds, close together, with that warm, faecal
stink that you never seem to get away from in the workhouse . . .
These workhouses seem all alike, and there is something intensely
disgusting in the atmosphere of them. The thought of all those
grey-faced, ageing men living a very quiet, withdrawn life in a
smell of w.c.s, and practising homosexuality, makes me feel sick.
But it is not easy to convey what I mean, because it is all bound
up with the smell of the workhouse.

Tobacco would have to be super-foul to beat that.

Around the time that he went down and out, Orwell began to
use the roll-up machines that became popular in the 1920s – and

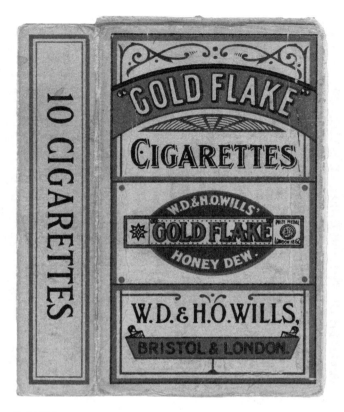

Gold Flake.

more so in the Depression years, when shop-bought packet cigarettes were out of reach for many. Even when he could afford ready-mades, Orwell liked the working-class statement that rolling your own made, as he liked drinking his tea from the saucer in the BBC canteen. It made a point.

Josh Indar has written an authoritative survey on Orwell's 'smoking obsession'.[1] His dabbling, for example, with 'green cigars' in Burma. There are 41 references, Indar calculates, to smoking in *Down and Out in Paris and London*, and the characteristically Orwellian comment, 'It was tobacco that made everything tolerable.' As a tramp, doubtless he picked up and smoked – along with Paddy – 'dog ends'. Part of the tramp's constant battle with authority was preserving a tobacco stash from the strip-searches when entering the spike. 'We would', writes Orwell, in his notes for *Down and Out*,

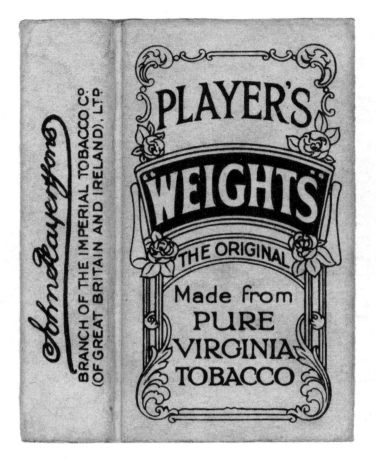

Player's Weights.

[smuggle] our matches and tobacco, for it is forbidden to take these into nearly all spikes, and one is supposed to surrender them at the gate. We hid them in our socks, except for the twenty or so per cent who had no socks, and had to carry the tobacco in their boots, even under their very toes. We stuffed our ankles with contraband until anyone seeing us might have imagined an outbreak of elephantiasis.

Note the 'we': smoking, and its paraphernalia, was one of the few things that put the Etonian on equal terms with the working-class man – symbolized by the pseudo-handshake of the 'offer'. If you couldn't smoke, you'd put it 'behind your ear', because your turn to offer would, in time, come.

The ever-present cigarette.

In *Keep the Aspidistra Flying*, Gordon Comstock comes close to nervous breakdown with only four ciggies to last him till payday. His brand is Gold Flake, with their distinctive canary-yellow packet. When 'short', however, he has to make do with Player's Weights (poor relative of the 'Player's Please', which were not quite so proletarian), so called because they were originally sold by the weight, not the number. The second paragraph of *Aspidistra* is one of tobacco-addiction torment:

> The clock struck half past two. In the little office at the back of Mr McKechnie's bookshop, Gordon – Gordon Comstock, last member of the Comstock family, aged twenty-nine and rather moth-eaten already – lounged across the table, pushing a four-penny packet of Player's Weights open and shut with his thumb.

He has four cigarettes left, and no money to buy a new supply for two days. 'Tobaccoless' hours stretch before the 'last member of the Comstock family'.

In *Homage to Catalonia*, tobacco is recorded by Orwell as being one of the five things a soldier in the trenches cannot live without. To paraphrase Napoleon, an army marches on its lungs. At a very low point the POUM ration sinks to five a day. The first thing Orwell did, on recovering from being shot in the throat, was ask his nurse for a cigarette. He writes:

> I wonder what is the appropriate first action when you come from a country at war and set foot on peaceful soil. Mine was to rush to

the tobacco-kiosk and buy as many cigars and cigarettes as I could stuff into my pockets.

George Bowling, in *Coming Up for Air* (between puffs, presumably), smokes cigarettes and, when he is feeling good, cigars, like the proverbial chimney. He had an early taste for Abdulla: 'the one with the Egyptian soldiers on it'.

As a mark of his new bipedality, the former pig smokes a pipe in *Animal Farm*. And most readers, particularly smokers who roll up, recall Winston Smith, in the first chapter of *Nineteen Eighty-Four*, forgetting to keep his wretched Victory cigarette upright, and the tobacco tipping out on to the floor.

Cigarettes were one of the things that kept the British sane during the Second World War. In his essay 'Books vs. Cigarettes' of 1946, Orwell calculates that he smokes six ounces of Player's tobacco a week, spending £40 a year to sustain the habit, £15 more than he spends on reading material. If most hand-rolled cigarettes contain about a gram of tobacco each, Orwell must have smoked close to 170 cigarettes a week, a little more than a pack per day. Empson, working alongside Orwell in the BBC, found the aura of 'shag' he generated 'disgusting'. But, he notes, it was preferable to the body odour of Orwell himself. J. J. Ross, the author of *Orwell's Cough*, concludes: 'A heavy smoking habit probably also contributed to his gaunt appearance.'

Gauntness was the least of it. Orwell was prepared to undergo crucifying treatment for the lungs he was abusing. And still smoke – even after he was diagnosed, authoritatively, with TB, in 1947. Hilda Bastian notes that

> Orwell had been given treatments that were common for tuberculosis in Britain at that time: 'collapse therapy' and other painful surgical procedures to keep the lung disabled to 'rest' it, vitamins, fresh air, and being confined to bed. The hospital staff confiscated his typewriter and told him to stop working – but they didn't seem to advise him to stop smoking!

Why did Orwell smoke so self-destructively? He was addicted, of course. But also, I think, he smoked for tobacco's deodorizing effect, and his morbid sensitivity about his own bodily smell. And, of course, because he loved the smell of tobacco.

APPENDIX II
The Smell Narrative of
A Clergyman's Daughter

The opening paragraphs of *A Clergyman's Daughter* describe Dorothy, the only child of the Reverend Charles Hare, Rector of St Athelstan's, Knype Hill, Suffolk, waking at 5.30, saying her bedside prayers and taking her cold bath, to be 'met downstairs by a chill morning smell of dust, damp plaster, and the fried dabs from yesterday's supper' (Knype Hill, like Southwold, is by the sea; fish smells abound).

Having fetched her father his hot shaving water, Dorothy goes to church to prepare for 'HC', Holy Communion: 'The church was very cold, with a scent of candle-wax and ancient dust'. There is only one communicant, as usual in mid-week, the decayed, well-off (but chronically mean) Miss Mayfill: 'A faint scent radiated from her – an ethereal scent, analysable as eau-de-Cologne, mothballs, and a sub-flavour of gin'.

Dorothy prepares her father's cooked breakfast and is given a message about one of the parishioners' children dying, of cholera: 'Well, Miss, it's turning quite black. And it's had diarrhea something cruel.' The rector is eating. He empties his mouth with an effort: 'Must I have these disgusting details while I am eating my breakfast?' he exclaims. Peaceful, post-prandial plumes of smoke float upwards from the rector's pipe. He does not visit the dying child.

Dorothy's work day begins – 'visiting' parishioners. 'She read chapters from the Gospels, and readjusted bandages on "bad legs", and condoled with sufferers from morning-sickness; she played ride-a-cock-horse with sour-smelling children who grimed the bosom of her dress with their sticky little fingers.' One visit in particular mines the pits of smell:

Dorothy knocked at the Pithers' badly fitting door, from beneath which a melancholy smell of boiled cabbage and dish-water was oozing. From long experience she knew and could taste in advance the individual smell of every cottage on her rounds. Some of their smells were peculiar in the extreme. For instance, there was the salty, feral smell that haunted the cottage of old Mr Tombs, an aged retired bookseller who lay in bed all day in a darkened room, with his long, dusty nose and pebble spectacles protruding from what appeared to be a fur rug of vast size and richness.

The Pithers' kitchen 'was decently tidy, but oppressively hot, evil-smelling and saturated with ancient dust'. Dorothy goes to the bedroom to 'anoint' with Elliman's embrocation Mrs Pithers's 'grey veined, flaccid', naked legs: 'The room reeked of urine and paregoric.'

Having done the round of visits her father should have done, Dorothy, released into the fields, experiences nasal ecstasy. It is orgasmic:

> In Borlase the dairy-farmer's meadow the red cows were grazing, knee-deep in shining seas of grass. The scent of cows, like a distillation of vanilla and fresh hay, floated into Dorothy's nostrils.
>
> Dorothy pulled a frond of the fennel against her face and breathed in the strong sweet scent. Its richness overwhelmed her, almost dizzied her for a moment. She drank it in, filling her lungs with it. Lovely, lovely scent – scent of summer days, scent of childhood joys,

The anthem to summer scent rises to a veritable rhapsody. But duty calls. Dorothy must go back to the church to make costumes, out of paper and glue, for the children's annual play – on the execution of Charles I (Orwell had done something similar at the Hawthorns): 'It was horribly hot in the conservatory, and there was a powerful smell of glue and the sour sweat of children.'

After Warburton's attempted rape Dorothy's mind goes blank. She wakes up in a shabby London street eight days later, in ragged clothes. In 'the strange, dirty sub-world into which she was instantly plunged', she picks up with street companions, Nobby, Charlie and Flo. 'Hunger and the soreness of her feet were her clearest memories of that time; and also the cold of the nights, and a peculiar, blowsy, witless feeling that came of sleeplessness and constant exposure to the air.' The quartet decide to walk to the summer hop fields thirty miles away to find seasonal work: 'After getting to Bromley they had "drummed up" on a horrible, paper-littered rubbish dump, reeking with the refuse of several slaughter-houses.' By contrast, the hop fields and the camp around them are redolent with more salubrious odours:

> When the wind stirred [the hops] they shook forth a fresh, bitter scent of sulphur and cool beer. In each lane of bines a family of sun-burnt people were shredding the hops into sacking bins, and singing as they worked; and presently a hooter sounded and they knocked off to boil cans of tea over crackling fires of hop bines. Dorothy envied them greatly. How happy they looked, sitting round the fires with their cans of tea and their hunks of bread and bacon, in the smell

of hops and wood smoke! . . . the bitter, never-palling scent, like a wind from oceans of cool beer, flowed into your nostrils and refreshed you.

The 'unspeakable' earth 'latrine' was not refreshing.

When the picking season closes, at the end of September, Dorothy finds herself 'dragged out and kissed by a young gypsy smelling of onions' and thrown into a hop bin. It's a ceremony, on the last day of picking. Back in London, virtually penniless, Dorothy takes refuge in a knocking shop, 'Mary's'. When she makes her way to her room, 'A cold, evil smell met her.' Soon she cannot afford to keep even Mary's roof over her head. There follows a nightmarish interval sleeping rough in Trafalgar Square. For warmth, she and other vagrants huddle together on a bench:

> They pile themselves in a monstrous shapeless clot, men and women clinging indiscriminately together, like a bunch of toads at spawning time. There is a writhing movement as the heap settles down, and a sour stench of clothes diffuses itself.

Mr Tallboys, a defrocked clergyman, rants about the noisome sulphur candles of Hell. 'Don't ole Daddy stink when you get up agen 'im?' says Charlie. Next morning he is drawn to the nearby fishmongers: 'Kippers! Perishing piles of 'em! I can smell 'em through the perishing glass . . . Got to fill up on the smell of 'em this morning.' Smell is all they get.

After ten days of the horrible communism of the Square, Dorothy is installed as a schoolteacher at the awful Ringwood House Academy for Girls, Brough Road, Southbridge (Hayes). She is rescued – gallantly – by Mr Warburton, who offers marriage, but she cannot surrender. It is the smell of sex:

> A wave of disgust and deadly fear went through her, and her entrails seemed to shrink and freeze. His thick male body was pressing her backwards and downwards . . . The harsh odour of maleness forced itself into her nostrils. She recoiled. Furry thighs of satyrs!

What, then, remains for Dorothy at Knype Hill? 'At that moment there stole into her nostrils a warm, evil smell, forgotten these eight months but unutterably familiar – the smell of glue . . . The smell of glue was the answer to her prayer.'

APPENDIX III

The Smell Narrative of
The Road to Wigan Pier

In the Brookers' spare bedroom,

> All the windows were kept tight shut, with a red sandbag jammed in
> the bottom, and in the morning the room stank like a ferret's cage.
> You did not notice it when you got up, but if you went out of the
> room and came back, the smell hit you in the face with a smack.

Orwell comes downstairs the next morning: 'The smell of the kitchen was
dreadful, but, as with that of the bedroom, you ceased to notice it after a
while.' He reflects:

> On the day when there was a full chamber-pot under the breakfast
> table I decided to leave. The place was beginning to depress me. It
> was not only the dirt, the smells, and the vile food, but the feeling of
> stagnant meaningless decay,

He concludes: 'It is a kind of duty to see and smell such places now and
again, especially smell them, lest you should forget that they exist; though
perhaps it is better not to stay there too long.'

In the mine, Orwell sniffs a more honest smell: 'Everything is grey
with shale dust; there is a dusty fiery smell which seems to be the same
in all mines.' There are rich smells associated with the home deliveries
of coal: 'Once a fortnight the coal cart drives up to the door and men in
leather jerkins carry the coal indoors in stout sacks smelling of tar and
shoot it clanking into the coal-hole under the stairs.'

Orwell moves to Peel Street, where he finds: 'Indescribable squalor
in downstairs room and smell upstairs almost unbearable. Rent 5s. 7 ½d.,
including rates ... the smell, the dominant and essential thing, is indescribable.' He moves on to Sheffield:

It has a population of half a million and it contains fewer decent buildings than the average East Anglian village of five hundred. And the stench! If at rare moments you stop smelling sulphur it is because you have begun smelling gas ... Many of the people in Sheffield or Manchester, if they smelled the air along the Cornish cliffs, would probably declare that it had no taste in it.

He indulges in further reflections, among them the most famous:

But there was another and more serious difficulty. Here you come to the real secret of class distinctions in the West. ... It is summed up in four frightful words which people nowadays are chary of uttering, but which were bandied about quite freely in my childhood. The words were: 'The lower classes smell'.

Orwell expatiates further, and further afield, on the theme:

In the West we are divided from our fellows by our sense of smell. The working man is our master, inclined to rule us with an iron hand, but it cannot be denied that he stinks: none can wonder at it, for a bath in the dawn when you have to hurry to your work before the factory bell rings is no pleasant thing, nor 'does heavy labour tend to sweetness' ...
      Meanwhile, 'do' the 'lower classes' smell? Of course, as a whole, they are dirtier than the upper classes.

He thinks back to his experience in Burma: 'Like most other races, the Burmese have a distinctive smell – I cannot describe it: it is a smell that makes one's teeth tingle – but this smell never disgusted me.' The British 'Other Rank' soldiers in Burma were particularly distasteful: 'All I knew was that it was "lower-class" sweat that I was smelling, and the thought of it made me sick.' He is similarly sickened by 'women and sandal-wearers and bearded fruit-juice drinkers who come nocking towards the smell of "progress" like bluebottles to a dead cat.'
      Orwell loves horses – workhorses, that is: 'Horses, you see, belong to the vanished agricultural past, and all sentiment for the past carries with it a vague smell of heresy.' That past, with all its hope, is gone – for ever, perhaps:

Socialism, at least in this island, does not smell any longer of revolution and the overthrow of tyrants; it smells of crankishness, machine-worship, and the stupid cult of Russia. Unless you can remove that smell, and very rapidly, Fascism may win.

A good note on which to end this book.

References

Preface

1 Daphne Patai, *The Orwell Mystique: A Study in Male Ideology* (Amherst, MA, 1984), p. 91. The 'sandal-wearers' diatribe is from *The Road to Wigan Pier*, and is much quoted.
2 Schiller's need for rotten apples was confided by Goethe to his scribe, Johann Eckermann. Goethe added that he, himself, preferred fresh air. Everyone to their taste.
3 Adrian Stokes, 'Strong Smells and Polite Society', *Encounter* (September 1961), pp. 50–56, www.unz.org.
4 Alain Corbin is authoritative on this subject in *The Foul and the Fragrant: Odor and the French Imagination* (Cambridge, MA, 1986).
5 George Orwell, 'Inside the Whale' (1940).
6 See Gilbert's post 'The Biochemistry of BO', on his olfactory blog, www.firstnerve.com, 30 April 2009.
7 George Orwell, 'Why I Write' (1946).
8 I'm grateful to my colleague Neil Rennie for pointing out Milton's nasal sensitivity. Once pointed out, *Paradise Lost* is read differently, I suspect.
9 The medical term osphresiolagnia rolls off the tongue less easily.
10 By Richard Ellmann, ed., *Selected Letters of James Joyce* (New York, 2003).
11 Simon Chu and John J. Downes, 'Odour-evoked Autobiographical Memories: Psychological Investigations of Proustian Phenomena', http://chemse.oxfordjournals.org, 30 September 1999.
12 George Orwell, *The Road to Wigan Pier*, as is the following quotation with its curdled disgust for innocent Welwyn Garden City and his warm reference to the persuasive power of 'one sniff of English air'.
13 Robert Butler, 'Orwell's World', *Intelligent Life* (January–February 2015).
14 The first Penguin edition of *Nineteen Eighty-Four* was published in 1955. I got hold of a Secker hardback from the public library.
15 The most robust explanation and defence of this 'snitching' – the source of much controversy – is given by Christopher Hitchens in *Orwell's Victory* (New York, 2002).

16 For some reason, the plaque is regularly defaced. By fast-food lovers, presumably.
17 The surviving Westrope literary remains are held by Hull University History Centre, and a biography is given on the Centre website.
18 One wonders whether the pathologically frigid wife of Winston, Katharine, is a bitter, possibly unfair depiction of Eileen. Something went wrong, sexually, with the marriage.
19 Published in 2002, Spurling's biography is a spirited defence of her friend Sonia, much maligned in her years as the Widow Orwell.
20 An authoritative account of the founding and running of *Horizon* – and Sonia's role in its spectacular success – is given in Jeremy Lewis, *Cyril Connolly: A Life* (London, 1998).
21 Frank Kermode, 'The Essential Orwell', *London Review of Books*, III/I (22 January 1981).
22 Orwell, 'Why I Write'.
23 Paul Foot, 'By George, They've Got It', *The Observer* (1 June 2003).
24 Notably *The Unexamined Orwell* (Austin, TX, 2011).

The Life

1 Orwell recorded this memory of his mother's conversation in his journal, in the last year of his life. Bernard Crick was the first to draw attention to it in his biography *George Orwell: A Life* (1980).
2 Bowker was the first to draw attention to this fact, in *George Orwell* (London, 2003).
3 George Orwell, 'Why I Write' (1946).
4 See the London tramping section of *Down and Out in Paris and London*.
5 George Orwell, 'Such, Such Were the Joys' (1952).
6 In what Orwell ironically calls the 'unhappy' (actually 'happy') ending, chronicled in ancient ballads, the dying Robin, having been treacherously bled to death by the nuns, *forbids* his outlaws from taking revenge on the priory.
7 The quotation is from Orwell's review of Arturo Borea's *The Forge*, *Horizon* (September 1941). The would-be flogger was many years later (the fact clearly stuck in Orwell's mind) identified as a Mr Simmons, a friend of Ida's.
8 The family moved into a larger house, in nearby Shiplake, when Richard retired in 1912, and downsized, moving again, in wartime 1915.
9 Cyril Connolly, *Enemies of Promise* (London, 1938).
10 The admirable life achievement of the young Wilkeses is recorded on the anti-Orwell website www.st-cyprians-school.org.uk.
11 This and subsequent quotations below from St Cyprianites, along with photographs and plentiful reminiscence – all favourable – about the Wilkeses, is recorded on www.st-cyprians-school.org.uk.
12 Connolly, *Enemies of Promise*. Published when it was, 1938, it would

be interesting to know what Orwell made of this unflattering pen portrait. The men nonetheless remained friends and colleagues on *Horizon*.

13 St Cyprian's website, www.st-cyprians-school.org.uk.
14 This, and Orwell's subsequent recollections of wretchedness at St Cyprian's, are recorded in 'Such, Such Were the Joys'.
15 Connolly, *Enemies of Promise*.
16 Crick in his biography, from interviews with aged survivors of Orwell's teaching (largely approved of by his pupils) at Hayes. See below for fuller account.
17 See www.st-cyprians-school.org.uk.
18 A scholarly summary of the evidence against Orwell can be found in Robert Pearce, 'Truth and Falsehood: Orwell's Prep School Woes', *The Review of English Studies, New Series*, XLIII/171 (August 1992).
19 There was mutual admiration between Mackenzie and Orwell in later life. And the other novelist, plausibly, inspired Orwell's late-life love of Scottish islands. Mackenzie was fanatic about the joys of living on them.
20 George Orwell, 'Good Bad Books', *Tribune* (November 1945); George Orwell, 'Raffles and Miss Blandish', *Horizon* (October 1944).
21 George Orwell, 'The Lion and the Unicorn' (1941).
22 George Orwell, 'Politics and the English Language' (1946).
23 The following account of Orwell's (Eric Blair's, as he was then) Eton career is largely taken from Crick's biography.
24 Bowker, who is the most diligent of the biographers on Orwell's sex life, gives a full account.
25 See Orwell's honorific essay, 'The Art of Donald McGill' (1941).
26 Spender delivered the lofty pronouncement in a memorial essay in *The World* (June 1950).
27 See Richard Lance Keeble, 'Orwell, Astor, and Me', www.orwellsociety.com, February 2012.
28 The clearest demonstration is the article Orwell wrote in April 1945, 'Antisemitism in Britain', in *Contemporary Jewish Record*. Bernard Crick notes that by this point he was 'fully purged of the mild and conventional but more or less clear anti-Semitism which appeared early in *Down and Out in Paris and London* and his wartime diaries'. The mischievous Muggeridge, surveying the many Jewish mourners at Orwell's funeral, maintained that he was 'strongly anti-Semite at heart', which seems contradictory.
29 A comprehensive survey of the BYT phenomenon is given by D. J. Taylor in *Bright Young People* (London, 2007). Eton is prominent but the book does not include George Orwell.
30 See Kathryn Hughes, who had a childhood connection with the Buddicoms, 'Such Were the Joys', *The Guardian* (17 February 2007). The above account is largely taken from her.
31 See, for example, D. J. Taylor, 'Orwell and the Rats', pp. 143–7.

32 Orwell, *The Road to Wigan Pier*, in the well-known passage excoriating himself as 'an odious little snob' in his schooldays.

33 For Orwell big-game shooting on a motorbike, with his pal 'Robbie' (Captain H. R. Robinson), see Gerry Abbot, 'Robbie and the Poet', SBBR, IV/I (Spring 2006), www.soas.ac.uk.

34 Crick has the most useful summary of Orwell's trial plans for this novel, which was very long in the writing and publication.

35 The conversation is recorded in John Haffenden's *William Empson*, vol. II: *'Against the Christians'* (Oxford, 2011). For more on this period in Orwell's life, and his relationship with Empson, and his wife, see below.

36 This anecdote was first turned up by Stansky and Abrahams. It has been made much of by subsequent biographers.

37 Caldwell was the bestselling author of such 25-cent shockers as *God's Little Acre* (1933) and *Tobacco Road* (1932).

38 So described in *Burmese Days*.

39 The memorable comment was first turned up in an interview by Crick. Arthur Koestler also likened Orwell to a 'Burmese sergeant'.

40 See J. J. Ross, 'Tuberculosis, Bronchiectasis, and Infertility: What Ailed George Orwell?', http://cid.oxfordjournals.org, June 2005.

41 In *Shakespeare's Tremor and Orwell's Cough* (London, 2012). Ross writes with a trained physician's authority.

42 Conor Cruise O'Brien, 'Orwell Looks at the World', in *George Orwell: A Collection of Critical Essays*, ed. Raymond Williams (Englewood Cliffs, NJ, 1974). O'Brien's charge is refuted vigorously by Christopher Hitchens in *Why Orwell Matters* (New York, 2003).

43 Lord Curzon of Kedleston was the vigorously reforming viceroy and governor general of India, 1899–1905. His influence was still palpable in Orwell's day.

44 Information taken from Michael Silvestri, 'The Thrill of Simply Dressing Up', *Journal of Colonialism and Colonial History*, II/2 (Fall 2001).

45 See George Woodcock's *The Crystal Spirit* (London, 1966).

46 Orwell took the word 'prole', a central term in *Nineteen Eighty-Four*, from Jack London's dystopian science-fiction work *The Iron Heel* (New York, 1908). A direct influence on *Nineteen Eighty-Four*, the title of London's work inspired one of the famous lines in the novel, when O'Brien tells Winston, 'If you want a picture of the future, imagine a boot stamping on a human face – forever.'

47 John Rodden, *The Unexamined Orwell* (Austin, TX, 2011), p. 300. Rodden is informative on this and other aspects of Orwell's life recently thrown up.

48 'Orwell's Fear and Loathing in Southwold', *East Anglian Daily Times* (26 April 2003).

49 This letter, and others of a similar intimate kind, were first made generally available in *A Kind of Compulsion: 1903–1936*, ed. Peter

Davison and Ian Angus (London, 1999). Some of the Orwell–Salkeld correspondence is still, apparently, withheld.

50 Bowker gives the fullest account of this unsettled period of Orwell's life and his tangled relationships with women.

51 No book has been written about Collings, although he deserves one. The best account of his life is given in the *Oxford Dictionary of National Biography*.

52 For background on Collings see 'Hubert Dennis Collings', www. zoominfo.com/p/Hubert-Collings/1337240949.

53 See my introduction to the Everyman Classics edition of *Brave New World* (London, 2014).

54 Pritchett made the much-quoted witticism in his obituary of Orwell, published in the *New Statesman* (28 January 1950).

55 For the florescence of expatriate literature in between-wars Paris, see Hugh D. Ford, *Published in Paris* (New York, 1975).

56 He confided the fact to his Hampstead friend, Mabel Fierz. See below for the friendship, which proved very useful to Orwell.

57 It was eventually published in Peter Davison and Ian Angus's *A Kind of Compulsion*.

58 As usual, Bowker is authoritative on this episode.

59 The authoritative life of Orwell's first publisher is Ruth Dudley Edwards, *Victor Gollancz: A Biography* (London, 1987).

60 For a concise account of Britain's idiosyncratic vagrancy laws, see 'A Short History of English Vagrancy Laws', www.southernafrica-litigationcentre.org/1/wp-content/uploads/2013/07/04_SALC-NoJustice-Report_A-Short-History-of-English-Vagrancy-Laws.pdf.

61 Malcolm Muggeridge, 'A Knight of the Woeful Countenance', in *The World of George Orwell*, ed. Miriam Gross (London, 1972). It was Crick's essay in this volume that induced Sonia to replace the tactically non-productive 'authorized' biographer, Muggeridge, with the very productive Crick.

62 See, for this and the following account of Orwell in Hayes, Crick's biography; and Mike Paterson, '"One of the Most God-forsaken Places I Have Ever Struck": George Orwell in Hayes', on the London Historians' Blog, https://londonhistorians.wordpress.com, 16 November 2011.

63 A useful collection of reviews of Orwell's published works is compiled by Jeffrey Meyers, ed., in *George Orwell: The Critical Heritage* (London, 1997).

64 A concise history of the ILP is given by Mordecai Ryan in www. workersliberty.org/node/5391.

65 See C. Wright Mills, *The Power Elite* (Oxford, 1956).

66 Orwell reviewed Connolly's novel, *The Rock Pool*, a study of rich bohemianism, a few months later. 'Mr Connolly rather admires the disgusting beasts he depicts,' he observed tartly.

67 Valerie Allen offers a fascinating account of the venerable history of social flatulence, acceptable and unacceptable, in *On Farting: Language and Laughter in the Middle Ages* (New York, 2010).

68 Alain Corbin, *The Foul and the Fragrant: Odour and the French Social Imagination*, trans. Miriam Kochan (Cambridge, MA, 1986).

69 See George Orwell, 'Antisemitism in Britain', http://orwell.ru, April 1945.

70 The authoritative biography of Burt, a highly controversial figure in his field, is L. S. Hearnshaw, *Cyril Burt: Psychologist* (Ithaca, NY, 1979).

71 In the preface to the Ukrainian translation of *Animal Farm* (1947).

72 The anecdote was turned up by the early-bird biographers Stansky and Abrahams, who were able to interview many still-living witnesses.

73 See, for example, www.orwelltoday.com/reader1984poemeileen2.shtml.

74 Geoffrey and Kathleen Tillotson, and Humphry House: three critics who went on to revolutionize Victorian studies.

75 Iona and Peter Opie, *The Lore and Language of Schoolchildren* (New York, 1959).

76 I am gratefully following here, and above, D. J. Taylor's analysis, quotation and interpretations of the letters, which he discussed in 'George Orwell: Another Piece of the Puzzle', *The Guardian*, on 10 December 2005, two years after his prizewinning Orwell biography was published. The letters have not yet, I believe, been published in full.

77 He confided this desire, and his experiment, to Harold Acton. See Gordon Bowker, 'The Road to Morocco', http://theorwellprize.co.uk.

78 See Taylor, 'Another Piece of the Puzzle'.

79 For example, the 'nancy poets' W. H. Auden and Stephen Spender, and their patron Nancy Cunard. See *The Road to Wigan Pier* and 'Political Reflections on the Crisis', *The Adelphi* (December 1938).

80 Taylor, 'Another Piece of the Puzzle'.

81 George Orwell, 'Spilling the Spanish Beans', *New England Weekly* (July and September 1937).

82 Bowker is particularly illuminating and informed on this episode in Orwell's Spanish sojourn.

83 Colls gives an extremely well-informed account of the Spanish episode in *George Orwell: English Rebel* (Oxford, 2013).

84 For the enigmatic relationship of Eileen, Georges and George, see Marc Wildermeersch, *George Orwell's Commander in Spain: The Enigma of Georges Kopp* (London, 2013).

85 Not, as Orwell seems to have thought, because of flies on the surface, but because the warm water there has higher oxygen levels.

86 I follow Bowker in this episode, working from Jackson's memoirs, written as 'Elisaveta Fen' (specifically *A Russian's England: Reminiscences of Years 1926–1940* [London, 1976]), and her literary remains, archived at Leeds University.

87 There is obscurity about this 'anonymous' gift. My suspicion is that it was the ever-generous Rees (proprietor of *The Adelphi*) and that the Myers story was a tactful fiction.

88 Taylor, 'Another Piece of the Puzzle'.

89 Here again I am indebted to D. J. Taylor.

90 I have written about it at length in *The Boy who Loved Books* (and hooks, I might add) (London, 2007).

91 See Stephen Cullen, *Home Guard Socialism* (Warwick, 2006).

92 One wonders whether Eileen's Trotskyist/ILP record led to her removal from the more sensitive censorship division, where she originally worked.

93 See Bowker's analysis in *George Orwell*, pp. 326–7.

94 There was a chronic shortage of stenographers and typists in the 1940s. Eileen was in this respect irreplaceable.

95 Taylor, 'Another Piece of the Puzzle'.

96 For an account of *Horizon* in Blitzed London and safe Cornwall see John Sutherland, *Stephen Spender: A Literary Life* (London, 2004).

97 For Peter Watson's central role as a patron and friend, see Adrian Clark and Jeremy Dronfield, *Queer Saint: The Cultured Life of Peter Watson* (London, 2015).

98 I had the story from Natasha Spender, who was there.

99 See Richard Lance Keeble, 'Orwell, Astor – and Me', http://bestof. blogs.lincoln.ac.uk, 8 December 2011.

100 See Richard Cockett, *David Astor and the Observer* (London, 1990).

101 The decision was later reversed, but the initial objection was symptomatic of the lingering distrust the BBC has for Orwell. John Peel, the disc jockey, they are happy to commemorate.

102 The preceding and following account of Orwell's wartime relationship with Empson is taken from John Haffenden's *William Empson*, vol. II: *'Against the Christians'* (Oxford, 2011).

103 Empson encouraged Hetta's promiscuity: 'I loved you in bed with young men, / Your arousers and foils and adorers,' he wrote in one of his poems. Orwell, alas, was not an arouser.

104 Denis Donoghue, 'Plain English', *London Review of Books*, VI/24 (20 December 1984).

105 Raymond Williams, *George Orwell* (London, 1971).

106 The windowpane analogy was actually made a couple of months later, in the essay 'Why I Write' (Summer 1946).

107 See Bowker, *George Orwell*, p. 368, for Orwell's pleasure in gutting animals he had slain.

108 Trotsky's birth name was Bronstein.

109 Richard was later put down for Westminster. He went to neither and – something that would have delighted his father – went successfully into farming.

110 Frances Stonor Saunders, *Who Paid the Piper?: The* CIA *and the Cultural Cold War* (London, 2000).
111 J. J. Ross gives the complex condition of his health in his last years, *Orwell's Cough*, pp. 216–17.
112 Richard Blair, 'Remembering Jura', http://theorwellprize.co.uk, 5 October 2012.

Appendix 1: Blair/Orwell's Smoking Diary

1 Josh Indar, 'Bumming Smokes in Paris and London: George Orwell's Obsession with Tobacco', www.popmatters.com, 18 June 2009. I gratefully borrow from Indar's witty account.

Acknowledgements

I owe a particular debt to Bill Hamilton, and through him the Orwell Estate. I owe another debt to Gillian Furlong, and the curators of the archive of Orwell materials at UCL. I am very grateful to Ben Hayes, at Reaktion Books, for encouraging what must have looked like a very strange book, and helping lick it into less strange shape. Martha Jay has been tireless in editing and re-editing the work. Anything which has escaped her eye is entirely my responsibility. Peter Davison I knew well fifty years ago. No one working on Orwell cannot be indebted to the majestic materials he has discovered, gathered, marshalled and published over the last half-century.

Photo Acknowledgements

The author and publishers wish to express their thanks to the below sources of illustrative material and/or permission to reproduce it.

© Collings, images courtesy of the Orwell Archive, UCL Library Special Collections: pp. 116, 165; Library of Congress Prints and Photographs Division, Carl Van Vechten photograph collection, Washington, DC: p. 19; © Estate of Donald McGill: p. 155; images courtesy of the Orwell Archive, UCL Library Special Collections: pp. 41, 44, 48, 53, 71, 78, 85, 86, 97, 140, 163, 200, 235.

Index